Under Northern Lights _____

UNDER NORTHERN LIGHTS

Writers and Artists View the Alaskan Landscape

Edited by Frank Soos & Kesler Woodward

Published for the University of Alaska Museum by the University of Washington Press

Under Northern Lights is published thanks to a generous contribution from Joseph Usibelli.

The authors and publishers have generously given permission to include the following copyrighted works: "The Island's Child" from *The Island Within*, copyright © 1989 by Richard Nelson (New York: Vintage Books, a division of Random House, Inc.; originally published by North Point Press); "What Everyone Wants You to Have" from *The Last Settlers*, copyright © 1998 by Jennifer Brice (Pittsburgh: Duquesne University Press); "Under the Tides, Under the Moon" from *Fish Camp: Life on an Alaskan Shore*, copyright © 1997 by Nancy Lord (Washington, D.C.: Island Press/Shearwater Books).

Library of Congress Cataloging-in-Publication Data
Under northern lights: writers and artists view the Alaskan landscape / edited by Frank Soos & Kesler Woodward.
p. cm.
ISBN 0-295-97924-0 (alk. paper)
1. Alaska—In art. 2. Arts, Modern—United States—20th century. I. Soos, Frank. II. Woodward, Kesler.
NX633.A37U53 2000
917.98—dc21 99-052227

The paper used in this publication meets the minimum requirements of American National Standard for Information Sciences-Permanence of Paper for Printed Library Materials, ANSI Z39.48-1984. ∞

CONTENTS

ARCTIC OCEAN

Barrow

Wainwright

Kaktovik

North Slope

Anaktuvuk
Pass

Arctic National
Wildlife Refuge

YUKON
TERRITORY

Point Hope

Gates of the
Arctic National
Park

Brooks Range

Arctic
Village

Old Crow

Chukchi
Peninsula

BERING STRAIT

ARCTIC   CIRCLE

Fort
Yukon

Kotzebue

Shishmaref

Diomede
Islands

Wales

Cape
Espenberg

Galena

Chena R.

Fairbanks

Pt. Spencer
King
Island

Port
Clarence

Tanana   River

St. Lawrence
Island

Gambell

Savoonga

Nome

Unalakleet

St. Michael

Yukon River

Mt.
McKinley

Wonder
Lake

Isabel Pass

Punuk
Island

Anvik

Shageluk

Tokositna
River

BERING SEA

Scammon Bay

Old Hamilton

Kwiguk

River

Denali
National
Park

Susitna River

McCarthy

Hooper Bay

Chevak

Qissunaq

Newtok

Nunapitchuk

Kuskokwim

Sleetmute

Mt.
Susitna

Eklutna

Anchorage

Lake George

Valdez

Copper
River

Mekoryak

Tununak

Akiak

Kasigluk

Bethel

Orca

Cordova

Mt.
St. Elias

Nunivak
Island

Nelson
Island

Kipnuk

Toksook
Bay

Togiak

Lake Clark
National Park

Cook
Inlet

Seward

Fox Island
Resurrection
Bay

Prince
William Sound

Gulf of Alaska

Pribilof
Islands

Katmai
National
Park

Alaska Peninsula

Castle
Cape

Chignik

Kodiak
Island

Attu
Island

Aleutian Islands

False Pass

PACIFIC OCEAN

Atka
Island

Unalaska

Haines

Klukwan

Adams
Inlet

Mendenhall
Glacier

Juneau

Icy
Bay

Glacier Bay

Hoonah

Chicagoff
Island

Kruzoff
Island

Sitka

Wrangell

Ketchikan

Klawock

Queen Charlotte
Islands

PLATES

FOREWORD

Aldona Jonaitis

FOUR YEARS AGO. when I told my friends that I had accepted an appointment at the University of Alaska Museum and would be moving to Fairbanks, some seemed happy for me but most were astonished. How could I possibly leave New York City to live 150 miles south of the Arctic Circle? What would I eat? Where would I shop? And, most importantly, how would I be able to consume culture at the edge of the earth? Fairbanks was, of course, a cultural backwater inhabited by illiterate hunters and boorish oilmen. My less polite friends thought I had lost my mind.

How little they knew of the cultural vitality of this community, and of Alaska in general. So many artists and writers have gravitated toward this northern land, enticed by its natural beauty, its wildness, its vibrant Native cultures. Many of them spent their early years "outside"—the term Alaskans use for the other states—and came to the Great Land where their creativity flourished. Others were born here and thus have within themselves the spirit of the land. I found the quality of the arts here extraordinary and soon wrote my disbelieving friends that I had become the happy resident of a place of great art and great writing.

This is in part due to Fairbanks's being the site of the flagship campus of a distinguished university. In addition to its world-famous scientific research institutes, the University of Alaska Fairbanks has an important creative writing program, an active art department, and an outstanding museum. All three contributed to the creation of this book. Kesler Woodward, head of the Art Department, and essayist Frank Soos of the English Department had for years spoken about producing a volume that would feature Alaskan art and essays. The University of Alaska Museum had begun a capital campaign for funds to build an extension that would include an art gallery for our fine collection of Alaskan art. Kes and Frank suggested that their book, to be illustrated with selections from the Museum's collections, might function as an interesting fund-raiser for the Museum. This seemed like such a good idea that I immediately contacted the University of Washington Press with the proposal that we copublish it. In addition to Kes's being a noted historian of Alaskan art as well as a major artist and Frank's being a distinguished and well-known writer, Barry McWayne—who had already taken the photographs for several University of Washington Press catalogs, including *A Legacy of Arctic Art* by Dorothy Jean Ray, *The Living Tradition of Yup'ik Masks: Agayuliyararpat* by Ann Fienup-Riordan, and *Looking North: Art From the University of Alaska Museum*, edited by Aldona Jonaitis—would be photographing the artworks. The Press eagerly accepted our proposal.

The only task left was to obtain the funding required to produce the book. One of the Museum's most devoted champions is Joseph Usibelli, Sr. He and his family have already named the Rose Berry Art Gallery in honor of his mother. He is the chairman of our Museum Expansion Campaign. He has a major collection of Alaskan works. He is a lover of literature. He was born in Alaska and cares deeply about it. When I approached him for help, he enthusiastically agreed. Frank, Kes, all of the artists and writers represented in this volume, and I thank Joe for his generosity and support. The combination of outstanding writing, superb art, and this wonderful philanthropic spirit demonstrates how Alaska is, without a doubt, a major cultural center.

■ ■ ■

Aldona Jonaitis

INTRODUCTION

Frank Soos &
Kesler Woodward

WHAT CAN BE SAID about the undeniable romance of Alaska? On a given day, Denali (Mount McKinley) may be visible to people in Anchorage, Fairbanks, and points in between. Over half the citizens in the state might turn and face this great lump of whiteness, a scoop of vanilla ice cream, sublime and out of reach. Yet for every dazzling landscape, every sacred place, there is the contrary desire to bring the far-off near, to make it comfortable and familiar.

How have we come to see this landscape? There's scarcely a souvenir shop, grocery store, or gas station in Alaska that doesn't offer a postcard view of Denali bathed in pink and lavender light, its image reflected in Wonder Lake. It's quite a sight. What that postcard doesn't admit to is the four-hour school-bus ride out along the bumpy park road, the possibility of rain and cold, and the probability of mosquitoes, the truth that the mountain is obscured by clouds more often than not. What it doesn't say is that the park bears ambling along the tundra can't possibly come up to all the bear tales, tall and true.

What does this place look like when you get beyond the picturesque and stereotypical? And where and how to find such views? We have wondered for much of the past year whether it might be possible to create a more expansive view of such a large and diverse region crowded under the single simple name Alaska by creating a sort of conversation between works of art and essays—a conversation that would be, if not immediately understandable, at least recognizable as a form of dialogue.

The Roman poet Horace understood a fundamental connection between writer and painter: they both start with the empty page. The American abstract expressionist painter Robert Motherwell once called the blank, white canvas the most beautiful and terrifying thing in the world. He has written about how the whole task of the painter is to destroy that awesome purity and then bring it back to an equal state of perfection. Writers who read his words know exactly what he meant. Jack London probably wasn't the first to use the snow-covered landscape of the Alaskan Interior as a geographic metaphor for that blankness.

How to approach the landscape as a painter? The word "landscape" itself evolved from a seventeenth-century Dutch term that originally meant a painting of a scene—a way of classifying a picture in a different category from, for example, a portrait or a still-life. As James A. W. Heffernan notes in *The Recreation of Landscape*, it took some time for the term to broaden beyond this technical usage, first to include a particular tract of land that could be viewed from a single viewpoint, as if it were a painting, and finally to its current meaning of natural scenery itself.

In our own time, the word "landscape" has been made to apply to different disciplines, and artistic landscape is no longer the only means of calling attention to the land. In this way, the task of the landscape painter is not very different from that of the writer—both start from observation and description of the physical, emotional, and conceptual world, and from those observations draw new insights and present new conclusions about that world.

When a writer moves into the Alaskan landscape, he is always pushing a wave of words before him. Words light on everything, illuminating rivers, mountains, frozen lakes, and trees, and provoking insights into doubt, fear, despair, and hope. These ideas arrived at through images are much the same for the writer and the artist, though writers are obliged, perhaps, to show a bit more of what goes on behind the creative act. There's a float plane that's just gone off and left you, or a canoe that has carried you down the river but could just as easily have tipped you over, or skis, or plain old feet that got people where they needed to go. There are plans, checklists, and precautions. The landscape, it seems, is still mostly *out there*, something to be approached. Maps help. Supplies matter.

Both artists and writers, however, are prisoners of the prevailing worldview of their time, place, and culture. They can't help but reflect unconscious cultural attitudes toward the land itself. What separates great artists and writers from ordinary good ones is the same thing that separates great scientists from their more respectable but more commonplace fellows—they begin to break out of those boundaries, and they bring on a slight shift in the prevailing view of things. It is through such discoveries—in reality more often the collaborative product of many seekers than the Eureka folklore of the lone genius—that the history of art and literature, much like that of science, lurches in an ungainly manner from one prevailing paradigm to the next. We can't see that shift when we're inside it, but we will see it looking back.

This sort of collaboration is what we had in mind in bringing artists and essayists together in a conversation—a conversation in which a work from one medium takes on a gesture from another and perhaps amplifies it, or pulls it in a slightly different direction, or even possibly reverses it with irony. The conversational links range from rather direct and clear to allusive and implicit, though our intent is to offer risks—and through those risks, possibilities—through varieties of indirection.

This volume is, in a way, a demonstration of that conversation. We wanted dialogues, not illustrations or captions. There's nothing wrong with illustrations. Rockwell Kent's images for *Moby Dick* are among the finest responses of a great artist to the words of a great writer, and they bring to the reading of the story a deeper poignancy and power, but they remain subordinate to Melville's words. Frank O'Hara's numerous catalog essays for his modernist painter friends Franz Kline, Robert Motherwell, and Jackson Pollock offer wonderful insights to their work, but finally they stand as captions, always at the service of the paintings. We wanted something different. Though the works of art from the collection of the University of Alaska Museum were *chosen* in response to the essays, they were not *created* in answer to the writing. They are, like the essays, responses to the Alaskan landscape itself.

As artists and writers, then, we try to question assumptions, both our own and those of our time and place. We try to break through those barriers. We've tried here to do the same thing in the juxtapositions of art and writing. The juxtapositions ask questions, some about Alaska and some about art.

Some of the questions are formal. How do you end a story? How do you know when a painting is finished? Can the character of words, the length of paragraphs, the shape of brushstrokes, or the colors of shapes carry the rhythms of the land as much as images can? What are the dangers of slickness, of technical facility, of too-easy acceptance of the picturesque? How can you respond thoughtfully to a landscape when you're standing open-mouthed in wonder at it? How do you say something new about a subject that's been talked—and painted—to death? These are issues faced, and answered in some way, by every painting, print, photograph, and essay.

Other questions are larger, more personal, and have to be answered not by single works, but by a life's work, if at all. What does it mean to be an Alaskan artist? Through what kinds of filters—historical, cultural, gender-based, political, personal—do we peer at the landscape? How different does that river look to a contemporary female, urban, recreational adventurer from the way it looked to an early-twentieth-century male pioneer in search of settlement and gold? What is the cost we're willing to pay to walk in this world? What has called us to be here? What is a homestead, and where is home?

■ ■ ■

Frank Soos &

Kesler Woodward

xiv

Under Northern Lights _____

Jane Gray

Kagamil's Children

Relief print,
tissue paper,
watercolor,
graphite
1980
UA85-3-39

THE WAY WINTER COMES   *Sherry Simpson*

THE WIND BLOWS from the northeast across the Arctic Ocean, exhaling the ache of winter into my nose and throat. Waves heave along the stony beach that fronts Barrow, as I scan the horizon for signs of pack ice. A milky nimbus brightens the margin between ocean and sky, and I say to myself, "Ice blink," a newfound term I learned from reading *The Illustrated Glossary of Snow and Ice* in the university library in Fairbanks. Ice blink means the white glare of ice reflecting on clouds. Surely there's an Inupiat word for this effect but I'm from Fairbanks and a stranger in the high Arctic. I memorized other terms from the book, more for their poetry than their science: frost smoke, frazil ice, water sky. I studied the black-and-white photographs of snow and ice, down there among the book stacks. But none of it seems to have anything to do with this thin wind breathing from an unfamiliar quarter. Tugging the flaps of my muskrat hat over my ears, I turn against the wind. It's mid-September and the first day of winter in Barrow. I don't like to be cold.

The blunt edge of Alaska slopes above me. Where the thirty-foot bluff rises from the beach, great hunks of earth have slumped and toppled into mounds of now-frozen soil. This is the turbulent rim of the North American slab, the place where the continent sloughs away into the Arctic Ocean. On maps the boundary between land and sea forms a crisp and static line, not this membranous, shifting

Mark Daughhetee

The Shaman

Toned gelatin silver photograph

1990

UAP92:006:001

negotiation between elemental forces. In my mental geography, I mark this spot on the beach with an X: "You are here." Below the X the continent flares and swells and finally stretches tight against the globe's belly. Somewhere above the X drifts the blank northern cipher of ice and magnetism and mystery.

Unsure whether I'm treading on the archaeological dig I have come to see, I step carefully into the tracks of other shoes as I climb a heap of soil for a better look. On the bluff's brow, just below the browning tundra, pink surveyor's tape flutters in the wind. Now I can see where, six weeks ago, archaeologists scraped away three feet of melting black soil and peat reeking sweetly of spilled seal oil.

The site lies on the periphery of Barrow, an Inupiat Eskimo town of about four thousand. I walked here from the Arctic Hotel, two blocks south of the beach. Stevenson Street runs just beyond the diggings; small frame houses line the bluff's edge. The junk of ages scatters about my feet, discards of Barrow societies past and present: a Pepsi case, cartoon-colored pull-tabs, a twisted bicycle wheel, the vaulted skull of a bowhead whale. I pick up a spoked whale vertebra steeped in the soil's organic juices until it turned ale-brown. I examine random sticks for signs of antiquity, wonder if a mud-covered object is the sole of an abandoned tennis shoe or an ancient hide slipper. Only the passage of time distinguishes artifact from litter.

Four little Inupiat girls romp down the beach, playing in the cellophane radiance of the afternoon arctic sun. "What are you doing?" one of them calls out, skipping up the mound. They are all about six or eight. The wind frisks black hair about their faces. "Just looking," I say.

Then I ask, "Did they find something here?" even though I already know the answer. "They say an old lady's body was found over there," one of them says, gesturing toward the bluff. "We live up there," says another importantly, pointing to a neat green house perilously close to the bluff's crumbling brink. "Let's go ice skating instead of climbing," one of the girls says, and they pick their way along the slope to find a puddle of ice. I wonder if I should say something; this is an archaeological site, after all, but they live here, and I don't. "Look what Aggie found!" one of the girls shrieks, and they all bend over and scuff at something in the mud. "Hair from that woman!" But it isn't really, and they know it. They keep climbing and disappear over the top.

It was not an old woman who emerged here, but a young girl aged between four and eight, already reburied elsewhere by the time I arrived. In late July heavy rains softened the bluff until huge chunks slid away from the continent. A passerby spotted a roundish thing jutting from the exposed slope, and something about it made him think of a human head. This was not the first time one of the people who used to live here squeezed out of the earth. Archaeologists excavating the abandoned village of Point Franklin down the coast came to Barrow to perform a sort of scientific triage, extracting the girl's body before it thawed and exploring the house site before it collapsed further. Now I scratch and poke around their work, hoping to learn something about the girl and the excavation. I want to know other things, too, things about the Arctic, and the way winter comes to us all.

The sea ice arrived a week ago, a cold chowder of slush and chunks that carried the season's first polar bear onto land. I read in the paper how townspeople drove the bear away with rubber bullets and how the ice retreated after a few days when the wind shifted. Soon it will return, thickening and gobbing and finally solidifying into a thick white pane bridging the ocean. Then the people will venture onto the ice to hunt seals, and polar bears will trek into town to hunt garbage and sometimes the people.

Already I've seen one way winter comes. This morning, a skein of ice skimmed the surface of lagoons that yesterday flowed free. All through the day, as I walked through town with head bowed against a blunt, fitful wind, I noticed the way ice coagulates into frozen sludge. From the glossary, I think it is called "grease ice." It seizes the shore and ripples outward, like an oil slick.

The cold seizes something in me, too. I think about my small house in Fairbanks and all the things I still need to do before snow shrouds the surrounding forest: insulate the door, buy straw for the dogs' houses, make a quilted cover for the upstairs bedroom window. Across Interior Alaska, birch- and aspen-covered hills flare into gold, and it was not easy to abandon the season's last mild days to travel north toward winter. My right index finger, the one I frostnipped years ago, feels numb. Inside my wool gloves I curl my fingers against my palm to warm them. Once winter grabs hold of part of you, it owns it for good.

Still standing on the mound, I turn back to the sea, hoping a little elevation will reveal more of the horizon and the white shimmer of pack ice I saw from the jet when I arrived. Long ago this bluff rolled in a gentle slope toward a shore that met the Arctic Ocean hundreds of yards north of here. From the hill, people looked across the water for bowhead whales and ice and whatever else the ocean brought. Once, they celebrated whale kills here during *nalukataq*, a festival of sharing and thanksgiving that continues as joyfully as ever on a different beach.

But the sea tears away great fleshy pieces of land along this reach. In recent years, violent storms have thrashed their way across the shallow coastal sea and beat against the bluffs, smashing them down and threatening buildings. Just a few hundred yards to the west, workers cracked a two-story building from its foundation last spring and carted it across the ice to another part of town before the ocean could take it. Souvenir hunters, archaeologists, the ocean, and the ground's restless movement have collaborated to expose and sometimes carry off ancient sod houses, artifacts, and the occasional body.

Archaeologists teased the girl's body from the frozen soil with streams of water trickled from the town's fire truck. She emerged curled within a lens of ice and wrapped in a birdskin parka. A baleen sled and a kayak skin lay on top of her. She died hungry; the autopsy found gravel and bits of animal fur in her upper intestine. Somebody laid her carefully in the sod house's meat cellar, a puzzling act because the Inupiat people traditionally carried their dead out onto the tundra and left them on wood platforms under the sky. Perhaps her family left her in the cellar because they had neither the strength nor will to carry her outside. No one can say.

The area where the girl appeared is known as Ukkuqsi, a part of the Utqiagvik settlement that predates by at least several centuries the modern Inupiat village of Barrow. From the new second story of Arctic Pizza, I look across part of Utqiagvik as it stretches along the bluff's edge. Old whale bones pierce the ruddy tundra where people once dug into the frozen earth and ribbed their partially submerged sod houses with bones and driftwood, and after the Yankee whalers came, with planks from shipwrecks.

Later walking over this rumpled ground, I admire the way Inupiats lived here using only what the earth and ocean gave them, yet never hesitated to adopt whatever technology served them. All of Inupiat culture, borrowed and invented, jumbles in the hard soil of Utqiagvik. The girl's body dates to 1200 A.D. but the archaeologists found harpoon heads on the cellar floor that date to 800 A.D., the time of the Birnirk culture and the first successful whalers. The girl's society, the Thule culture, was shifting again when she died. The landscape appears so impassive that nothing seems to move, but the people changed all the time, creating a better fit for themselves here. But even today, tempered by jet service, grocery stores, natural gas, water and sewer lines, insulation, oil money, and other amenities, life in Barrow seems difficult to me. A person who lives here contentedly must be at ease in a world planed by land, sea, and sky, where the perpetual daylight of spring and summer drains as swiftly as the thousands of birds that pour overhead when the north tilts toward winter.

I wonder what people here know that I don't. I grew up in Juneau, on the southeast coast, where winter stages a wet and blustery melodrama. After ten abrasive winters in Fairbanks, 150 miles or so below the Arctic Circle, the dry cold still scrapes against me. When fall equinox tips us into a deep well of darkness and cold, I count to myself the months of hard winter: October, November, December, January, February, March. Then I recount them, thinking how half my life is winter.

Only a trembling rind of flesh separates us from the dark embrace of cold. Winter reminds me every moment how weak is the flesh that rides our bones, how quickly fervent blood retreats from limbs and puddles deep inside, trying to delay the chill that reaches steadily toward the heart. The body becomes a frail vessel of heat that must be shielded in a soft armor of down and wool and fur. It is a cruel science, learning how to dress properly so that sweat will not freeze me in my own damp salt, so cold will not steal fingers or toes or ears, searing them into a white deadness that will blister and blacken and swell. A delicate balance is required. The coldest I've ever been was in Barrow several years ago as I stood on the pack ice for a few hours, watching efforts to rescue three trapped gray whales. The cold slowly percolated from the ice through my boots into my feet, until the sensation of rising numbness twisted my stomach with nausea. When I finally

■ ■ ■

Sherry Simpson

8

thawed out, I nearly wept from pain as the cold relinquished me. That same day, another woman out on the ice fainted from overheating; she had swaddled herself too tightly and thickly.

Winter weights the year so heavily that it nearly develops a personality. Every summer seems akin in its radiance of heat, green, and light, but winters I recall individually. The winter a Siberian cold front mired us for two weeks in temperatures of minus fifty and sixty degrees. The winter a foot of wet snow dropped in September, bending and freezing the slim birches into permanent arcs. The bloody winter the moose escaped snowdrifts by walking the railroad line. Summer carries you away, but winter inhabits you.

Somehow the landscape abides within the terms of this perpetual imbalance, in which heat always yields to cold. Under the spongy tundra lies a mantle of permafrost, the name given to permanently frozen ground. The top layer freezes and thaws each summer, but permafrost remains ever solid. At Barrow, the ground may thaw only five or ten inches deep in the summer; in some places permafrost delves as far as twelve hundred feet below the surface. South of the mountains, pockets and ribbons of permafrost course beneath much of Alaska's bulk, but north of the Brooks Range, permafrost sheaths the landscape, extending below lakes, under rivers, even beneath the Arctic Ocean.

Permafrost contours the land. Water cannot permeate it; it pools against the frozen layer, wicking back through the vegetation to create bogs. The ground does not freeze uniformly, either. Frozen particles saturate some regions that scientists call "ice rich." Elsewhere vein ice pierces the ground in runnels and splinters. As frozen ground contracts, it cracks the earth. Meltwater fills the seams in the short warm season and then refreezes, spawning ice wedges that swell and jostle underground like uneasy molars. Just as sea ice demands its own nomenclature, an entire vocabulary exists to describe the way permafrost agitates the landscape: ice lens, frost shatter, pond ice, aufeis, pingo.

Permafrost does not bear insult well. Scratch through the delicate protective layer of vegetation, and the exposed ground melts and sinks, leaving gutters of mud. If the archaeologists had not carved the frozen girl from that bluff, the melting permafrost eventually would have eased her out, coated in stinking muck.

Drive an all-terrain vehicle or a tractor across the tundra, and the scars remain for good. It is the old enemy, winter, that best shields the land from damage, and it is permafrost that preserves ancient treasures.

But everywhere permafrost troubles the living and the dead. In Fairbanks, people choose carefully where they build homes. Erect a house on land that harbors an ice lens, and years later, when the building's reflected warmth raises the ground's temperature, the land will heave and buckle and shift, and so will the house. I once lived near an abandoned suburban home twisted and jarred by permafrost into some cubist fantasy. I always wanted to sneak into the house and brace myself against the tilt and jangle of geometry gone bad. Eventually the empty house became a research site. For many summers, until the property owners razed the building for fear trespassers would injure themselves, tour buses daily hauled visitors past it so they could snap photos of something you don't see every day. The house served as a reminder that frozen earth will have its way.

The old prospectors knew what permafrost could do, and it's said that many didn't care to be buried in the north, where their coffins might later lunge from the ground. Today Fairbanks inters its dead on birch-covered hills where permafrost is less likely to exist. Still, it's impossible to bury the winter's deceased until the ground thaws enough; coffins are stored in concrete bunkers on the edge of the cemetery until spring arrives to accept the dead. Sometimes I feel the waves of frigid air cascading off the windows surrounding our bed, and I shiver thinking of the way cold must radiate through the earth. Each January, when winter air becomes something fluid that pools against the landscape, I remember to tell my husband I wish to be cremated when I die.

In Barrow, where the ground is always frozen just beneath the surface, people use mechanical equipment to auger graves, to scrape some room in the earth for the departed. Probably they'll remain in their deep hollows, but those old ones laid out on the tundra occasionally return. Some bodies eventually merged into the shallow organic layer that freezes and remelts each season, and the earth thrusts their bones back into the open air. When people from Barrow find exposed ancestors, they tell local authorities, who consult with the elders. "Give them a Christian burial," the elders advise, for Western religion is one of those innovations many Inupiat have accepted, and the skeletons are reburied with benedictions from the modern world. It seems a shame somehow to return them to the very earth they eluded, but it disturbs those of us still walking about on the surface, still tracking the sun's comings and goings, to stumble over bones.

So it is with the little girl, whose dark passage through the centuries was interrupted when the land rubbed away and freed her. Once the archaeologists probably would have shipped her off to the catacombs of some university or museum, but these days Barrow's Inupiat elders have a say in what happens to their people. Eskimos are no longer considered artifacts, no matter how old or dead they are, and the elders decided the little girl should be reburied in a simple Christian ceremony. Still wearing her feather parka, she was placed into a small casket and given back to the earth that yielded her.

One afternoon during my brief stay in Barrow, I visit a class of third-graders from Ipalook Elementary. They've been learning about the little frozen girl, whom they named Agnaiyaaq, meaning Young Girl. They spend the morning "excavating" tools of their own creation from boxes filled with sand. From pastel clays they fashioned things their grandparents and great-grandparents once used: harpoon heads, seal oil lamps, needle cases, labrets to decorate lips, bolas to knock birds from the sky. Even though the children already know what they made and buried, it thrills them to retrieve their belongings from the sand, to mimic swinging the bolas over their heads or piercing a bowhead with pale blue harpoon heads.

While the children dig up their instant history themselves, I study a display titled "Our Ancestors." Dewey wrote that his mother is from Ruby, an Athabascan village on the Yukon, where her family has worked at the Big Eddy fish camp for one hundred and sixty years. "My dad is a cowboy," Dewey said. "My dad's family has had the ranch for over two hundred years. I am half Indian and half cowboy." Lillian's great-great-grandmother Miriam was a hunter who had braided hair and a tattooed chin. Both of Nayuk's great-grandfathers were whaling captains. One also delivered U.S. mail along the coast with a dog sled; the other was a reindeer herder and great hunter. Matthew's great-great-great-grandfather came to Barrow on a whaling ship around 1895 and married an Eskimo girl named

Iggilasuk. Shamans, magicians, ivory carvers, carpenters; immigrants from China, the Philippines, Italy, California—their blood stirs here still, in this brightly lit classroom on the edge of the Arctic Ocean.

The children themselves are too shy to talk with me. Finally a young white girl named Ashley marches up and presents me with a brightly crayoned illustration of a tennis shoe. A few moments later Jerry, his dark eyes looking down, hands me a drawing of himself riding his orange snowmachine across the tundra. Everything is white except Jerry on his snowmachine, flying along that glowing margin between the sky and earth.

I ride on the school bus with the third-graders to the new cemetery out on Freshwater Lakes Road. At the cemetery the kids climb off the bus carrying bright paper flowers, also handmade, to leave at the girl's grave, a lumpy pile of turned-over frozen dirt so humble that the children and grown-ups occasionally forget you shouldn't walk where people are buried. The teacher coached the students about proper graveside behavior and encouraged them to think a "special thought" while standing at the burial site. But most of the children are more interested in frozen water than frozen girls. They slide gleefully across ice puddles, skitter across the tundra, and shout into the sullen sky. Three months have passed since the last time they played on snow and ice, and while I think, "Winter so soon?" they think, "Winter at last!"

The girl's grave faces south, across the arctic coastal plain, where countless lakes and ponds freeze even now, where frost stiffens russet grasses, reindeer moss, and sedges. Fine snow powders the ground, hardly enough to bear a footprint. The wind scours us. Six gigantic satellite dishes poise across the road, listening for electronic messages whispering over the horizon. Around us headstones mark a few gravesites, wooden crosses the others. Artificial wreaths and bouquets heap the graves and quiver in the wind, the harsh blues and reds and yellows no colors ever borne by the fine plants woven tightly into the matted tundra. The Alaska Commercial Company of Barrow sells the wreaths upstairs in the housewares department. The plots lie in no particular arrangement; the streets and lots of Barrow do not adhere to any noticeable sort of zoning, so it seems unfair to expect order from the dead. I like the random way graves also scatter

Anonymous

Polar-bear-head knife handle

Punuk period archaeological ivory

UA77-66-13

among the streets and houses of Barrow, implying a companionableness among the living and not-living.

The girl's grave huddles next to the remains of a previously resurrected group of prehistoric bodies from Utqiagvik that everyone calls the frozen family. "Now they're really frozen," jokes an employee of the North Slope Borough. She props up a tall, blank wooden plank, rounded at the top, that will serve as a grave marker; later, a bronze plaque will memorialize the girl's return to living memory. The woman shivers in her wolverine-trimmed parka and stamps her feet on the hard ground. I'm cold, too; I watch the kids play and think longingly of my good down parka left behind in Fairbanks.

The way these children love winter makes me consider my own struggle to embrace it. Lately I've been thinking about what winter requires of us. I long for reconciliation because I will spend the rest of my life in the north, never far from winter. This means relaxing into the land and the weather, recognizing that blind resistance to the way things work can lead only to the same jumbled dissonance that twisted the permafrost house in Fairbanks. Winter's beauty is not hard to locate in the rosy dream of mid-day light, in the brilliant swell and fall of the aurora, in the comfort of downy snow falling through the trees at night. But there is some deeper feeling in the way the constancy of winter presses against me, turning flesh into a membrane that allows cold to permeate, connecting me more intimately and uneasily to the outside world than does any other sensation. Winter clothes me in awareness, so I can admit that by allowing the cold and dark to seep into me just so far, far enough that my own heat and desire for life will cause me pain, I find a fierce joy. Perhaps surviving winter demands yielding some part of myself.

A few students, helped by a father, dig and scratch at the earth so they can erect the grave marker. A local video crew tapes the scene. Out on the tundra, other children spin and slide and swoop like little birds. The teacher asks for a few special thoughts from those gathered. "Thank you for showing us your body," one boy offers. "We're sorry you died," another suggests.

I stand there wishing I had seen the girl's body. I wanted to see how in death she curled back into the shape she assumed in the womb. I wanted to see the way cold earth can hold and release us, perhaps more tenderly than life itself does. I suppose I wanted to see what awaits me in the future as much as I long to understand her past.

But whether seeing her could tell me these things, I can't say. There's so much I don't know about the Arctic, about Alaska, so much I'll never know. In every direction I turn on the tundra, the compass needle bobbles and jitters, pointing only to uncertainty. I yearn for ways to bind myself to the landscape, to press closer to some essential mystery I can't even articulate. Meanings arrive the way ice does, forming silently, congealing and crystallizing almost beyond vision until suddenly the surface shimmers and I need new words to describe what I'm seeing. Ice blink. Shuga. Brash ice. Icebound.

If there are answers, they lie somewhere in the living margin between ice and blood, between permafrost and sky. Sooner or later, flesh and land become the same. What we bury, the earth gives back. What we hide, the ocean finds. What time takes, it returns. I learned one thing in Barrow: People can be born again and again, emerging from the earth covered in rich, organic muck, here where the land ripples and convulses with ice and bone and flesh, where winter lies always just beneath the surface.

■ ■ ■

Brian Allen
If Beavers Had Bulldozers
Gelatin silver photographs
1981
UAP83:037:001

FINDING A PLACE ON THE SEAWARD EDGE

Carolyn Servid

IMAGINE THIS, and you will have painted yourself the Southeast Alaska scene I look at each day from the windows of our house. A crowded landscape, one of thick forests hugging hillsides that rise steeply from rocky shorelines to the alpine limits of the craggy mountains that are squeezed into the confines of Baranof Island. There is no open level ground within view, and there is not much within any proximity. Everything gives way to slope, and most slopes are covered with a density of trees. The sense of space here is created by water—the bays, inlets, coves, and open channels where the North Pacific Ocean moves in to fill geological voids carved in the land. Fractures and rifts and chasms that cut deep into this massif of rock and earth create a convoluted shoreline. Still there are stretches along the island's edge where the land slopes more gently to meet the water and offers a perch for a house like ours and a bench big enough for a town like Sitka. As the tide rises and falls—as much as sixteen feet—both the land and those spaces across water shrink and swell accordingly. The predominant orientation here is toward that open watery space, with the island's steep slopes at our backs.

Our house falls into suit. Its front corner of windows faces due south and looks out over Thimbleberry Bay and beyond into Eastern Channel, a prominent passage out to open ocean. It is tucked into a hillside and a sheltering stand of cedar, hemlock, and Sitka spruce, and is rimmed by a profusion of red huckleberry. The land in front of the house falls away to a rocky beach thirty feet below. The trees and berry bushes push toward the water's edge, putting down roots wherever they can find a bit of soil. Eventually they give way to the tidal zone and the barnacled rocks that are washed by remnants of ocean swells or waves kicked up by a breeze. Behind the house, the trees climb a hill that continues steeply skyward to terminate in the triangular rock summit of Mount Verstovia, three thousand feet above the water. The road into town cuts across the mountain's extended slope a hundred feet above our house, and we make our way to it each day by way of a trail that meanders through the trees. Standing on the beach rocks with my rubber-booted feet in the water, I sometimes try to fix my place in that steep-sloped reach—the sea floor falling away beyond me, the barnacles underfoot, the huckleberry just above me, the trees towering above those bushes, the shoulder of the mountain looming toward the clouds, and that stone summit soaring over all. The small stretch of rocky beach is one of the few natural open spaces between the water of Thimbleberry Bay and the high rock that crowns Verstovia's sharp rise. I pick my way cautiously, tentatively over the broken shoreline to a little ledge in a sloping face of stone where I can sit. Then I ease myself down, lean my small back against the mountain, and try to soak up some of its certainty.

A few feet from where I sit, that seaward sweep begins, the coastal deep that breaks up this compact, sharp-crested, forested land. While that watery openness gives me breathing room, its expanse limits my wanderings. It separates me from a contiguous part of the island, from the spiky summits of the Pyramids and the rounded ridges of Mount Longenbaugh across the way. The enclave of Thimbleberry Bay is somewhat protected by the Marshall Islands a half mile out, but just beyond them Eastern Channel offers a straight shot at the North Pacific. That oceanic horizon, not quite in view, extends itself over a third of the globe to the shorelines of Siberia and Japan and China. Baranof Island hangs on the Pacific's eastern rim, its own complex piece in the three-hundred-mile straggle of islands that shape this northern coast. Here on its western edge, this rock, this beach, this forest, this slope are my vantage points. I am grounded here with the mountain against my back. This island's edge is home.

My allegiances here are not rooted in birthright or family ties to the place, nor are they linked to a local cultural tradition. Strictly speaking, I am a visitor here, a short-timer. But my choice to come here to live was a deliberate one. It grew out of a subconscious longing to be possessed by a place on earth. A yearning to be steadied by tangible realities outside myself. At the time I decided to move, I couldn't put words to this desire. My friends and family shook their heads when I took my backpack and the thousand dollars I had saved and got on the ferry in Seattle. Where was I going? Well, I thought to Sitka. What was I going to do? I didn't really know. I couldn't explain it to them. I am only now—years later— coming to understand it for myself.

No landscape had truly worked a spell on me until my first trip to Alaska the summer of 1979, the year before my move. The journey was a reckless one for me. I quit two jobs to go off on a three-month escapade with a companion I hardly knew but thought I loved, through country that left me speechless and afraid. He had set out on a camping and mountain climbing tour of the north and I was along for the ride—up through the Southeast by ferry, out to Glacier Bay, then into Alaska's interior in the vintage Volkswagen bus my friend had packed with an array of equipment, minimal comforts, and supplies. A canoe and kayak were strapped on top. I added my pack and clothes to the contingencies, settled into the front passenger seat, and worked on figuring out the protocols. Routines with tent and camp stove and food weren't hard to learn, but ropes and ice axes were not familiar to my hands. My skills on a rock face or snow ridge were limited. But being along for the ride meant I went along with the plans.

That journey took me to places I could not have imagined beforehand. I had never seen the retreating blue caverns of glacial ice. I had not sat face-to-face with a mountain range that rose three miles high out of the sea. I hadn't pictured myself cutting steps across a vertical slope of snow hanging hundreds of feet above a valley floor. Or walking a tenuous snow bridge spanning the sheer ice walls of a deep crevasse. I had never felt my life start to give way to the strength of a rising river. I was shaken again and again by the challenges we mounted against the land. My attempts at courage were attempts to feel significant, and again and again I failed. None of them had anything to do with the place itself.

Those conceited ventures were staged against the abiding backdrop of nature's detail and scope. The turquoise milk of a glacial inlet. The quiet watchfulness of a seal. The yellow burst of cinquefoil on a ledge of rock. The graceful fork in the

James Schoppert

Spruce Needle

Spruce panels, paint

1982

UA83-3-33AB

tail of an arctic tern. The rosy light of a three o'clock dawn tipping sharp mountain crests and spilling a blush down their cold white slopes. And north of the coastal ranges, the vastness of the land—a horizon stretched as wide as one could see by distant mountains, an immense green rolling away, stubbled by black spruce, sculpted by the cutbanks and braided strands of far-flowing rivers. The foothilled rise of a few landmark snow-capped peaks emerging like mirages before our eyes. Above all, the daunting blanket of silence that came down with the pressing expanse of sky.

I confronted this landscape each time without words. Often my body ached and my heart had been wrenched small, and yet here was a presence I could not face down—powerful, indifferent, complex, staggering, sublime. Its lack of humanness offered a curious comfort, a perspective that let me imagine, for the first time, the boundaries of my life being defined and supported by the earth. The magnitude of this northern countryside was its own silent force, opening my mind to the land on its own terms. The human scale I was accustomed to was diminished here. Our tent, our canoe, our Volkswagen were my measure and protection, but their adequacy was an illusion. They disappeared against the face of a glacier, were hardly visible on the slender thread of the Alaska highway stretching off across the distant expanse. The occasional human habitation we came to—perhaps a group of houses, a gas station, a few other buildings clustered at outposts along the road—seemed huddled together in refuge from the enormity around them. The whole huge place breathed the question: What is the appropriate relationship between human beings and this land?

While our adventures took their place as stories in my memory, it was this question that needled its way in deeper. It rekindled another, latent since adolescence, about my own relationship to Creation. That quest had always been posed in terms of my belief in a Christian god—an omniscient creator—and my willingness to live by Christian standards. It had never been posed in terms of my relationship to the earth. And it had never been posed *by* the earth. I had never considered the possibility that the earth could pull me toward understanding. I had never let it fill me with longing. As poet Robert Hass has written, we say longing "because desire is full of endless distances."

To be possessed by a place on earth: that was the heart of my longing. The word *possess* has Latin roots in *potis*, "a master of," which comes from *potesse*, "to be able" and, hence, strong. Mastery implies authority and dominion, but when those characteristics are given to the earth rather than human beings, they take on a different aspect. To be possessed by a place on earth might mean that I submit to its authority. Rather than taking a dominant role in a given landscape, I might leave that to the locals—the plants, animals, weather patterns, geological formations. I might come to know their habits, designs, and histories, let them teach and direct me. By becoming possessed, I myself might be enabled, given strength, perhaps even faith. I might then feel myself to be part of the place—part of Creation—rather than removed from it. Though I couldn't acknowledge this at the time, I left Alaska after that summer journey with some inkling of it in my mind.

That longing led me here, to this island's edge, where I find myself these many years later leaning against a mountain, looking out to sea, and thinking about notions of inhabitation. This place—Baranof Island, Thimbleberry Bay, Eastern Channel, Sitka Sound—is inhabited by eagle and brown bear, by raven and deer and chickadee, by squirrel and mink and otter. It is a summer place for salmon and thrushes and warblers and hummingbirds. It is a winter place for humpback whales and herring and loons and scoters. Orca, Canada goose, harbor seal, and sea lion know this place too. And humans have known it for a long time. Archaeological evidence puts human populations in Southeast Alaska 9,500 years ago. A piece of a basket found recently on south Baranof Island confirms that people were in this area around 3200 B.C. The fragment suggests a utility basket similar to more contemporary ones used to collect fish. Archaeologists don't assign the basket to a particular culture, but the Tlingit, the indigenous people living here when eighteenth-century European explorers came up the coast, would claim the basket as part of their history. Their oral tradition does not give exact dates for their arrival in these parts, but their stories put them here "from time immemorial." Tlingit villages and fish camps spread up and down the Alexander Archipelago and as far north as Yakutat. They moved inland too, to communities in southwest Yukon Territory and northwest British Columbia. The Tlingit that settled on this island called it Shee. Sitka is an Anglicized version of their name for a place on the island's outer, or seaward, edge.

Among the many things that are noteworthy about the tenure of the Tlingit in this area is the fact that they left little mark on the land. Archaeologists don't have a lot of material evidence of their occupation in part because they didn't leave much that lasted—woven baskets, wooden boxes and tools, and cedar clothing mostly decayed back to the earth. What they did leave was an ecosystem that was intact, one that had not been significantly altered. They settled here because life was abundant, and they seemed to know that their own continued well-being in this landscape was inextricably tied to the well-being of the place itself. They knew from years of experience the habits of herring and salmon and how to catch them, prepare them, store them. They caught halibut with elegantly carved wooden hooks that floated just off the ocean bottom. They learned when and where to hunt for seals. They recognized spruce trees that offered good roots for baskets. They knew how to take the bark of a cedar without damaging the tree. They figured out that the roots of a devil's club plant had medicinal value. They identified the seaweeds that, when dried, would provide good nourishment through the winter. They inhabited this ecosystem as an integral part of it. They were a people possessed by a place. The present-day Tlingit are here as witness.

On a 1995 visit to Sitka, Dan Kemmis, then mayor of Missoula, Montana, gave a public talk that incorporated ideas about our ability to inhabit a landscape well. He was referring primarily to the dominant Western culture and began with a consideration of "charismatic megafauna." The term is one coined by biologists and others trying to help us think about our relationships to whole ecosystems. As the term implies, charismatic megafauna are animals with charisma, ones we find compelling—the bear or wolf or elk or eagle. Our attention to them reveals our bias toward the extraordinary in nature and our ignorance about the more subtle complexities of whole ecosystems. But Dan Kemmis wanted to fix on this bias for a moment and look at some of the characteristics we find in these animals—power and majesty and grace. He suggested that they convey a sense of sovereignty because of the very way they inhabit their own landscapes. The characteristics we admire in them lose their poignancy for us when those animals are extracted from the place they belong. Their power and majesty and grace are shaped by context, by their fundamental relationship to the land. The qualities we recognize in these noble animals are not mere human qualities. They are measures of beauty that arise out of nature itself.

Kemmis went on to pose the question of what it would mean for humans to be seen as charismatic megafauna. What would it mean if we were to behave in such a way that we were recognized by other animals—perhaps by nature itself—as having majesty and sovereignty and grace? How might we think about ourselves if we acknowledged first and foremost our fundamental relationship to the land? How might we live our lives if our standards of quality were measures of beauty that arise out of nature itself? As I listened to Dan Kemmis formulate these ideas, I recognized the now-familiar longing that instilled itself in me during that first precipitous journey through Alaska. What is my fundamental relationship to the land? Can I recognize those measures of beauty? What does it mean to live by them? How might I balance humility and dominance, ignorance and grace? Do I know what it means to inhabit a landscape well?

The Tlingit oral tradition is rich with stories of consequence stemming from human interactions with nature. The cultural prescriptions they describe outline a sense of appropriate relationship and regard to both animals and the land. A Glacier Bay history, recounted by Tlingit elder Amy Marvin of Hoonah, tells the story of a young woman entering puberty who taunts a glacier by calling to it as though it were a dog, and prompts the massive river of ice to heave its way forward toward her village. The people of the village manage to escape, but the young woman and the village itself are destroyed. The story "The Woman Who Married a Bear," as told by Tom Peters, an inland Tlingit from Teslin, begins with a woman who steps in a pile of bear scat, slips, and spills a basketful of berries. Her immediate response is a comment insulting to the brown bear, and the ensuing events—her disappearance, her marriage to the bear, and her people's search for

John Bartlett

Standing Raven

Wood, metal, glass, acrylics,

mountain-goat horn

1990

UA94:010:001

her—result in the death of her brown-bear husband and in lessons in appropriate respect and reciprocity toward animals that give themselves to humans.[1]

I can't help but think of these stories as reflections of the Tlingit understanding of how to inhabit a landscape well. Perhaps our stories are a measure of our sense of belonging to a place. The roster of Tlingit creation stories with Raven as the central figure are specific enough to places in southeast Alaska that one gets a sense that the Tlingit world is contained *here*. Though they acknowledge arriving here at some ancient time, presumably from some other place, it is *this* place that possesses them. This place is their home. The creator of their world is in their midst. His black form soars overhead in feisty flight. His watery clucks and raspy croaks reverberate through the forest. He sits in a beach-edge tree and calls across the water, his voice rebounding like that of the owner of this grand estate.

I came to Tlingit country ignorant of their rich tradition. I came, unknowingly, for the same things they value about this place—its abundance of life, its wildness, its demand for regard and appropriate relationship. Their stories and art and lifeways have all enhanced my sensibilities, but I can't claim their ways of knowing for myself. The Tlingit history poses a strong presence here. I hold it respectfully in mind. It helps me think about my own settling, my own reconciliation with the longing that brought me to this place.

That settling has been given shape by the seven-acre slope of land between the edge of Thimbleberry Bay and the shoulder of Mount Verstovia, where I've been lucky to live most of my time in Sitka. It is a piece of land that was purchased by Jack Calvin in 1953, the year I was born, and is still owned by his widow, Margaret. My luck began with the fact that the Calvins were people who lived by principles inherent in the questions that brought me to Sitka. Over time, four houses have been added to the one that existed on the property, one up close to the road, the others at the water's edge, each occupying a niche no bigger than necessary. But for the most part, the property consists of the forested hillside. From the back cor-

1. *Amy Marvin, "Glacier Bay History," pp. 261–92; and Tom Peters, "The Woman Who Married the Bear," pp. 167–194; in Nora Marks Dauenhauer and Richard Dauenhauer, eds.,* Haa Shuká, Our Ancestors: Tlingit Oral Narratives *(Juneau: Sealaska Heritage Foundation; Seattle: University of Washington Press, 1987).*

ner windows of our house, I look up the slope into the dark tangle of boughs that is as high and deep as it is green with cedar and hemlock and spruce, part of the largest remaining temperate rain forest on earth. I make my way through those woods each day along a trail that marks our human passage here, a quarter-mile amble from the house to the road into town, from this waterfront refuge in the trees to the civilized world of Sitka.

My ritual in the morning before engaging the day is to stand at the floor-to-ceiling windows that face the water and look. If the early temperature and breeze aren't too bracing, I'll step out on the deck so I can hear as well as see. I like to get a sense of the company I keep. The color of the day is first, yet another variation on gray, perhaps, to accompany the rain that saturates this forest. Sometimes the clarity of the sun's fiery light has pushed every shred of cloud out of sight and gilt the tops of the peaks across the bay and the trees on their slopes. Or perhaps an opaque shroud of sky has come all the way down to rest on the water, obscuring everything but itself. Then I look to the nearby trees and rocks, the frame of stability for everything else that is in flux. A slight breeze rustles in lower boughs, and a slack tide swirls and gurgles against the shore. Up the hill, a winter wren's chattery song breaks in. Beyond it, the trilled whistling note of varied thrush. Chickadees flit back and forth from the feeder, juncos scuffle about on the ground below. Our resident red squirrel scampers headlong down a cedar to the porch to close in on any sunflower seeds left behind. The fog on the water rises and I make out the nose of a harbor seal stretched into the air. From somewhere distant, the cry of a gull. Then the other water birds—goldeneyes, mergansers, sometimes mallards close to shore, grebes and scoters and cormorant a ways out, now and then a pair of buffleheads, now and then a pair of harlequin ducks. Once, in a late-season snow storm, four tundra swans.

When the view is clear out to Eastern Channel, I watch the water for spouts. Recent winters have sent a couple hundred humpback whale to Sitka Sound. Through a telescope I watch eight, ten, fifteen towering white shots of breath appear there, there, and there. The slick dark backs catch a glint of light before they sink down. Spout again and the back reappears, dorsal fin peaking the heavy black arc, its curve continuing almost in slow motion to bring the giant winged flukes above the surface and send the whale deep. In its wake, a flurry of sea lions nosing the air, looping back into the water, a slippery throng of hungry, lithe bodies on the trail of the whale's feed. Occasionally, a tall, pointed fin appears with shorter curved ones beside, a pod of orca cruising through, pushing a swath of danger in front of them and pulling it behind. All who can clear out of their way, and they move on.

Most days a flock of fish crows will join us for breakfast. A dozen or more of them congregate in an alder tree rooted on the beach and scan the rocks for any scraps we may have thrown out for them. If the scraps are fishy enough, the crows may be joined by an eagle or some gulls. Raven comes too, hulking his shoulders, hopping from branch to branch, then down to the rocks, often making off with a sizable share of the goods.

My frame of reference shifts when I have to head to town and walk the trail up the hill. I trade light and space, then, for the time-worn company of trees, centuries of wood towering around me, their high boughs creating a filigree sky. They are too tall for me to be able to crane my neck and see their tops. These are not the old-growth trees for which this rainforest is known. Woodsmen's saws and axes of the previous century left some of those as remnant stumps, now a green-russet mingling of mosses and lichens and rotting wood. They've nurtured new generations of spruce and hemlock and cedar, some old enough to be two feet in diameter, others younger, trunks solid or fluted, bark scaly black or shaggy gray-brown. They grow out of a cushiony forest floor of humus and moss. The summer carpet hosts deer heart, twisted stalk, foam flower, single delight, skunk cabbage. Above those a tangle of huckleberry and menziesia fills things in. Up close to the road, a swath cleared for powerlines is thick with bunchberry, bramble, ferns, and golden thread. Young trees are crowding their way back. Everything is damp with the hundred inches of rain that fall here in a year. Everything is green, everything is alive.

All this is familiar to me now. I've come to expect all this life. It has infused my days, wrapped itself around my imagination and my heart and steadied me. Still, I try to keep it all from becoming ordinary. I try to imagine the essences, the intrinsic qualities that shape this abundance. I can acknowledge the conditions of climate, ocean, and geology that each play a part, the role of evolutionary function, but beyond that groundwork are those ineffable measures of beauty. I get hints from particularities: a merganser's claret bill against its dark green head; the spray of white on a certain whale's flukes; a seal's ease of motion and its deep, watchful eyes; a red stem of blueberry against white snow; the breath of flight under a chickadee wing; the agility of the squirrel on its branchway through the trees; the soft green unfurling of deer heart stalks in spring; the strength of a hundred-year-old hemlock swaying violently in a storm. To live each day in the face of these is to live in the grace of Creation. To inhabit such a landscape well is to take my cues from the indigenous knowledge of the place itself, the power of limit and proportion and relationship.

These seven acres where I live are part of a contiguous forest that rims the parameters of Baranof Island. It jumps the waterways to establish itself on nearby smaller islands as well as larger ones to north and south. It continues on up the coast until massive tidal glaciers get in its way, but it jumps those, too, and settles itself around the rim of Prince William Sound and down to Kodiak Island. South of Sitka, this forest finds its way all the way down the coast of British Columbia, Washington, Oregon, and into northern California. For some two thousand miles it takes root in the land and creates a home for other living things. It is not exactly the same forest everywhere, but its variations are like kith and kin, related households that accommodate species shifts and ranges. When I venture out to other places, I find that away-from-home comfort in familiar thrush song, recognize bunchberry or wood violets like old friends. If I'm lucky, I come across the elders, the three- and four- and five-hundred-year-old cathedral trees that frame the sacredness of their place. They are both worshiped and coveted, the prized riches of this forest. If I stand beside one and stretch my arms out as wide as they'll reach, I can't begin to encircle the tree. Instead, I lean my back against it, as I do against the mountain, and look up through its branches to the sky.

All along this coast, the forest is under human pressure. An increasing population and the demands of a global marketplace are diminishing it. Its contiguous two thousand miles are checkered with shaved patches, clearcuts, some of them hundreds of acres in size. The pressure has not only pitted people against the forest, but it has pitted them against each other. It has encouraged some indigenous peoples of the Northwest Coast to betray their cultural traditions. It has created whole communities and bureaucracies based on assumptions of ownership and propriety: This forest is ours. To many people, it is not a forest, but a resource from which they expect to make a living. It is pulp, it is lumber, it is cellulose, it is paper, it is fine furniture or wooden crafts. All of these ignore what Canadian poet Pat Lowther calls "the plainness of first things." [2] *First* things. Those trees that were here. That forest, which has allowed humans to settle here. That forest, which nourishes and shelters us. It *gives* us a living. If the living we were to make from the forest were any kind of match for the one the forest gives us, it might be a very fine living indeed.

In the introduction to his book *The Good City and the Good Life*, Dan Kemmis recalls his boyhood fears about the atomic bomb. They were fears shared across a generation for whom childhood was imbued with the stark prospect that there might not be a future. Kemmis looks back now from that threatened vantage point at how this shared fear shaped the psyche of his generation. "Is it not possible," he asks of his peers, "that we have always known, in some collectively unconscious foresight, that a world so wounded, so near the mirror of its own annihilation, could only be well inhabited by developing some ways of being together which would differ radically from those forms which had created the crisis that was our world? If we did end up with a world to inhabit, to govern, to pass on, might there not have been a kind of species wisdom that would have told us, however faintly, that the task of carrying life forward could only succeed if we learned to call much more broadly on the human potential of everyone?" He goes on to consider the current political framework that shapes our culture and society—that of the nation-state—and acknowledges its dehumanizing nature and its inability to "restore our deeply severed trust in the very future of life." Looking for a better framework, Kemmis suggests, "It is the deep and varied bounty of life that we dimly but fervently seek to nurture and secure through politics, and it is by this measure that we might judge any framework within which we conduct our human affairs. If we make the abundance of life our focus, we can see that we have

Carolyn Servid

30

2. *Pat Lowther, "Coast Range," in Gary Geddes, ed.,* Skookum Wawa: Writings of the Canadian Northwest *(Toronto: Oxford University Press, 1975), 2.*

already begun to view the human situation in a framework which has everything to do with life and little or nothing to do with nationhood."[3]

Kemmis' idea startled me with its clarity. What if we took it seriously? What if we conducted our human affairs in this forest in such a way that the abundance of life was our focus? Not money in the bank or global markets first, but the abundance of life—*here*. What if we took on the task of reimagining how we inhabit this place? It might allow us to picture a future for the forest that could heal the rifts we have created between ourselves, one that might restore indigenous traditions, one that might include us as charismatic megafauna, as acknowledged integral parts of the ecosystem, made whole by the forest that surrounds us. In many places, this possibility has passed us by. We have taken down the trees and are left with a wounded world. We are faced with the ache of poet Robert Frost's question of what to make of a diminished thing. But elsewhere, the forest still stands. It gives us life. Within the power of its limits and proportions and relationships, it gives us room to imagine a new metaphor of inhabitation, a way we might balance our dominance and indebtedness, our ignorance and grace.

On a wintry November morning, I am up just as dawn brings on the day. Narrow streaks of slate blue light are framed by heavy clouds above and the dark irregularity of mountains below. The trees move slightly in a breeze that riffles the water. From a cedar just outside the house, Raven calls. He modulates his voice from a hollow, watery *kloke, kloke, kloke,* to a raw, grating *kaw*. There is in that voice the centuries-old story of this place, an image of his black form sitting in a tree at the edge of the dark wood or soaring overhead, scanning the countryside below. He spots something that triggers his curiosity, circling down, tail fanned out and flicking him into balance, wingtips curved up. He circles again, puts his legs down, arcs his wings and lowers himself to the ground. In one Northwest Coast story, it is a giant clam shell he finds with little humans inside, struggling to make their way into the world. I listen this morning to his voice move away as he flies out across the water. Today he is off to see just how we are doing.

---

3. Dan Kemmis, The Good City and the Good Life (Boston: Houghton Mifflin Co., 1995), xiv–xvi.

Todd Sherman

Silent Forest V

Acrylic on canvas

1990

UA95:057:001

AVALANCHE LILY

Peggy Shumaker

WHEN NEW SNOW won't hold on to the mountain face, won't stick to an ice field or adhere to the base pack, an unstable area becomes avalanche prone. Any disturbance, wind or voice, footstep or gunshot, can unleash a frozen tsunami, scouring down the slope, suffocating any breathing being in its way. Once three radio-collared wolves from a pack inside Denali National Park disappeared. Rangers tracked their unmoving signals to the base of a mountain remade by snowslide.

Avalanche lily—that's the shape left after an avalanche, after the snow lets go and careens in a deafening thunderhead of white down the mountainside. Avalanche lily—fluted, those sharp edges unfurled like just-opened petals.

The snowfield, contained, conceals itself until release allows the new self to be seen—the uprooted, transformed, avalanched self. The avalanche lily exists already, underneath, disguised by what it contains.

Avalanche Lily

Any disturbance, particle
or wave, footfall or

word, can loosen the cornice,
grease the slide, send crashing

breathless snow spume
thunderheads to edge

the sharp-rimmed space
no one ever saw before,

here, where restless
earth releases

at once all urges held back,
magnified, till

pure force carves
a new face

transformation mask opening
to reveal a fresh self

masked and slippery
unstable lily

cradle of absence
rocked by loss.

On a transformation mask, one face opens to reveal another, and sometimes another. These are all true selves, some revealed, some kept inside.

In one disastrous summer, eleven climbers died on Denali. One was Muggs Stump, a veteran mountaineering guide. Imagine being one of the two novices he was guiding. Moments before, they were roped to the man they'd just seen swallowed by a crevasse so deep they can't see bottom, so twisted no echo returns. I don't mourn Muggs. He died the fitting death for a man most alive on the mountain. But imagine being one of those other two, not quite so adventurous anymore, and certain about only two things: (1) they don't have the experience to make it off the mountain alone, and (2) Muggs ain't coming back.

During the breakup of the Soviet Union, Joe Enzweiler built a serpentine wooden walkway to his outhouse, which has no walls. It does have a roof, to keep snow off the styrofoam seat and off the patron of the moment. Joe named his walkway the Perestroika Bridge to Tomorrow. I walk it at Goatfest, a quarterly celebration, one of the galas for each change of season. In September, it's the Saws of Autumn. *Bring your own chain saw*, the invitation reads. *If you do not own a chain saw, one will be provided for you*. We take a group photo. Joe's holding Lefty, his Stihl with a thirty-two-inch bar. My saw's named Cash Up Front, because I once made the mistake of telling Joe I'm a cash-up-front kind of woman, and he's never let me forget it. One year we pose with scythes instead, as grim a pack of reapers as you're likely to see cavorting on a hand-hewn cabin porch.

After twenty years in Interior Alaska, Joe has driven his ancient Toyota pickup to Kentucky to find a "hot tomato." After all, he can't spend his whole life flirting with the bee-hived waitresses at June's Café, who bring him, before he even asks, a chili burger, extra onions, gravy on the fries.

Breakfast at the Old F. E. Company was worth the drive to Chatanika. We'd recruit a whole crew, a dozen or more, and head out past Fox, past the Poker Flat Rocket Range, on the road you'd take to Arctic Circle Hot Springs if you were headed that far. About thirty-five miles out, set amid rusting behemoths of antique mining equipment, the corrugated metal siding of the mining camp buildings poked out of the snow. The cookhouse once fed three thousand miners a day, when Chatanika was a going concern. Up to ten thousand souls camped in this valley, while they tried to scratch out a living till they hit the mother lode. Running sluice boxes with snow melt, or operating dredges days after breakup, the old timers knew about cold deep in their bones. Their rough-died tools and oiled broad saws hung around the unplumb walls of the dining hall. For years a round, grumpy woman and her bearded husband who stayed in the back and cooked put on the best spread next to an elder's potlatch. Any given weekend, they'd haul out platters of sourdough pancakes, reindeer sausage, gravy, hot biscuits with Alaskan blueberry jam, eggs to order, thick homemade- bread French toast, fruit compote, hash, salsa, fritters still sizzling. Outside a red shoat waited none too patiently for handouts.

Japanese investors saw potential for an aurora-viewing paradise, way beyond town lights, perfect. They invested upwards of $750,000 and built a string of modern cedar cabins and a glass-walled "Aurorium." Before long, locals were offering Japanese tourists dogsled rides, snowmachine rentals, guided cross-country ski loops, and, most popular of all, the chance to shoot a gun—a dollar a bullet.

The round woman and her silent husband had neglected, though, to pay off the lien on the property. They owed a pittance but fell behind, and the former owners foreclosed and won. And won again, on appeal. So somebody, I'm not claiming to know who, dismantled the pretty cedar cabins in the woods, trucked away every beam and pane of the aurora-viewing center, and took every object on the place that could be lifted by four guys onto a flatbed. We're talking about the old tools and oiled broad saws, of course. Also the doors to the rooms in the bunkhouse, the pig's watering trough, the pig, the light fixtures.

The new/old management still holds outhouse races once a year, but it's not the same. My favorite contender was a slow plywood privy set on wide skis, with hot-rod flames licking up both sides and over the roof. It's not there any more.

One of the few objects handed down to me when my mother died is a small, rectangular locket engraved with a spray of wildflowers. Might be gold, might be plate, I don't care. It was hers. In her high school graduation portrait, it rests in the hollow between her new breasts, nestled in folds of angora. Inside, a miniature photo of her, very young, her smile wide as the Milky Way. On the other side, all sleek muscles and slicked-back Wildroot hair, grins a boy, a young man barely, cocky and sure he's good-looking, so why not cut his eyes at the camera, why not lean back on two legs of his chair? The sun's out, he's got gas money and a pretty girl, surf's up, man.

During the long fifteen years of their marriage, my parents yelled at each other, didn't even agree on a topic, just yelled in general. I took solace in the knowledge of that young man, imagined he was my real dad, lost to war or adventure, his presence there next to her heart a repudiation, male and sexy, of every reproach my father could throw at her. The self she carried in that locket grinned, eternally joyous, sassy as a skirt of giant kelp, stinging bare midriff and thighs, salty as her first good kiss, not shared with my father. Nobody recalls that boy's name now— not my grandmother, not my mother's high school friends, not Uncle Harry.

And my father—what did he carry, man with no amulet to protect him, and the heavy freight of his Nazarene father always on his shoulders? Pressed down on his knees in surrender to a god he never really met, my father shook off his father's oppressively zealous palm and knelt between the knees of any willing female. "Never pass up a chance at pussy," he told Harry, who knew even at thirteen there was something basically wrong with that advice. He wasn't sure what, though, because all the other guys were laughing and nodding, blowing smoke rings and French inhaling. He was the youngest one there and counted himself lucky to be allowed to tag along. So, Harry told me, he swallowed the hard knot in his throat and made himself think about motorcycles, baseball, ham, pistachios, anything but how his sister's, my mother's, face would look when she found out whom she'd married.

Along one wall in the hallway of the elementary school on Unalaska, children have put together a town. In this town they construct stories, building in all they know and what they feel about the forced evacuation of the Aleuts during World War II. One commander, following orders, gave families only twenty minutes to get on the boat. He felt terrible when people evacuated from other islands on the chain showed up with most of their household goods. Some of the people from Unalaska did not even have bedcovers. Behind one door a little girl has scrawled carefully, "My grandma doesn't want to talk about it, ever. She said not to ask her again."

We round the corner, and high up, over our heads, a cormorant spreads wide its wings. In "Volcano Woman," the Aleut carver John Hoover has retold the story

John Hoover

Salmon Woman

Wood, brass, paint

1979

UA82-3-32

of how the Aleutians got populated. Each of the Aleutian Islands rose from the sea, pushed up by volcanic forces from below the waters. From one volcano a beautiful woman emerged. A flock of cormorants witnessed this amazing apparition. The cormorants changed into human form, made babies with the volcano woman, and shape-shifted back into birds. They flew around and put babies all over the islands. Hoover says, with a little laugh, "I'm not sure how the Aleuts feel about having cormorants for grandparents. But that's the story."

Hoover's carving combines grace and endurance, plus spectacular mythic unpredictability. His whole life, Hoover has been both a fisherman and an artist. After thirty years of painting, he moved to carving, then to sculpture. His calling card now is the triptych, modeled after Russian Orthodox traveling icons with wings that fold in to protect the Madonna. His works, though, hinge on images from very old stories combined with the fresh combinations and ideas in his contemporary imagination.

After the war John Hoover captained one of the boats that brought people back to the islands. He ran a power barge in the harbor craft detachment and delivered one hundred tons of coal so the people on the Pribilofs would have something to burn when they got home. Many of their homes had been burned down already by U.S. forces determined that the Japanese would not take comfort there.

When the Native people arrived back in the Pribilofs, nobody had killed any seals for five or six years. "There were thousands and thousands," Hoover said. "They had to clean house." He stayed for the killing and ate some of the good food it provided. "Got to know a lot of nice people," Hoover said.

In Dutch Harbor I wake at sunrise to the yapping of a neighborhood dog deviling three eagles come to fish the stream out back. They tolerate him as if he were a slow-witted cousin.

In the crevices on the hillside, tiny orchids grow in summer.

We stop by the waterfront house of Gert Svarny, the Aleut carver who began making art in her fifties and now, in her sixties, has more commissions than she can handle. Her grandchildren are preparing for Russian Christmas and take great joy in telling us who'll sing what and which treats to expect at which house. Gert's carvings show storytellers and dancers, people braiding hair and preparing food. I wonder aloud how many carvers represent Aleut daily life in their work. Firmly, Gert says, "*I* do."

Without much comprehension of the ritual, cultural, and religious implications of such a prohibition, wildlife officials outlawed the use of many feathers in artworks. Eagle, raven, loon, and several others are off limits. One of Gert's carvings shows a dancer in full regalia. It's titled "Give Us Back Our Feathers."

When I get back to the bank manager's overheated house where I'm a guest, I'm giddy, filled with wide arcs and swooping-down talons of eagles in falling snow. My host, unimpressed, tells me, "To us, they're big pigeons. Make a mess everywhere you go."

How often we turn away from what's in front of us every day.

In his hillside cabin on Unalaska, Jerah Chadwick keeps Persian rugs rolled up in the loft. There's not enough floor space, and anyway, who'd want to track up the intricate patterns tied by tiny fingers halfway around the world? From every wall, on every horizontal surface, goddesses watch over us—opulent, fleshy fertility goddesses, the Virgin of Tlatilco and bawdy, ferocious Sheila Na Gig. The goddesses watch as Jerah rolls out each rich rug, stories interwoven generation by generation, stories of suffering and blindness, stories of patterns handed down within families, stories of colors that carry songs of survival, songs of protest in their boldness. Under inhumane duress, the human spirit not obliterated makes beauty.

Four inches of fresh powder disguise the snow pack. I back out of the lane, gun the engine for a running start up the big hill, crest it, then coast around the corner to Old Nenana Highway. I'm on my way to a potter friend's art show. This potter pushes things into wet clay—seashells, bolts, wood chips, nubbly cloth. The spirit of each vessel reveals itself (as this potter does) via geography. I'm thinking how I'll want to touch each piece and how that's not allowed, thinking, too, about six priests mutilated and shot—six Jesuits, their housekeeper, and the house-keeper's daughter, cut and beaten and burned. With each broken tooth, their captors, their neighbors, their brothers tried to make them something else, some-thing not human, certainly. They cried out when they had to, they sweat, pissed, prayed, bled. The attorney general of El Salvador blames the archbishop and the other bishops. He warns them to go far away. They know there is nowhere far enough away.

I take a slick curve too quickly—the Honda swivels like the seat on a barstool. I tap the brake and break contact, skiing a grand slalom with no poles. Turn into the skid—the trees rush up. Turn away—the rear end whips around in front of the front, backwards downhill too fast to the edge—snag the berm, skid turn, stop. That fast. My lungs lunge for air.

The car is pointed uphill, planted rear-end first in a deep bank of snow. My mit-tens uncurl from the wheel. Lifting on one elbow, I can check out the angle—I think the front wheels are still on the road. All my weight against the door jams it open. I step out and sink waist deep in soft snow. I dig myself out and start the walk home, snow melting in my boots and clothes. The impression I've left will warn others. I know that I'll warm up soon and stop shaking, that I'll get help to dig out, that there's no harm done.

I wonder as my fingers sting, wet and stiff as I walk home, how the soldiers live. How do they imagine they can destroy other people without disappearing them-selves? How do they think they can press hot metal into human flesh and not sear their own souls beyond recognition? My government sends fabulous wealth to El Salvador every day to make sure this can happen. They want the whole place to settle down and get back to business.

A clutch of ravens gathered over a fresh kill at the roadside clatters into the trees as I draw close. Their tracks write a story I want to know how to read. The entrails of the red squirrel, steaming and glossy, spangle the snow. The ravens watch as I pass by, chilled, hunched into my garage-sale coat, then flap back down. They brace themselves to rip off bits of meat small enough to swallow. They swallow the flesh, the blood, their communion simple, well suited to their species.

In deep winter I expect ravens and redpolls, chickadees and jays. But this morning, without warning, in fly two sturdy woodpeckers, wintering over.

The hairy woodpeckers batter rapid tattoos on the heaped remains of a turkey carcass boiled already for broth. They rap hard even when their meal isn't concealed under birch bark. Red slashes mark the backs of their heads. Their fronts look ashen in winter, but their white backs blend with bark and snow, and their spotted wings resemble patches of lichens and broken growth spots on the paper birch. Morse code now, messages I wish I could decipher.

The woodpeckers breakfast alongside chickadees, black-capped and boreal, who nest as they do in the hollowed heartwoods of the old stand of alders down the hill. The woodpeckers ward off a squirrel with high-pitched squeaks of a child's cheap squeeze toy. As soon as they take off, Canada jays take over, looking burly with their down puffed against the air's still minus thirty.

Snow. Barely any this year. So it's a thrill to watch it, snow so light you have to look twice to be sure it really is snow taking its time drifting down out of the sky. So quiet. Quiet until I walk out, that is. This is the time of year that every footstep crunches and creaks. Remember how it feels to test first before committing your whole weight, even when you have on your boots with the best traction? You try for something solid under this new cover, try for the layer that lets you hold fast and push off without whoop-bam, flat on your back, take a good look at the stars.

The air's so crisp breath freezes onto the little hairs in your nose so when you come in the house you have to find a tissue quick even before your glasses uncloud. Everybody automatically takes off boots at the door so nobody has to mop up puddles of melted snow. Then you get to see who cares if his socks match and whose toes have poked through her warm wool raggs. It's solstice. We're gaining light every day.

They say that panes of freshwater ice let light into early arctic dwellings.

The light changes every day. So the way we see the world changes, too.

Henry Wood Elliott
Seal Drive Crossing
Watercolor
1872
UA482-2

When the barn gates open, light floods the dank arena. Astride the prancing white Andalusian Orion, the bride holds her head regally high. Orion cross-steps around the ring, brilliant, little purple asters braided into his mane and tail. Swathed in fur, the bride has carrots woven into her bouquet, carrots we unwire after the marriage kiss and feed to the horses. In this solstice season, the groom pledges to his new wife to share the depths of his soul forever. The bride also does some pretty fancy talking about love everlasting. I'm on Perfect Note, a tall first-level dressage sorrel the stable kids have obligingly saddled western. When the couple exchanges rings and kisses, the congregation breaks into mad applause. Ten horses rear and skitter, dodging anything big enough to make a noise like that. I hold on. I hold on, realizing that I could not with a straight face claim much of anything forever. Love for my grandmother, sure, easy, as long as I live. What part of forever is that? Just the glimpse one life allows. My toes are little blue nuggets of ice.

On the way home from the reception, full of grape leaves and sushi, Gruyere-with-pistachios and spanakopita, all prepared with love by the couple's friends, I give a ride to the three kids who live at the stables. Jackie, the oldest, says she'd like to be a vet tech. Lizzy, the little one, says, "You'll have to dissect a horse, then."

"I've already done that, almost, on Sammy," Jackie claims. Lizzy shuts up, quick. Sammy was her pony, who suffered colic, then a twisted intestine, then an obstruction so massive her bowel burst. The kids report this like business news—they're serious but not worried. Lizzy tells me she keeps bunnies now in Sammy's stall, because "outside they'd freeze to death."

At sunrise, these girls take all the horses, shaggy in their winter coats, outside to their paddocks. After dark, they bring them back in. Near winter solstice they barely have time to throw sawdust on the pee spots and to rake in clean straw where they've shoveled out fresh horse biscuits.

Near summer solstice the light will spend the night. We talk of a camp-out trail ride for one of those nights when the light will stretch into what we call tomorrow. We'll ride away after our daily chores to sleep outside under the midnight sun. Around the fire each story we tell will shed light on some facet of self, selves we claim, ones we're aiming for, selves we're trying on, those we don't yet suspect or admit. We'll cook over that fire and tell stories till we can't laugh any more, tell stories till we can't keep our eyes open.

The light changes. Every day. So the way we see the world changes too.

James H. Barker

Storm Crossing the Board Walk

Gelatin silver photograph

1976

UAP90:015:001

RAIN, DRIZZLE, FOG CONTINUING . . .

Leslie Leyland
Fields

"... *THROUGH THURSDAY*, through Friday, and the outlook for the weekend, more of the same," the reporter announced in professionally modulated tones, not giving away frustration or boredom or despair. I felt all of those, despite my tenure in Kodiak and my well-practiced, sharply honed laissez-faire. The fog had already grounded "my" plane that morning. It was "my" plane because it was "my turn" to get off the Rock, as Kodiak is affectionately termed by those who have lived here too long. Just a simple flight to Anchorage for a long weekend had marvelous, restorative powers, but the fog . . .

The fog was driving us all mad. On Kodiak Island we know about rain. Our vocabulary for "snow" is limited, but we can name two dozen different drizzles, speak a thesaurus of terms for all the many precipitations. But this fog, this obliterating, suffocating fog that had already devoured our spring and summer was something new in its persistence and ferocity. It was some kind of giant Alaskan subspecies, grown huge on the doughnut of currents and meteorological forces that continually spin the Gulf of Alaska into our laps. Those same forces should have blasted it straight out again, kept it moving, but it parked, took up residence, applied for citizenship. We drove with headlights on in the middle of the longest, lightest days of the year. Planes sat. Boats motored tentatively. We forgot why we lived here.

This fall day promised nothing different. Then a sprite of a wind kicked up, a good thirty-knot northeast. Everything quickened, hope most of all. The stands of spruce began swaying like a herd of furred beasts, the ocean frothed and spit, the beach sizzled, grass quaked, everything mirrored life and response. I was packed and ready to go, but even more, I was ready to see the harbor again, the mountains, to see color, the world intact and shining, to remember just as I was leaving why I lived here.

But the fog did not move. It did not lift; it did not disperse; it sat, inert, passive as a fortress the entire afternoon while the wind puffed and blustered impotently through it. I did not make it out that day, or the next.

I've never counted all the flights I've missed in and out of Kodiak because of weather, the days stranded in airports, how many trips canceled. If I did, I would arrive at some kind of cumulative total as a shorthand code for part of what it means to live here. And if I did, the number could be seen as a negative integer, "trips lost, days gone," counting me backwards to the left of zero.

But I don't want to know that number, and I will not tell it. Because this is not about loss, as though something that belonged to me, to us, is taken away. We only imagine that we control our lives. Instead I will tell of the weather's mark upon my life, the life of my family through these few stories. As the clouds shift, winds arrange and rearrange the skies for the next blow. We, too ready to turn, flex, resist, shift yet again . . .

The terminal, a long grey hall with pinball machines at the far end, was almost empty when we arrived. We were late because of the weather report we had heard, but the plane wouldn't leave without us since we were its only passengers that morning. There were six of us, constituting a full flight for the Piper Cherokee we were chartering. The pilot watched as we stumbled into the hall with boxes and bulging black garbage bags for luggage. Of the six, three were children, the youngest just turned two, the oldest six. Myself, my husband Duncan, and our longtime friend Ron finished the group.

The pilot looked at us questioningly. We knew him from years in a small town, from countless flights before.

"You're going out to Larsen Bay this morning?" he asked, puzzled.

"Yeah, we're going to fishcamp for the week," Duncan answered. "The weather's good now, but have you heard the forecast?"

"We heard yesterday it's supposed to blow southeast sixty."

"How about southeast eighty to a hundred?" the pilot said with a subtle lift of his eyebrows. For a bush pilot, it was the equivalent of wild gesticulations.

This was news. I raised my eyebrows too. Although, as I thought about it, how much worse is eighty- or ninety-mile-an-hour wind than sixty?

"Why are you going out there this time of year?" he asked, looking at the children.

"For spring break," I replied as blithely as possible, trying to sound like a happy vacationer. The careful listener would have heard a hint of sarcasm.

It had not been my idea. Our island, on the west side of Kodiak Island, eighty miles from town, was remote, uninhabited, accessible only by water or plane, and was the site of a grueling four-month marathon named euphemistically the "commercial salmon season." To spend spring break at fishcamp sounded to me like coal miners picnicking down in the shafts. One friend was going to Greece for spring break. Other years we had gone to Hawaii, to Florida, to Mexico.

There were other reasons for my hesitancy, though. I could list four right off the top, and did, as the subject came up between December and March. They had names and also very young ages: Naphtali, Noah, Isaac, and the last we were still waiting on—three months to go. It wasn't the ideal pregnant vacation. Gradually, though, I began to see the sense of it. This time we would go and just play, and maybe when we got tired of that, work on the many projects we never got to in the summer. High on my list was a plumbing system and running water. That alone sold me the trip.

But now, eighty to a hundred? Kodiak sees blows like that at least once a year, but we don't usually plan a vacation around them. Still, the weather was clear and calm as we stood there. It was cold, about eight degrees, but the winds either were still traveling or they had veered off elsewhere.

Duncan and I looked at each other, calculating. The flight was only thirty-five minutes. We would be there within the hour. Once there, in the village, we had to find and then launch our skiff, then make the final leg—a thirty-minute skiff ride out to the island. If all went well, we could be at the island in three hours.

"What do you think?" Duncan broke the silence, addressing the pilot. "We can beat it if we leave this morning, don't you think? It won't hit until later today."

"Yeah, if we go right now we'll probably beat it," he agreed.

By the time we landed in Larsen Bay, the wind had begun, a biting, insistent breeze that promised more. An hour and a half later, the skiff had been found and launched and we were on our way. The breeze was now a genuine "blow," registering a solid thirty miles per hour. At eight degrees, with our forward motion plus a thirty-knot wind in our faces, I didn't need a wind chill chart to know it was cold. We all wore almost our entire closet of winter clothing. Still the wind sent us under a tarp, huddled together, backs walled against the gale. Isaac, the two-year-old, sat on my knees. Noah pressed against my side, my other arm cinched around him for comfort and warmth. The oldest sandwiched herself between Noah and Ron. Duncan ran the skiff, standing upright in the stem to see over the high bow.

The trip was longer than usual. Halfway through, feeling less embattled, I poked my head from the tarp and caught my breath—the wind was tearing the top of the waves off, the spume spilling out so white, so blindingly white, and the sun, a vacation sun. There was no warmth in it, only an icy brightness, but it lit the work of the wind, igniting colors. . . . And later as we rounded the last cape, we saw whales spouting. The tempest seemed for that moment only a unanimous frolic.

The wind steadily increased the rest of the day. We were on solid ground by then, safe on our island, but we were not warm. The house was five degrees inside. With every heat source flaming—the wood stove, all burners of the propane gas stove, the propane heater, the oil stove—it took twelve hours to warm just the front room to fifty degrees. We had built the house, Duncan and I, six winters before and prided ourselves on how tight it was—the insulation, the thick walls, the Anderson windows. But that day and the next two the walls felt like cheesecloth. The wind hissed through the window moldings, wailed through the door-jambs, devouring our heat as fast as we could make it.

Shelley Schneider

Ocean Wave #1

Cibachrome

1985

UAP86:018:001

We didn't sleep much that night, the kids piled up on one bed, the adults on couches in the one warm room. The stovepipe to the woodstove, rising twelve feet above us, cranked and shimmied with every blast of wind, threatening rupture and fire at every moment. The nearest person was eight miles away by water. Not that it mattered. Were we only half a mile from a neighbor, no one could move. All the world was paralyzed, pinned to the ground.

By morning, we guessed the wind to be near the hundred mark, the wind chill about seventy below. The vista out our front windows was unrecognizable. The distinctive colors of browns, whites, blues, and grays had blurred into a single color: the color of wind, a streaked white erasing all boundaries among elements—water, sky, clouds, mountains, air, house—all dissolved into howl and smoke, moan and scream.

For three days we read, recited Mother Goose with the kids, nursed and voodooed our heat sources, and, most of all, hunched in front of the windows, watching. We saw our own insignificance and saw too the equal force of mercy.

The morning of the fourth day we woke to silence. It was over. We walked outside, not ready yet to repair the damage, but just to breathe air that was still. We were exhausted, and somehow, too, the air felt limp, depleted. The winds as they swept over our island had taken something with them.

We didn't get much done those next days before we packed up and headed back to town. A little work—some siding put up, a drain for a future bathroom sink, a room rearranged for the new baby. We hiked to the top of the mountain, scouted the beaches for firewood in the skiff. It almost didn't matter what we did. The real event had happened already. Somehow we knew without saying it that nothing else mattered. We were alive, we were together, and whatever the storm had taken from us, it gave all of that back.

Four months later, July, all of us stood again in the same terminal facing the same decision. This time it was fog. And this time there was one more in our family—the new baby, now ten days old. The fog was lifting—the plane would go, and on it Duncan and the three older children to return to fishcamp. The salmon season was in full swing and his brothers, already overworked, were working harder to fill his absence. I would stay in town for another week or two with the new baby and then join them.

Ten minutes later they were gone. I hugged and kissed them off into the Caravan, with my husband now Father Hen over seating arrangements, seat belts, when and how much gum was apportioned. I stood and watched first the fog, then the plane rising into it, the splayed wings and wheels, though so small and vulnerable, the only solid object in a hazy dream. Too soon they disappeared through a tunnel.

This fog was patchy, alternately thick and then gauzy, not the solid, definitive stuff that sent airline employees home, that even silenced the phones usually ringing with questions, uncertainty—"Are you flying today?" Today's fog was the ambiguous kind—maybe yes, maybe no. Maybe, maybe. Maybe they'll get to Larsen Bay, eighty miles away over mountain peaks; maybe they'll get as far as Port Bailey and have to turn around. Maybe they'll fly the usual route, or if the clouds are too low they'll fly the shoreline for forty-five more minutes. Everything hangs on the moment, the lift of wind and wing the minute they enter the crucial passes. Everything hangs on the pilot, how long he's been here, how tired he is, the map in his head.

My first trip out to fishcamp this season, just three weeks earlier, before the baby was born, had been just as uncertain. I didn't make it out the first day—fog. All flights had been canceled. The next day, when I got there at 8:30 A.M., the fog was more than halfway down Barometer Mountain, our literal barometer for gauging the likelihood of flight. We were on "weather hold" again. This time, compelled by hope, I waited at the terminal instead of going straight home— maybe the fog would lift.

Three hours later the pilot appeared, faced the five of us who were determined to get to the other side of the island for various reasons, and said, "We'll give it a try," with an offhand wave of his hand. "We'll go up and look around. We may turn right around in five minutes. We'll just see." We were locals, we understood. No commitment, no promise of anything: maybe. Maybe we would get through. Maybe anything. We had to think it, all of us, each of us, anyone who flies regularly in Alaska, and especially Kodiak. You do not have to live here long before

Rain. Drizzle.

Fog Continuing . . .

53

you know someone who dies in a plane crash. If you have lived here any length of time, you can tick off pilots and friends, using up all the fingers and rounding them again.

We made it that day in a single try. It was not our usual route. The fog pressed us low to the ground; some passes were inscrutable, the clouds like veils alternately revealing and concealing. But the pilot nosed his way through, picking and choosing, rising, dodging, until finally the village emerged through a rend in the cloak. As we circled to land, I could see below, near the gravel runway, three tiny figures in raingear, faces to the sky. A maybe flight that ended in yes. Not the kind of loud, two-fisted yes.that exultantly yanks air to your sides: this a yes that you breathe, a prayer.

Two weeks later a flight over the same route ended no. It was fog, again. The pilot successftilly maneuvered his three passengers across the treacherous interior of the island. Five miles from the airport, through the last pass, where on a clear day you could see the runway, the wingtip hit ground. Someone planted four crosses there, on a burnt piece of ground just two hundred feet from the road.

No one asks, Why was the plane so low?

A few springs ago my mother made her first to visit to Kodiak. She flew up from Florida for a month-long stay and arrived just at the start of the spring rain. That year happened to be one of the worst on record: fifty-five days literally without sun; fifty-five days of rain nearly every daylight hour. After twenty-some days, even the local paper began keeping track. Worse, the house we were renting was tucked behind a hill higher than the sun's hypothetical arc. Mold grew on the windows; in the middle of the day we needed every light bulb blazing.

Why do I live here? she wanted to know.

I had explained the meteorological facts already: the Japanese current, the warm, wet air stream that clots our skies with clouds and persistent rain; that we really have only two seasons—the wet season and the rainy season; that we average only thirty clear days a year. All this she believed.

How do I tell her the rest, that gratitude can be found anywhere, that every geography erects a scale of gains and losses? It could be so much harder: fifty below in Fairbanks, seven-month winters in Anchorage, double our rainfall in Ketchikan, ten feet of snow in Whittier . . .

But what about Florida or California, or the Southwest? she asked.

I tried to explain. There is virtue here, discipline, perseverance. To have any kind of weather we want, to have sun every day, denies our essential helplessness, our lack of control over forces beyond us. There is a principle of scarcity at work, and as simple and as clichéd as it is, it does work. Because I live here, I love the sun.

There is consistency here as well. The climate I live in corresponds to the other choices I make for my life, in areas where I have almost complete control. I could eat Häagen Dazs chocolate chip cookie dough ice cream for breakfast every morning if I wanted to. I could drink double tall hazelnut lattes all day. I could take a bubble bath every night, subscribe to thirty magazines, buy all my clothes brand new, but I choose to do none of these.

My mother is unconvinced. Thirty days into the siege, she left, relieved. I am sure her Florida sun shone more brightly that next month—at least at first.

I know about clouds, wind, and fog, too, by their absence. Ten years ago I crossed the Sahara Desert in a truck along with twenty-two others. It was part of a four-month trip that took us from Egypt down into the heart of the rain forest, then straight east through to the coast of Kenya. For the four weeks it took us to plunge and grind our way across that empty expanse, we never saw a cloud, not a single one, not a wisp of fog, not a spit of rain. Description of the desert crossing is simply a catalog of dearth. No roads, only telegraph lines. No villages or people, no vegetation, no animals, no food, almost no water, no landscape, and no weather. It is easier to list what we did see—sun sand sky, the sun like a great fire breathing on our heads, the ground a copper coin, and everything else a neutral blue expanse. Never did the formula vary: sun sand sky. Each night we pitched our tents in the cool dark and woke the next morning knowing the texture of the day to follow—sun sand . . .

It should have been heaven, and all the more so because it was January. Back home I knew a maelstrom of gales, squalls, snowstorms, hail, and winter rain

Gail Niebrugge

Perkins' Paradise

Acrylic on canvas

1983

UA85-3-2

hovered, descended, attacked. Snow tires had to be mounted, windows taped. It was the season of black ice, frozen pipes, nights that bled too far into day . . . but there, just the steady bake of sun into bones.

We took some minor precautions that first week—wearing sunblock, hats, sitting under the roof of the truck. But the sunblock tubes were soon squished empty; we lost our hats and then sat carelessly on the roof of the truck as we drove. No shade either for our canteens; the water boiled; we were constantly thirsty; the wells marked on our maps were mostly dry. Ten days in we were on rationing. We never ran out of drinking water, but our evening dole of bathwater evaporated to a liter, then half a liter, then a single cup for all our washings: teeth, clothes, hair, bodies, faces, all lacquered in dirt from twelve hours of dust and sand, merely got swiped at with a damp rag each night in the privacy of our tents. And we were thankful for it.

But it wasn't this that wore me out. It was the blankness of it all. Without the dozen different kinds of damp and rain, without fog, without clouds or wind, it felt a kind of blindness. There was nothing to quantify or measure, and worse yet, nothing to name, nothing to which language could be assigned. Most, I missed the clouds and learned this: Clouds map the sky, give us words, perspective, dimensions. They are both the script and the passion that fills it. Without them, the book has no text, the universe is inscrutable. Without them, without a sense of weather, time counts for nothing, the sky is dead.

■ ■ ■

Rain, Drizzle,

Fog Continuing . . .

Robert Swain Gifford

Icy Bay, Alaska

Oil on canvas

1899

UA81-3-116

THE ISLAND'S CHILD

Richard Nelson

THE PEAK OF KLUKSA MOUNTAIN, brightly corniced with last winter's snow, probes up through a bank of fog so thick it looks like an avalanche rolling across Haida Strait. I stop the boat before reaching it, carefully set a compass on the seat, take my bearings, check my watch, and head on again. Within a few minutes I've sliced into the vaporous wall that stretches away in either direction. Beads of moisture prickle against my cheeks and lips. The boat seems suspended in a pool of gray water, closely surrounded by nothingness.

At first the intensity of the fog is exciting. But then anxious thoughts creep into my mind. Claustrophobia. A complete absence of direction. The possibility of running into a log or another boat. I slow the engine and watch the compass, telling myself to trust the needle but wondering why I didn't wait for the fog to burn away. With every landmark gone, even the most stable elements of the world seem unreliable, as if the island might drift off and let me wander out into the Pacific. For once, I wish there was a breeze. When I hunted walrus with the Eskimos, they told of finding their way through Arctic Ocean fogs by holding a constant angle to the wind. What they feared most was a calm. Luckily I have the compass, but a steady wind would seem more reliable than this little trinket, more like an elder guiding me toward my destination.

I also remember the Eskimos' advice that a fogbound hunter should never aim straight toward his destination but to one side of it, so he knows which way to turn when he finds land. With this in mind, I bear left to make sure I'll reach the island above Tsandaku Point. From there I can work along the shore and cross the narrow passage to Kanaashi Island. Trying to head directly for the pinpoint of Kanaashi would be foolish under these circumstances.

An unusual number of fork-tailed storm-petrels haunts the waters of Haida Strait, perhaps because a recent gale pushed them from their offshore feeding grounds. They look like miniature gulls, dove-sized, pearly gray, with geometric patterns in their wings. Most of them sit on the water until the boat comes within a few yards, then lift up as if it's startled them awake. Wonderfully light and dainty, they loop back and forth in a fluttering air dance, delicate moth wings almost touching the easy swells. A few dart close to the stem, apparently curious, watching with dark, sad eyes. They seem to fly in a daydream, visitors from a fairy world, too pure and innocent to be real.

The birds make me feel less alone, less anxious about groping deeper into the fog. They also seem like a good omen, as if they're escorting me to Kanaashi Island. Watching a petrel weave into the mist, I feel a twinge of excitement about the night ahead. If I can ever find my way . . .

Sometime later I check my watch and realize I should already have reached the shore. An empty circle of water closes around the boat. I wish for the security of Shungnak's company, but it seemed inappropriate to take a dog into Kanaashi's nesting bird colonies. I imagine myself far off course, riding into the trackless sea. I wish I could laugh about my dilemma, the way Eskimos sometimes do when they make mistakes or find themselves in trying circumstances. But at the moment I feel more like a fool kid than an Eskimo.

When I'm about to shut down the engine and wait for the fog to lift, three dark blotches appear in the haze. Tufted puffins. This means I've gone off course, missed the island's shore and run past Tsandaku Point; but it could also be a sign that my destination is somewhere close. I peer ahead, idling slowly, listening for the slosh of surf on rock. Soon afterward the fog darkens. Then a gray wall rises from the water thirty yards ahead. "Kanaashi!" I announce the name in disbelief, realizing how lucky I was to intersect this pinpoint of land with an empty expanse of ocean beyond.

I ran the boat slowly along the quarter-mile of Kanaashi's outer shore, savoring my little adventure and forgetting the errors that caused it. Perched on the steep palisades are hundreds of herring gulls, clucking and moaning, adding to the beauty of a lost, misty island. Swells ride up against the vertical rocks, rising to the height of their crests and sucking down to the depths of their troughs, making dozens of miniature cascades. Even with these lazy seas, the nearby waters are scrambled with backwash and colliding waves. Ironically, a breeze begins wafting the fog away, shredding it to patches that writhe against the slopes, gradually unveiling the whole length of the island.

The waters around Kanaashi are strewn with flocks of tufted puffins. Squadrons of them flap across the surface ahead of the boat, struggling to get aloft. Their chunky bodies are hardly aerodynamic and their short wings are compromised by the need to serve as flippers. Some sputter along for a hundred yards before they finally become airborne, then circle back for a closer look. I wonder if they do this out of simple curiosity or if there is annoyance in those expressionless faces. A few have apparently eaten so much they can't get free of the water even after long takeoff runs. Finally they stop and watch nervously as the skiff approaches, turn their multicolored parrot-beaks this way and that, then flip their tails skyward and dive to safety.

At its outermost end, Kanaashi Island is a massive sculpture of deeply gouged cliffs, pinnacles, and buttresses, shouldering against the sea. Grassy overhangs along the top edge are densely populated with tufted puffins, who launch out by the hundreds from their burrow entrances. Beneath them, cormorants roost on a sea stack, indigo feathers shimmering in the hazy sun. They twist their sinuous necks and lift their tails to eject milky excrement as I pass. Farther on, the precipice bulges over a keyhole-shaped grotto about eighty feet high and fifty feet wide, with an elegant natural arch suspended between the walls. Every ledge and protrusion is jammed with common and thick-billed murres, perhaps a thousand in all. Some are apparently brooding eggs, and the others are either mates standing by or younger birds roosting with the multitude. The atmosphere is decidedly urban, the smell definitely organic.

Murres could be considered the northern hemisphere's equivalent of penguins (which are only found on and south of the equator). They're the size of small ducks, erect-postured, with black backs and snow-white bellies; but unlike penguins, they use their wings to fly above the water as well as beneath it. They fill the grotto with a bedlam of raspy, staccato voices that sound like mad laughter. When I bring the skiff close they begin taking flight, but instead of bursting from the rock all at once, they stream out in an orderly formation, as if each one jumps a split second after the other. The mass of birds plunges down in an elegant inverted arc, levels off, and sweeps over my head, surrounding me with a shower of wings. Staring into them, I feel like a space traveler hurtling through a swarm of asteroids.

The murres wheel out over the sea in strings and skeins, then circle back past the cliff and away again, making a huge, spinning necklace of birds. Eventually, some pass closer to the grotto, then peel off from the rest and flutter up to their roosts. But most stay with the circling flock until I ease away.

On the lee side of the island, I unload my camping gear in a tiny rockbound cove, then fasten the skiff to the kelp offshore and paddle the catamaran punt back in. This done, I carry the gear to a narrow ravine with a patch of level ground for the tent, protected from wind yet open enough for midday sun. A little stream seeps off the slope, but the water is full of green slime and has a smell to match. Kanaashi is so permeated with bird droppings that I wouldn't consider drinking any of its water. The supply I've brought from home can be replenished by collecting rain or refilling from a Kluksa Mountain stream just across the passage.

After setting up the tent, I walk out to have a look around. A brief but auspicious sunbreak glitters on the blue water between Kanaashi Island and Tsandaku Point. It's odd to think of myself groping through the fog such a short while ago, where now everything looks bright and inviting. I trace the far shore with binoculars—the familiar coves and beaches, the forested mass of Kluksa Mountain, the sweep of land that sinks down beneath the passage and rises again to shape this monolith of basalt. Although a stretch of water lies between, Kanaashi is a part of the island, born from one of its ancient eruptions. Several islets that hug the distant shore are like sisters to Kanaashi, made from the same rocks, chilled and split against the same seas.

But in some ways Kanaashi is a very different place, an isolated, cliffbound fortress surrounded by a moat of perpetually thrashing swells. Steep and solitary, with feed-rich waters all around, it supports an incredible abundance of bird life. During the summer nesting months its estimated population is over half a million seabirds. The air around this nucleus of rock is constantly awhirl with wings. Few places I've seen burn so intensely with the heat and motion of living things. Fertilized by nutrients birds carry in from the sea, the island is covered with lush, almost hypertrophied vegetation. Even the winds seem stronger and more alive here, the seas heavier, the currents more powerful. Although Kanaashi is a small island, you can somehow feel the sheer hulk of it, feel the weight of its great, furrowed bluffs and pillars of rock. Some intangible, undefinable power seems to permeate the island and arise out of its fecundity. Koyukon people speak of places in their homeland that are sensitive, temperamental, full of spirit and awareness. I only know that something draws me here, as surely as it draws these multitudes of birds.

Excitement surges inside me as I begin this first exploration of Kanaashi Island. I've been here several times before, but never stayed long enough to develop a real sense for it. Following the shore, I come onto a shelf of flat, bare rock with stacks and steep-sided ridges standing above tide pools shallow enough that I can puddle through them in rubber boots. Swells occasionally burst over the seaward edge, sending cascades and rivulets into the pools. Along one stretch I find millions of tiny snails and periwinkles covering dry rocks and crawling over a bed of emerald algae in a few inches of water. I do my best, but still feel like the Shadow of Death stalking across the snails' world with gigantic, crushing feet. Perhaps this is the hatching season, judging by the minuscule size and incredible numbers of snails.

The pools are richer than any I've encountered before, bright with living colors, fertilized by the steady fall of bird droppings. Everywhere I move, the water scuttles and frets with creatures. Hundreds of shells have been taken over by miniature hermit crabs, who forage among mazes of barnacles, mussels, and anemones. They twitch along erratically, duck inside their borrowed carapaces when I loom down for a close look, then forget about me and resume their business. In one place I find an unusual thing—a cone-shaped limpet, alive, upside down in the level shallows, with its round, white "foot" exposed to public view. How does a rock-hugging limpet, one of the least gymnastic creatures on earth, manage to get flipped over like this? An oystercatcher calling nearby gives a clue. Perhaps I interrupted its meal. Turning the limpet foot-down, I offer a self-serving comment about how lucky it was I came along. On any other day it would have been a goner.

Several pools look quite ordinary from a distance, but instead of being mere puddles they plunge down ten to fifteen feet, and the water in their depths is a fluorescent cobalt green. One of these ponds is situated beneath a natural arch riven through a narrow stone ridge. Clinging to a shelf along one side, I move under the arch, then lean over the pool and gaze down through my reflection. The glowing, viridescent water has a deceptively tropical appearance, and I'm almost overwhelmed by an urge to dive in. I can feel myself stroking down through that radiant light, peering into the crannies, searching under the burnished fronds of kelp, running my hands over the nest of cold, smooth boulders that covers the bottom, staring up through the glittering water and longing for the wind, the lost world of clouds.

The rocks and pools end against a steep slope, topped by the forested plateau that makes up the center of Kanaashi. As I walk toward it, a bald eagle glides from a snag above the cliff, swoops down to the edge of a tide pool, hunches its back, and extends its talons. I have my binoculars up when it lands, but it's half hidden by a curb of rock. The bird lurches and struggles, leans forward with its shearing beak, and bends back against something I can't see. A fish, perhaps, but more likely a young gull or a kittiwake distracted for a fatal moment by the ruckus of the flock. I circle behind a grass-covered knob, trying to sneak closer. But the eagle has gone, and no torn feathers or shining scales mark the place where it landed—not even a fleck of blood. It seems strange that a life ended here just minutes ago, yet there isn't the slightest sign, as if the rocks have been vacant forever. In fact, over the run of time, millions of lives have ended within sight of this spot, all without leaving a visible trace. I gaze up into the sky filled with birds, where the exultation of life carries on.

A cliff reaches out overhead, spilling with puffins, echoing gull voices and the high, thin whistles of pigeon guillemots. Its shape is that of a stupendous breaking wave, seventy feet high, ready to plunge back toward the very seas that shaped it. I clamber along the frozen curve of its face, worrying that a loose rock might give way above, but knowing I'll probably get nothing worse than a minor white-washing. Two oystercatchers fling up from the shore, unleashing a barrage of staccato peeps. They land, take off again, and finally settle almost invisibly on the rock. Unconcerned about camouflage, they strut back and forth, looking over-weight and ridiculous. The dish-shaped cliff focuses their shrill voices where I stand, as if I've leaned under the hood of a car with a child at its horn. The noise is punishing but beautiful, a pure incantation of this northern shore, arising from the dark rocks, the chill gray waters, and the slick fronds of kelp.

By watching the oystercatchers I manage to locate their nest. They erupt in pan-icked calls when I walk toward it, and fly past within a few feet, glaring at me with red, reptilian eyes. The tempest is over a single brownish, speckled egg in a grav-elly pocket among the rocks. I half expect the egg to shake and hop like a Mexi-can jumping bean, if the chick inside is anything like its parents.

Toward evening, I find a comfortable seat on the rocks and watch salmon trollers stream in from the fishing grounds off Cape Deception. About fifty boats have crowded into the anchorage behind Kanaashi, their crews bedded down for a few hours' sleep. Earlier this summer I joined an old friend aboard his commercial troller, the *Narwhal*, for a day's fishing out beyond the Cape. We'd hardly dozed off when Joe's alarm blared at 3:30 A.M., but we wasted no time crawling out and getting the engine started. Some boats had already left and oth-ers were clinking their anchors aboard. Half an hour later, in full daylight, we joined a scattered line of trollers headed out for the "morning bite." Once under way, we had a simple breakfast while Joe discussed fishing strategy with young Wade, his only crewman.

In an open skiff the low, irregular swells would scarcely have been noticeable; but the *Narwhal* rolled and pitched, and before long I was ready to lean over the side. Taking mercy on his landlubber guest, the captain administered medication for seasickness. It was pretty embarrassing, especially on a day when the boat's ra-dio was dominated by talk of calm seas and lovely weather.

Off Peregrine Point, Joe and Wade lowered the fishing lines, baiting them with brightly colored lures. For the next few hours Wade kept busy pulling up the gear at short intervals and gaffing bulky coho salmon aboard. Because the fleet had already reached its seasonal quota of king salmon, Wade gently released the few we caught. Some must have weighed over fifty pounds, and in the open season our day's catch of kings would have brought at least two hundred dollars. During quiet periods, Joe and Wade arranged fish on the deck, gutted and cleaned them, and packed them into the ice-filled hold. A knot of fulmars and gulls trailed off our stem, squabbling over bits of offal.

Several times during the day, Joe experimented with lures of different styles and shades and ran them at various depths, hoping to find ones that matched whatever the fish were feeding on. Compared with net fishermen, who work closer to spawning areas and take hundreds or thousands of salmon at once, trolling might be considered "inefficient." But it produces fish of the highest quality, because they're in prime condition far from the spawning streams, and each one is handled individually as it's caught. Aside from their skill as fishermen, what impressed me most about Joe and Wade was how carefully they tended to every salmon, ensuring that it would bring top price from the buyer in town.

By midmorning the bite had slacked off, but there were still enough fish to keep the crew and landlubber busy. We took turns at the wheel, and during slow spells we sat together in the cabin, snacking and swapping stories. Joe had an endless supply of trade secrets about lures, currents, feeding patterns of fish, and ways of dealing with competition on the water. The radio blared with constant banter between fishermen, covering every imaginable topic of importance to life at sea or ashore. I was especially fascinated by the private codes used between friendly captains to tell where they were fishing and how well they were doing. One discouraged-sounding voice reported, "Not doing much today, only a zebra. Heard from Sandy though. She's up where you and me fished last year at this time. Said she had a giraffe yesterday and same the day before. If it stays like this, I guess I'll move that way." Tone of voice was the only hint of how many fish a "zebra" might be, but that could have been part of the deception. Joe and a friend fishing nearby had a different strategy. By programming their radios to odd frequencies, they could talk freely about hot spots and numbers of fish, certain that no one was listening in. They were also spared the need to affect that gloomy, hardship voice

Richard Nelson

66

so common among fishermen, even when they discuss their plans to spend next winter in Hawaii or Costa Rica.

It was a slow day for the *Narwhal*: about 75 cohos plus a few chums and humpies, compared to catches of 100 to 120 on previous days. So after fourteen hours on the grounds, Joe decided to pull the gear and head in. Only then did he relax and show his tiredness. He spoke about the pleasures of fishing: the challenge of hunting the sea for salmon, the freedom of exploring these far stretches of the coast. But he also talked of the loneliness: being apart from his wife and longing to see his little girl. During the day, it was obvious how much Joe loved the troller's life, but as evening came on I could also sense the emptiness he felt during these months away from home.

As I watch the fleet of lighted boats riding placidly beyond Kanaashi's shore, the same emotions sweep through me—the emptiness of being alone, and the pleasure of solitude amid this wildness. I climb a ridge beside the camp ravine, find a patch of dry grass, huddle there against the growing chill, and watch the sunset. Kluksa Mountain darkens until the green above timberline is lost and all that remain are streaks of snow on fields of dusk. The clouds cool away and dwindle, promising clear skies tomorrow. Late flocks of murres and puffins drift toward the cliffs. Nothing moves except a few restless gulls. The soft, swaddling grass lulls me asleep as I await Kanaashi's night.

Sometime later—perhaps a few minutes, perhaps an hour—I'm awakened by a voice seeping up from the ground a few yards away. It sounds like a stream of air squeezing through compressed, liquefied earth, arrayed in an incredibly complex pattern, so different from anything I've ever heard that I can only hold a shadow of it in my memory. At first the voice is scarcely loud enough to hear, but it becomes stronger as the minutes pass. When I listen closely, it resolves itself into an endlessly repeated sequence of bubbling sounds that rise up the scale, with an undercurrent of tonal grunts and high-pitched wheezes, reminiscent of the way bagpipes are played on two levels at once.

Moving on my hands and knees, shining a flashlight into the grass, I follow the voice to the cliff edge. Then silence. Shortly, I find a small burrow, about four inches across, with bare dirt at its entrance. I peek inside but see nothing.

Whether the sound is a hatchling bird calling for its parent or an adult calling for its mate, I may never know. But I'm sure that the burrow belongs to one of the two species of storm-petrel that nest on Kanaashi.

At 11:00 P.M., night covers the sky except for a lavender glow toward the north. A gentle flurry of wings comes out of the silence, followed by a sharp buzz like the sound of a nighthawk. It's entirely different from the voices in the burrows, but must be a petrel. I can make out the shadow of a bird whisking across the sunset horizon. Shortly there is another, then there are several, and then more. Soon the calls come every few seconds, and they're of two distinct types. One is rather plain: a raspy sequence of sounds, a bit like smooth rubber squeaking against itself. By a lucky coincidence, I catch a fork-tailed storm petrel repeating this call as it flies in the flashlight's beam. The other is musical and bubbly: a precise pattern of about ten quick, stuttering notes, varying in tone from one bird to another. By the process of elimination, it must be the leach's storm-petrel.

At 11:30 the air is swarming with petrels, like feathers falling in a whirlwind. I can still pick out individual birds against the dimly lit sky, darting back and forth, swift as hunting hawks, delicate as dancing butterflies, agile as looping swallows. If their wings make any noise, it's lost in the clamor of calls. At first I focus on the voices close at hand. Then I become aware of the background noise, a swollen chant that comes from everywhere over and around the island: the combined calls of a hundred thousand petrels descending like a storm cloud, raining voices into the darkness of Kanaashi.

Whispering in amazement, I ease down the slope and make my way back to camp. The ravine is filled with birds, wheeling between walls that trap their voices and magnify them to an almost maddening cacophony. When I shine the flashlight the whole swarm lifts up until birds spill over the edges and flick through the maze of trunks at the timber's edge. But when I switch it off they descend, sometimes to the level of my shoulders. Every few minutes a flurry of noisy wingbeats marks the arrival of a rhinoceros auklet, darting straight in toward its burrow, apparently oblivious to the petrels.

Each returning petrel has spent several days offshore, while its mate stayed in the burrow with their egg or hatchling. Now, in the safety of darkness, they are changing shifts. Somehow the birds locate their own nests despite the whirling throng and the profusion of burrows. Perhaps they do this by an exchange of calls between mates, though it would take a remarkable ear to pick out a distinct voice amid this pandemonium. Also, the nest is sometimes left unattended for a day, yet the petrels manage to find it again.

There are no burrows in the bottom of the ravine, so I scramble up the slope, turn off the flashlight, and stand amid the brush and trees. After a minute, airy phantoms begin flitting so close I could touch them. Then I feel wings brushing past my face and touching my clothes. When a bird lands nearby I flick on the light—a fork-tail, soft and gray, smaller than a robin. It cringes against the ground, pulls down its head, and stares into the beam, black eyes glistening like droplets of ink. Finally the little bird flies away, frustrated or alarmed by the light. For the next bird, a uniformly dark leach's petrel, I try a quick flash every few seconds. Apparently unconcerned, it creeps toward a burrow and disappears inside. This also works for a rhinoceros auklet that whizzes past my knees and thumps down beside the closest bush. It's almost as bulky as a puffin, plain gray except for two white plumes on each side of its face and an upright "horn" at the base of its bill. Clamped crosswise and side by side in its beak are two shiny needlefish.

In 1896, a naturalist named Joseph Grinnell found himself stranded overnight on Kanaashi: "Thus, in anything but a voluntary manner, I was given an opportunity to observe the Petrels, which I would probably not otherwise have had." His report was published in a journal devoted to nidology, the fashionable science of bird egg collecting: "As the gloom grew deeper the Petrels became more numerous. Those which had been out to sea all day began to arrive among the trees and were even more awkward than those leaving. They flew against branches and bushes and into my face. . . . The chorus of their cries was curious, and depressing to one's spirits, and the chilly air was constantly being fanned into my face by their noiseless wings."

Later in the night he became frustrated by his situation and tired of his feathered company: "As I began to feel cold and likewise hungry, the novelty of these strange experiences naturally wore off. After considerable searching for dry fuel, I started a smoldering little blaze, which lighted up the dusky surroundings, together with the flitting forms of the birds, thus disclosing a very impressive scene. But presently several of the Petrels were attracted by the light and flew pell-mell into the fire, extinguishing the feeble flames in short order. After several similarly frustrated attempts, though partly on account of the damp wood, I gave it up."

Reflecting on Grinnell's night in the bird-infested woods, I feel lucky to close down the tent flaps and zip myself into a cozy sleeping bag. When I've just begun to snooze, a petrel smacks into the peak of the tent, flaps partway down the side, and takes off again, apparently unhurt. Near dawn I briefly awaken and listen once more—the ravine is still raucous and echoing with calls.

There is a different island in the night. I could have spent a lifetime of days here and never imagined anything like this. Islands are more like people than I'd thought; their nights are filled with dreams.

Sunshine warms the tent walls and embroiders them with shadows of tall grass. I open the sleeping bag, luxuriate in the peace of bird songs, and contemplate the good fortune of awakening in this cradle of rock. There is no hint of petrel voices, as if the whole thing was some kind of fantasy. The morning sounds are dominated by gulls wailing outside the ravine. A rufous hummingbird squeals and ratchets near the tent; a fox sparrow pours out fluid notes; and a varied thrush rings softly from the forest above the slope. I haven't noticed the varied thrushes much lately. During the spring they sing conspicuously in open places, but in midsummer they retire to the deep woods, while gaudy singers like hermit thrushes inhabit the edge. Perhaps varied thrushes suffer a twinge of vanity, so they hide away when the heavy competition arrives.

Crouched outside the tent, I fix a bowl of cereal and soak up the early sun. Again I compare my fortunes to those of the hapless Grinnell. When his long night was over, he dipped into the treasured puffin eggs he'd gathered and ate some for breakfast. His report neglects to mention how he cooked them, or if he was forced to eat them raw. In the midst of this thought, a winter wren appears in the salmonberry bushes a few yards away. He moves soundlessly, like a tuft of cottongrass on the breeze, and flips his head so first one eye sees me, then the

Alvin Eli Amason
*I Could Watch You Until
the Stars Come Out and
I Can't See No More*
Oil on canvas
1983
UA83-3-63

other. The wren hops to the end of the closest twig, where I can almost reach out and touch him. There he sits, blinking. He's scarcely larger than the humming-bird that whizzed up to inspect my cap a while ago. His brown feathers are patterned with fine, dark reticulations; his unnaturally short tail perks up so it seems permanently ajar; and his beak looks too small to serve any purpose.

The wren does a flip turn and flies back into the thicket. Though his wings blur almost like a hummingbird's, his flight is actually quite slow. Shortly after he van-ishes, a burst of wren song rattles out like the babbling of a madman, ranging wildly up and down the scale, loud as a robin and intricate as the signals that run computers. How can lungs that fit inside a bird not much bigger than my thumb throw out such a labyrinth of sound? A close look at tiny creatures like wrens and shrews and hummingbirds reveals exceptional power and energy. Koyukon people have a clear sense for this. They emphasize that all animals are something to be reckoned with, regardless of their size or their importance in the human scheme of things.

Outside the protected ravine, there is a light breeze from the northwest, and last night's fog clings against the water. It's not the kind of fog I remember from muggy mornings in Wisconsin, lying across summer lawns like a velvet robe. This is a sharp mist that tingles like a sprinkle of icewater. I amble across the bare rocks toward the cliffs of Kanaashi's middle plateau. The anchorage is now empty. Gulls cover the whitewashed rocks and ridges in numbers beyond estimating; feathers float on the wind's breath; and the air is heavy with the acrid smell of droppings. I suppose they're attracted here by the congregations of needlefish around Kanaashi in summer. Whatever the reason, the result is wonderful. Who could ever get enough of gulls?

A rock spur reaches down from the cliff like the root of an enormous tree. I make my way up its edge, trying not to look down, until I reach the shoulder-high grass that grows in dense tussocks along the top. This gives way to a snarl of salmonberry bushes rising above my head as I force my way in, leaning my whole weight against the clumps until they bend down or pry apart and let me through. On the first of several tumbles, I find myself face to face with the explanation for this rich growth—an organic compost riddled everywhere with petrel burrows.

If the soil behind our house looked like this, even I might be able to grow a successful garden.

Stopping to catch my breath, I see a few orange and purple salmonberries amid the clouds of leaves. It takes some extra struggling to reach them, but there is ample reward in the sweet, juicy taste of this year's first berries. Perhaps the fertile soil accounts for their early ripening, but I suspect it's more the weather. Surrounded by the relatively warm ocean, Kanaashi has less snow, fewer frosts, and an earlier spring than we do in the sheltered bay at home. Grasses and other plants like cow parsnip appear weeks earlier on Kanaashi, and the leaves open before those in more landbound areas. Even in the cove behind Tsandaku Point, just across the passage, plant growth begins somewhat later than it does on Kanaashi. There are thousands of little climates within the larger climate that encompasses them all, another way in which every speck of the earth's surface is unique unto itself.

Something else in Kanaashi's climate, perhaps wind and salt spray, must account for the sparse numbers of berries. I can only find enough for a snack, but the ritual of gathering and eating them means as much as the food itself. Each time I come to the island across the way, I try to find a few berries, an edible plant, or at least a freshet to drink from—some way to bring a bit of it into myself, a little communion, a physical sharing of body with that place.

Blundering over a quagmire of logs and stumps, I finally break through the underbrush into the shaded luxuriance of forest. The trees are heavy-bunked spruce, squat and gnarly where the winds beat against them, but tall and elegant farther inside the woods. Spread out beneath them is a dense and varied understory, dominated by masses of shoulder-high ferns that look like a solid wall but are actually quite easy to walk through. Here and there, sunlight flakes down through holes in the high boughs and gives the fronds a luminous glow. Scattered among the ferns are patches of Angelica, water hemlock, twisted stalk, and stunted elderberry bushes. Impenetrable salmonberry brambles cover the few openings where trees have fallen in storms. And in the dusky swales beneath heavy timber, there are fields of smaller, shade-tolerant ferns and oversized wild lily of the valley growing on carpets of moss.

As I walk deeper into the forest it becomes greener, more lush and moist; the heavy air drifts with flower pungence; boughs and branches droop in the steamy wet. The atmosphere is still and thick, a summer broth of living trees and soft mulch. I move through silken threads of spiderwebs and little swarms of hovering insects, mouth closed and eyes squinted to keep them out. Though it stands above the cold waters of the north Pacific, the forest is pervaded by an equatorial lushness. Bird sounds intensify in the dense, windless gallery of trees, especially the cawing of the ubiquitous crows. They show little fear and land in the boughs above my head to scold incessantly, upset by this rare intrusion. A Swainson's thrush song rises from the undergrowth like a phosphorescent pool of flame. Woven through it are the high, sweet voices of song sparrows and golden-crowned kinglets. And occasionally the liquid gurgling of a petrel issues from a burrow underfoot, like the chanting of a spirit voice, the shaman island singing to itself.

I become absorbed in the process of moving quietly, staring ahead through the variegated leaves and branches. I feel the air against me, like a body of clear gel—invisible flesh that fills the space inside the forest and covers the hard bones of rock underneath. The maze of tree trunks, branches, boughs, and needles penetrates the flesh of air as a web of veins. I move through them like a microorganism swimming inside a huge animal. I touch a spruce bough and sense it feeling me, as if it's become a nerve inside my own body, or inside the larger body that encompasses us. Just as the branches stimulate my senses, I stimulate the senses of the forest. We move within each other and feel each other's movement. During these moments, the notion of separating myself from the forest seems as untenable as crawling out of my own skin.

The forest floor is a soft, richly scented loam, permeated with guano and feathers and decomposed bird flesh. A handful poured on rock might draw itself into some amoeba shape, tremble and swell, breathe deeply, and ooze away. The soil is so honeycombed with burrows that it sponges under each step. There are entrances everywhere: in the flat, mossy ground, along the edges of fallen logs, beneath clumps of ferns and bushes, and especially around the buttressed roots of trees. The island is a living hive, with a network of tunnels woven through its surface. I imagine hundreds of birds hidden in the earth all around me, open-eyed in the blackness of their nest chambers—the hot, breathing nodes of Kanaashi's veins.

The invisible colony seems perfectly tranquil, but there is ample evidence it has moments of violence and death. Every few minutes I come across a patch of gray petrel feathers, and occasionally a pair of disembodied wings still connected by the shoulder bones and cartilage. I also find two dead rhinoceros auklets, one rotting in the entrance of a flooded burrow and the other lying on bare earth with no indication of what killed it. River otters, which are common along this coast, might sometimes prey on Kanaashi's birds. Last spring I found their tracks on wet snow near the camp ravine, but I've seen no otter sign today.

Only one other predatory mammal has been reported here. In the summer of 1912, a wildlife agent named G. Willett discovered that a brown bear had excavated at least five hundred burrows and eaten the birds inside, "feathers and all." Much to his relief, it left the island before he arrived; this would be a terribly small place to share with a brown bear. Nowadays, the fishing activity around Kanaashi probably discourages any bears from swimming across.

In all likelihood, bald eagles account for most of the bird remains scattered through these woods. There are at least a dozen eagles perched in trees around the island, about evenly divided between white-headed adults and mottled brown adolescents. Besides the usual diet of fish, Kanaashi eagles regularly hunt for birds. Those connected pairs of wings are telltale evidence of their activities. During the gloom of dusk and dawn, eagles sit on low boughs deep within the forest, owl-fashion, waiting to swoop down after petrels muddling through the brush near their burrows. Even at midday, I'm startled several times by a commotion in the nearby branches, as a black specter flaps off through the trees. The first time it happens I catch myself thinking, "Only an eagle." Then I realize people once thought that way about buffalo on the prairies, elk in the forests of Wisconsin, and wolves on the outskirts of Washington, D.C. Somewhat later I stalk close to an eagle, by staying where the tree trunk screens its view of me. The whole time, it stares intently at the ground, craning its head this way and that, waiting for something to move in the tangled vegetation.

I stop to rest in a copse of particularly huge trees, and wonder if Joseph Grinnell might have sheltered himself for the night beneath one of them. He spent the daylight hours somewhere in this forest, digging petrels from their burrows, collecting eggs, and killing birds for specimens. He wrote: "On being handled, both species of Petrel disgorged large quantities of the yellowish oil with a musky odor, so characteristic of this family. This oil rapidly saturated the plumage of the head and breast, and the birds had to be caught and killed with great care or else they became almost spoiled for specimens. I finally found that the best way to manage them was to hold them head downward until they had vomited most of their oil, then to kill them by compressing the thorax, plugging the bill and throat with a copious amount of the damp soil."

Like many naturalists of his time, Grinnell carried out his predation in the name of science. He sent the petrel skins to a museum, where a taxonomist studied and measured them to find their fit within the burgeoning Linnaean system of classification. During this era, scientists traveled throughout the world and killed thousands of animals—some so rare they were never seen again—in a competitive quest to identify new species. This infatuation with taxonomy eventually faded, and modern biologists depend far less on the shotgun as a research tool. But wild creatures of every sort are still routinely killed for scientific studies—for example, when an ecologist "collects" animals to examine their stomach contents. It seems a bit odd that a quest for deeper understanding of nature could involve killing an animal to find out what it had for its last meal.

The question of research ethics comes to mind again when I spot a painted wooden stake in a snarl of underbrush. It was placed here last summer by a team of biologists assessing the numbers of each bird species on Kanaashi. Most of the estimates were based on visual counts, but for burrow nesters like the storm-petrels more intrusive methods were used. I watched the researchers lay out a study plot, one of many scattered randomly around the island. They first marked the corners with stakes and stretched bright cords between them, then examined the ground within each plot, crawling on hands and knees, counting burrows and probing inside for adult birds, chicks, or eggs. Some of the tunnels were long and deep, putting the nests beyond reach. To increase the reliability of their count, the biologists dug out a percentage of these.

Gently as possible, they pulled storm-petrels from the burrows. The birds squealed and complained at first, then settled down like tame doves, blinking against the glare of daylight. Many nests also yielded a creamy-colored egg or a chick. The nestlings were impossibly cute, ranging from miniature tufts of gray fuzz to wriggling, rotund puffballs whose frizzy down made them appear larger than their parents. I felt a little heartsick, wondering how the petrels and chicks would fare after being returned to their damaged burrows. And I wondered if the researchers, who obviously loved birds and treated them with great care, felt a similar twinge of conscience. All of us had been taught that certain sacrifices can be justified. In exchange for the discomfort or death of a few birds, the information they yielded might someday assure the protection or even the survival of this entire colony.

When I lived with Koyukon people, they sometimes mentioned wildlife researchers who had worked near their villages, capturing animals and tagging them, putting radio transmitters on them, or relocating them to start new populations. Sarah Stevens once told me, "We never fool around like that with animals, because they have a spirit, and if we treat them wrong we might suffer just like they did." At first this seemed inconsistent, given that Koyukon people live mainly by hunting and fishing. But later, as I learned more about the code of respect governing their relationships with animals, I realized how carefully they seek to protect the dignity and integrity of every creature. My Koyukon teachers held a spiritually based covenant with all members of their natural community. According to this covenant, animals give themselves to feed and clothe people, but with few exceptions it is not appropriate to manipulate them, control or confine them, or entertain the illusion of understanding them.

Most of the adult petrels and chicks pulled from their burrows fouled themselves by regurgitating viscous oil, apparently in self-defense. The biologist in charge said this concentrated, nutritious oil is produced from tiny invertebrates the petrels catch at sea and store for days to maintain themselves and feed their young. The intrepid Joseph Grinnell had an opportunity to sample this oil: "In going back to Petrel-curing, I found a couple of hard-tack in the cotton in my collecting basket, and I lost no time in putting the crackers where they were of the most use under the existing circumstances. I noticed that they had a peculiar flavor, but that didn't bother me much at first. Finally I closely examined the crackers, and found that in killing the Petrels and putting them in the basket, the hard-tack had become sprinkled with the odiferous oil from the birds. So I had the 'rare and wonderful' experience of eating hard-tack soaked in Petrel oil, or possibly more correctly Petroleum!"

Naturalists of Grinnell's era often laced their reports with such delightful asides, illuminating the human dimensions of scientific endeavor and giving a fuller expression to the world as they found it. Reading these accounts is a striking reminder of how desiccated and mechanical most scientific literature has become. Grinnell and his colleagues not only wrote differently from the way biologists do today, they also had very different goals. It was their purpose to observe nature as meticulously as possible, to acquire knowledge through direct experience, to rely principally on their senses as the source of information, and to publish their results in richly descriptive field reports.

Inspired by the writings of such naturalists, I began college with a biology major. But I eventually realized I had little affinity for the kind of science I encountered there, with its emphasis on quantified data, controlled experiments, technological monitoring devices, and theoretical analysis. Because I was unable to comprehend and appreciate this work, I felt incapable of understanding what really mattered about nature. But I found a refuge in anthropology, where the descriptive approach had persisted like an orphan child, and where the study of Native cultures revealed traditions of natural history that seemed richer than anything accessible in Western science. Through ethnographic literature and the experience of Native American life, I gradually realized there are many paths to a meaningful sense of the natural world.

Among the Koyukon people, I experienced an attitude quite different from that which prevailed in academic science. Elders like Sarah Stevens and Grandpa William carried their vast and insightful knowledge of the natural world with great humility. I never heard them speak of how much they knew, but of how little, and of how much there was to learn, how difficult it was to understand even the smallest mysteries around them. Anthropologists working among traditional peoples are often told that they have learned very little about the culture they've come to study, even after their research has gone on for years. Unfortunately, the rocks, plants, and animals are unable to give the same appraisal to those who study them, although its humbling influence might be of great benefit.

Slivers of blue sky appear between tree trunks as I work my way toward a clifftop overlooking the passage. A freshening northwest wind furls down the side of Kluksa Mountain and scrawls dark gusts on the whitecapped water. Beyond Cape Deception, a prodigious bank of fog rides coastward on the sea wind. Only the island's mountain wall keeps it from engulfing Kanaashi, rolling in across Haida Strait, and burying the mainland shore. Fog lies through the saddle between Kluksa Mountain and Crescent Peak, and stretches across the other side like the tongue of a glacier. At first glance it seems inert and motionless, but a closer look reveals that it pours endlessly downhill and dissolves over the sun-warmed land. Occasionally during the summer months, high pressure systems with brisk northwesterlies build the fog bank to a height of two thousand feet. The fog wraps around Kluksa Mountain so only the peak is visible, as if it's poked up through an advancing sea of meringue.

Sitting in a patch of grass, I gaze at the clouds and revel in the absence of purpose. Two ravens sail along the cliff, mirror wings shining in the sun, pinions flexed against the breeze, tails flared and twisting, indigo beaks turning toward me as they pass. Then they draw together, dip their wings in unison, circle and lift, staring from first one side and then the other as they veer above the precipice. "Found me again," I whisper; but then I wonder if they've noticed me or care in the least that I'm sitting here. Perhaps they've seen something behind me, or want me to *think* they've seen something behind me. Mr. Willett's bird-eating bear looms from the underbrush of my imagination.

A born sucker, I play the game, turn and look into the thicket. Empty. And the ravens soar away, croaking jubilation.

Evening creeps up the eastern sky and smolders on the mainland peaks. The mantle of fog rises, opening a dark crevice along the face of the Pacific. Clouds wrap in around Kluksa Mountain and Crescent Peak, cover the island, and march across Haida Strait, blackening the waters below. Perched on a hillside near the camp ravine, I huddle against the cold wind and contagious gloom. Only a few trollers are anchored behind Kanaashi, clustered tightly and vaned into the northwester like gulls on a rock. After pounding all day in the gale off Cape Deception, many captains headed for town to sell their fish and find shelter in the harbor. Even the birds have abandoned these brooding waters and hidden themselves away, except for a few stragglers still circling in the deadened light.

Unlike yesterday, with its bright sunset and reverie of birds, tonight Kanaashi has an empty feeling, like a barren rock in a northern sea. The misty breeze chills my face and cuts through my layered clothes. I instinctively turn to look for Shungnak, to touch her fur and pull her close to me. Her absence sharpens my loneliness and brings on the deepest wish to be with Nita and Ethan.

Sometimes I feel burdened by the shapeless desire that brings me here. Yet each day at home I long for the island, much as I now long for the tenderness of human company. And while the island can be a lonely place, it also gives an elemental comfort much like shared human love. As with any love, it can seem almost imaginary, like wandering through a far paradise, savoring pleasures too rich and sweet to exist beyond fantasy. But at other times it seems entirely commonplace, filled with the ordinary but indispensable satisfactions that also strengthen the bonds between people. Perhaps this is the essence of connectedness with place and home: bringing nature and terrain within the circle of community, joining with them in a love that is both magical and ordinary.

Comforted by these thoughts, I let the wind embrace me. The island's whispering breath—it is company enough.

No shadows of grass on the tent walls this morning, but the clouds have thinned and brightened, which means they'll probably evaporate by noon. Last night's wind has slackened to a breeze. The muffled rhythm of an increasing swell drifts into the ravine and amplifies in its confines. The forest rings out with thrush songs.

I remember awakening before dawn, when another petrel hit the side of the tent. Hearing wind in the trees, I dressed and walked out to check on the skiff. The sky was overcast, except for a few breaks showing a faint glow of sunrise.

Petrels whirled around the island like bees, and I stood on the rocks watching, mesmerized by the flickering of wings. Once again, the air was laced through with bird voices, thick as mist in the darkness, the night anthem of Kanaashi. It was a long time before I could sleep again, and as daylight came on the voices faded.

Slipping outside, I notice a spatter of droppings on the tent; if the petrels were still flying it would be wise to eat breakfast under cover. The cool temperature encourages activity, and since the drinking water is about gone I pick up a container and head for the skiff. Swells wrapping around Kanaashi surge against the walls of the anchorage. Guillemots strut and wheeze on the nearby rocks. I fetch the punt, wait for a break in the swells, climb down onto a ledge, and launch when the next surge rises around my boots. After bailing the leaky skiff I untie it from the kelp and ride out into the passage.

It doesn't take long to reach the nearest anchorage, a cove protected by a levee of tide-washed rocks. After viewing the island from Kanaashi these past days, it feels good to step ashore. A warm sensation of familiarity spreads through me, as I climb a hillside behind the cove. Scanning the length of Hidden Beach through binoculars, I pick out the sperm whale carcass we found some weeks ago. Now a mottled, creamy color, it stands out against the black rocks, inviting a closer look. Partway down the beach, I wonder about the wisdom of this little expedition. A female bear and her yearling left their tracks in the sand after last night's tide, heading toward the whale. And higher up the beach, prints of two other bears lead the same way. Although I'm carrying a rifle, the abundance of fresh sign unnerves me a bit.

Sunshine breaks through the dissipating clouds, glistens on the sand, and makes spindrift rainbows above the breaking waves. Across the passage, Kanaashi's cliffs are patterned with gleam and shadow. The scattered bear tracks converge near the end of Hidden Beach, making a well-traveled highway that vanishes where the rocks begin. I find a high spot on the shore, away from the woods, and watch for movement around the carcass a hundred yards ahead. There are two gaping pink concavities in the whale's belly, and it isn't hard to guess who made them.

In the midst of this thought, a dark shape rises on the far side of the carcass.

The bear looks my way, disappears, and then ambles into the open. Even from this distance I can tell she's a big one. She lifts her snout and probes the air, gazes myopically along the shore, and comes around to the belly side. Shortly, the yearling scrambles out to join her, and they gnaw halfheartedly at cratered spots in the whale's hide.

Then something catches my eye in the background. A third bear, medium-sized, lifts up from a hollow in the rocks where he's been resting. He paces back and forth like a caged animal, reaching out hungrily with his nose, slowly and indirectly approaching the whale. The big female glares for a moment, then swaggers toward him. He takes the hint and sidles away, casting meek, frustrated glances over his shoulder. Perhaps the female's perfunctory feeding indicates she's not really hungry but wants to claim the entire carcass. The unwanted bear roams at a safe distance, sniffing and pawing among the rocks, apparently resigned to waiting until she leaves.

I empathize only too well with him, as I stand faint-heartedly in the distance, grateful for every inch of ground that separates us. It's a luxury to see bears at all, so I try to relax and watch, like a kid peeking at the overlord through a hole in the fence. The mere presence of bears here demonstrates their absolute domain. It's a good reminder, because I sometimes feel possessive about the island when I see a boat anchored in a favorite cove or a streamer of campfire smoke rising from the woods. Watching these animals, I can hardly ignore my own standing as a visitor here.

I feel a drift of wind at my back. A moment later, the female lifts her nose and takes a few steps in my direction. She peers toward me, sways back and forth, then lofts up on her hind legs, extending her forepaws for balance. There must be a tingle of fear inside her, but it couldn't possibly match the spasm that runs through every nerve in my body. I can't decide if I should skulk toward the trees, which seem a long way off, or hold tight on this open ground. The last time I felt so tiny and vulnerable, Mom towered overhead and I'd been caught in the act of a childhood crime.

But this time I get off without a punishment. The bear drops down and swings away, glances back, then rambles into the woods with her cub close behind. The other one seems reluctant to leave at first, as if he's not sure what frightened her and sees his chance to work on the unattended carcass. But finally he accepts her judgment and hurries up into the trees.

I wait a while to make sure they've really gone, then walk cautiously ahead, staring at the carcass in case yet another bear is on its opposite side or resting somewhere among the rocks. My attention turns to the whale, which looks like an enormous, half-emptied, chalk-colored sack sprawled over the shore. Just above it is a short stretch of salt-and-pepper sand, a mix of pulverized basalt and seashell. The whole thing is a mess: scrambled, trenched, and ploughed by the bears. They've dug several big hollows in the sand—places to rest and cool off between feasts. Chunks of styrofoam are strewn all over, torn from a large block that drifted ashore and became the cub's plaything. One pie-sized heap of droppings looks extremely fresh. I put my hand on it, wanting to feel the heat of a bear; but instead it feels cold, gooey, and unpleasant.

The carcass is pretty bedraggled. Aside from the sag and stench of decay, it shows the effects of considerable scavenging. Bears and eagles have reduced the flukes to remnants of shredded hide and blubber. They've gnawed a hole the size of a football into one side of the head. Much of the lower jaw is gone, bone and all; and the tongue is a stump of mangled, purple flesh. Apparently the bears prefer blubber and meat, because they haven't eaten through the two belly craters to reach its insides. There is a large excavation in a patch of sand below the dorsal fin, but my investigation stops short of crawling underneath to see if they've chewed into the body there. Claw marks all over the whale make me jittery, and I keep an eye on the trees in case a bear comes back to take ownership. Once again, I find myself wishing Shungnak were along, to keep watch and to provide the illusion of safety in not being alone. Rather than press my luck any further, I head back for the beach, keeping a constant lookout behind.

In the anchorage cove, I fill the water jug from a stream that runs down across the rocks. The tawny muskeg water is like an organic tea, steeped in saturated moss, filtered through acres of roots, enriched by dissolved nutrients, permeated with the island's essence. Rising tide has partly covered the barrier rocks and the swells roll over them, setting up a lively rollick inside the anchorage. My pants are fairly soaked by the time I've paddled to the boat, but clearing sky promises sunshine to dry them.

The lee side of Kanaashi is glassy calm, but steep, silent swells loft the skiff, fall away, then rise again, in a sickening, irregular pattern. To prevent queasiness, I keep my eyes on the horizon as much as possible. The water is littered with diving seabirds—an enormous concentration of them—arranged in singles, pairs, clusters, bunches, and swarms, sometimes mixed together in congregations of several hundred auklets, puffins, murres, cormorants, and murrelets. Mingled through the crowd and floating overhead are flocks of glaucous-winged gulls and herring gulls, apparently waiting to snatch fish from the divers' beaks. When I arrive, the closest birds scatter to a safe distance, and for several minutes others pop up around the boat.

Finally they resume their feeding. The only sounds are intermittent croaks and whistles, wings flapping against water, and waves sloshing against the boat. Then a strange noise arises through the quiet, like static hissing from inside the water, and I notice a dark rippling patch on the surface. As the ripples come closer, I peer down through curtains of fractured sunlight that shiver in the depths. Then the water starts glittering with needlefish, millions of them, in a school so dense that a tubful would contain hundreds. They crackle against the surface, making tiny bubbles that sail briefly on the slick water and then pop.

I lean over the side, watching the school drift slowly underneath, dizzied by the frenetic motion. Each fish is a silver minnow, three or four inches long, scarcely thicker than a pencil. Suddenly, the school begins shimmering intensely. A sharp swirl disturbs the calm along one edge, and a spatter of needlefish bursts up through the surface. The spasm circles at incredible speed, then veers off in a straight line, as if a runaway beam of electricity were shocking the needlefish. By a quirk of luck, it runs right past the skiff, and I see a school of pink salmon slicing through panic-riven knots of needlefish.

I grab my spinning rod and fasten a small lure on the line. By the time it's ready, both salmon and needlefish have gone, but during the next hour the same thing happens again and again. Each time, I run the boat close and cast toward the disturbance, but not one fish bites. When a gull or kittiwake flies over a school, terrified needlefish erupt under its shadow like a gust flinging the water apart, accompanied by the tinkling sound of pebbles being thrown against a sheet of glass. Surprisingly, the birds take no notice, though it seems they could plunge down for easy pickings. Perhaps they've already had their fill, or they might prefer the ease of stealing from the flocks of divers.

Unable to catch salmon, I run the skiff back to Kanaashi Island's anchorage and fasten it to the kelp. At high tide, strong surges are rising and falling against the ledged shore. For once, I'm glad Shungnak isn't along, because she hates water and would have no taste for clambering up these sheer, slippery rocks with surf licking at her paws. I tie the water jug to one float of the catamaran punt, cinch on my backpack full of wetsuit gear, kneel on the other float, and paddle toward shore. One side of the anchorage is fronted by a high cliff with a flattened cave at its base. The opening is about twenty feet wide and five feet high. At low water this morning it was dry, so I could see its floor of rounded boulders, sloping up toward a lightless chamber forty feet back. As the tide rises, this dark, dripping cavern gradually fills to the ceiling. And when conditions are right, it alternately opens and closes with each swell, making a powerful, horizontal blowhole. I've never seen it better than today, and I can't resist the temptation to have a closer look.

I paddle tentatively toward the cave, keeping a cautious distance until I've watched a few swells roll in. Each time, a thick column of spray spews out thirty or forty feet and expands into a cloud of mist that drifts and dissipates along the cliff. Growing bolder, I move in and float beside the cave's mouth, using the paddle to fend off the rock wall when a surge runs up against it. From here, I can sense the *life* of the thing. Each time a trough draws down inside, the expanding chamber breathes in with a great, prolonged sigh, and little streamlets of water that trail off the roof are sucked back into its throat. The crest that follows rises against the ceiling and shuts it off, then runs back inside, compressing the air until it explodes through the top of the wave and blows out a cloud of atomized water.

After watching for a while, I have a perverse inspiration to put on my wetsuit, swim inside, and experience it from there. But a glimmer of common sense makes me realize it could implode my eardrums at the very least or pulverize my body at the worst.

So I opt for the next best thing. During a quiet spell I paddle just outside the mouth of the cavern and position myself directly in its line of fire. The first few swells are only medium sized, but the noise, the blast of air, and the mild soaking are enough of a thrill to keep me there, instantly addicted, waiting for more.

A long lull is followed by a couple of small blows . . . and then I see the big one coming. I quickly realize this swell is much larger than any since I got here. My whole body tingles with adrenalized fear and excitement, as the shining mound of water comes inexorably toward me. During the final seconds, I wish I'd stroked out of the way; but I turn and watch the cave, grinning like a madman about to be executed. My little craft drops down into the trough; the cavern yawns open; and there is a deep, protracted moan as it inhales.

The next fragments of time move as if the friction of their intensity slows and magnifies them, so that everything registers in perfect detail. As the wave's front slope heaves up inside the cave, there is a slow, building exhalation. Froth and spittle fling out from the ceiling amid a basso grunt that becomes a deep bellow. The swell forces itself like a plunger into the lung of rock. I watch the smooth, hunched, glossy backside of the wave roll in. And I stare, wide-eyed, into the blank, white geyser that explodes outward with a boom that reverberates into the surrounding bedrock. I am utterly, perfectly, exquisitely in its path, struck by a blinding maelstrom of salty mist, blown backwards and nearly capsized, drenched, breathless, and ecstatic.

I've never been kissed so vehemently. It's moments like this that fire the deepest passion for being alive.

Dripping wet and satisfied, I make my way to the landing place and head for camp. The sun-filled ravine is gloriously warm and calm. Hummingbirds and bumblebees hover around clustered flowers on a rock face beside the tent. Fox sparrows sing from perches among the salmonberries. I drape my soggy clothes on the bushes, then struggle into my wetsuit.

Sweating inside the neoprene outfit, I hike over the sun-heated rocks carrying mask and snorkel. Finally I reach a series of tide pools, some small, some large,

Al Sanders
Untitled photograph
Gelatin silver, selenium toned
1980
UAP85:084:001

ranging in depth from a few inches to fifteen feet. The water feels refreshingly cool as I drift along the surface from one to another, peering at the rich life below. Each pool has its own assortment of plants and animals, its own lavish pastel colors, its own array of exotic twists on the shapes of living things, its own intoxicating beauty. Especially where shallow water lies over dark rocks, the pools are warm enough to encourage a careful, deliberate inspection. The bottom of each pool is filigreed with shimmering crystal lines from sunlight falling through the ripples. I drift silent and weightless above my own shadow, like a cloud passing over forests of red and green anemones. When I gently poke a finger into their bellies, hundreds of soft, sticky, translucent tentacles close tightly around it. Spiny sea urchins bristling in the crevices react to my touch by sending up dozens of tube feet. The slender appendages explore my skin so delicately that I can't even feel them. There are also broad swaths of barnacles, rhythmically sweeping the water with feathery nets like tiny hands, groping for invisible microorganisms. Clinging here and there are outcrops of horse mussels, blue shells the length of my hand, adorned with white clusters of barnacles.

The cone-shaped limpets and hunched chitons regard me, if at all, with a studied indifference, although they seem to clutch the rocks a little tighter when I touch them. Multicolored starfish creep along at a contemplative pace, combing the rocks for shellfish to slowly pry apart and digest by extruding their stomachs inside the opened shells. They have a lively counterpoint in the dainty brittle stars, who writhe away when I pick them up, like five prickly snakes fastened to a button. Loveliest and most fascinating of all are the nudibranchs—who look like slugs dressed up for carnival in Rio de Janeiro. Though only an inch or two long, their stout build, brilliant colors, and elaborate shapes make them appear much larger. Most remarkable are the fleshy gills that festoon their backs like decorative fringes. Most of them are frosty, translucent white on the body, with fluorescent orange stripes on their gills. Others are tinged with vibrant yellow, lemon, vermilion, scarlet, mahogany, or black. Nudibranchs are strangely inconspicuous despite their garish colors. Perhaps it's because they crawl over the wrack and algae with the liquid grace of water itself, or because they're so gentle and delicate they can hide within themselves, like an inward secret.

How many other secrets does Kanaashi Island hold? The more I look, the richer it becomes, the more deeply penetrated with life, like a stone colossus touched and made animate. Last night I listened to the island chant with myriad voices. This morning, I felt the island shiver when the swells broke powerfully against it. At midday I looked into the island's throat, heard it shout, and took the cold wind of its breath against me. And now I float like a speck in the island's opened eye. Adrift between sun and rock, I gaze down inside the eye that watches and contains me.

In late afternoon, I hike along Kanaashi's outer shore, clinging to narrow ledges and working my way around massive formations of striated rock—pinnacles, spines, chasms, amphitheaters, and cliffs. Standing in the shadow of an enormous, wave-polished facade, I imagine the seas that explode against it and roll back into the sheer-walled clefts nearby. Over thousands of years, the storms carved this shore into an expression of themselves, like an ocean's song made visible in stone.

Even today, swells heaving against the shore make it impossible to walk around the island's far end, so I decide to follow the clifftop instead. First, I climb a ridge that narrows to a spine with hollowed walls dropping a hundred feet on either side. Near its summit I lose my nerve and back slowly down, pressing my face against the cold rocks, reenacting the terror of a foolish childhood adventure. After some reconnoitering, I try again, this time angling up a steep-sided ravine, digging my feet into the soft dirt and clinging to wads of vegetation. When the slope becomes gentler, I crawl like an insect through head-high tussocks of grass and a scramble of salmonberry, wild celery, and elderberry.

Once on top, I hike to a headland that plunges sharply into the sea. Sitting on a grassy shelf beneath its edge, I can stick my arm out into a rush of wind deflected upward by the cliff, while my little nook is completely calm. A steady flow of birds weaves back and forth in front of me. Murres launch from a nearby colony and circle monotonously before landing again. Puffins flap by just beyond reach, red feet and beaks blazing in the sunlight, beady, golden eyes unblinking, creamy head tufts streaming like banners celebrating the exuberance of natural design. A bunch of crows glides along the forest's edge. They spot an eagle in a treetop, harass it off its perch, and follow it away, pitching down in turns against its back. I once saw a bunch of kids do the same thing in a city park, running around an old man, teasing and tormenting him, dancing away from the clumsy swings of his cane, then dashing off when two of us hurried toward them.

Glaucous-winged gulls swoop and soar in the updraft, as if it's taken possession of them. Some hover a few feet from my ledge, as if they've chosen to show this landbound creature what wings are for. I've never been so close to the dream of quiet flight. While each gull drifts past, downy feathers on top of its wings lift and ruffle, pulled up by the same vacuum that holds the bird aloft. Sitting in the midst of these gulls, I feel as dense and ungraceful as a stone. They float by like leaves in a clear mountain stream, inviting me to abandon this complex life and stumbling body, launch out from the precipice, and spend my days riding the sea wind.

A huge gathering of puffins and murres rafts on the rippled water off Kanaashi's lee, fretting with constant motion. Dozens of little squadrons flow around and through each other like processions in a Chinese pageant. At the same time, scores of birds are diving, bobbing up, and flapping their wings dry. I can imagine what's going on below—birds driving down through the shadowy columns of water, toward a school of needlefish that trembles like aurora in the night sky. And salmon flinging like meteors at the school's lower edge, cutting it off from escape into the depths. Birds and fish, island and ocean—all knitted into one living fabric that encompasses them all. I wonder which is the organism: the bird or the flock, the fish or the school, the insect or the swarm, the tree or the forest . . . the animal or the island.

Life saturates Kanaashi, flows so richly through the waters and over the rocks that the island seems almost magical. For a moment I find myself believing that nowhere else on earth could match this beauty and perfection. Then I hear the sweet, clear voice of a song sparrow, and I remind myself that the same sound rings nearly everywhere along this coast, nearly everywhere across the breadth of this continent. I remember the song sparrow's voice from summer mornings in Wisconsin, mingled through a chorus of bird songs that swelled up from the farmlands and the forest. Those midwestern dawns were as rich and lovely as any I've ever experienced. Perhaps there are no inherently special places, only places made special by the relationships people sustain with them—wilderness or city, mountain or prairie, desert or swamp, forest or farmland. In this sense, all places on earth are equal and identical, waiting only to be *known* as Koyukon people know their boreal forest homeland.

Across the passage, a bank of clouds flows around Kluksa Mountain and trails out to streamers that vanish over Haida Strait. A black flicker materializes against the timbered slopes, then takes the shape of a raven flying toward Kanaashi. Carried along by the wind, he soon comes close and flares up through the mingled colonnade of gulls. I'm certain that our eyes meet as he passes, opens his beak, and lets out a series of toneless, garbled, vainglorious squawks, rising curiously at the end: "*Gwaaaaawk?*" And for some reason, I think he's asking: "What is this pale, wingless, stumbling creature trying to *do* here?" A gust takes him around the headland, but his voice drifts back once more, as if to remind me of a question that must be answered. Sparsely trained in the natural sciences, caught between two deeply different ways of seeing the world, and guided by nothing more than a love and fascination for the out-of-doors—what can I really hope to learn by coming here?

I lie back against the cushion of grass to think it all through again. And this time, perhaps because I've finally kept at it long enough, the answer comes with surprising clarity: I haven't intended to carry on research as a naturalist or ecologist, nor to gather scientific observations of any animals or plants that live here. My purpose, which has emerged gradually and of its own accord, is to understand myself in relationship to a natural community of which I am, in some undefinable way, a part. I've come seeking a better sense of how I fit into this place, not only as a visitor and watcher, but as a participant. From the beginning I've had a nebulous idea of "studying" the island or of exploring a world that seemed external to myself. But the exploration has turned inward, and I have slowly recognized that I am not an outsider here. Like every other human in every other place, I am an inhabitant, a member of the community largely defined, an organism who differs very little from the others around me. The island is not just a place to pleasure my senses—it is my home, my ecological niche, my life broadly defined.

Slow-minded Norwegian, it's taken me all these months to figure out what

■ ■ ■

The Island's Child

91

I'm trying to do here. This is the first time I've thought seriously about the idea of home, what it means to choose a place on earth and live there, to be a member of the community whose boundaries extend beyond the human enclave. I wonder what it would mean if each person, at some point in life, set aside a time to become thoroughly engaged with a part of the home community: a backyard, a woodlot, a pond, a stretch of river, a hillside, a farm, a park, a creek, a county, a butte, a marsh, a length of seacoast, a ridge, an estuary, a cactus forest, an island. How would it affect the way each person views herself or himself in relationship to the natural surroundings, or to the earth as a whole? And over a period of generations, how would it affect the collective worldview of Western culture? There are clues, I believe, in the thoughts and lifeways of people like the Koyukon.

As I look out from the clifftop, I hear the raven's distant, querying voice once more. I suppose I'll never understand how we belong together here, but even the wondering may be purpose enough; and if I spend the rest of my life on this little stretch of coast, some deeper answers might yet emerge. I used to dream of traveling to distant places, thinking that would be the best way to understand the process of living on earth. But perhaps I could learn as much by staying within the horizon visible from this island's edge, focusing on the world close at hand. It's a very old idea, which I never comprehended until now. Modern thinkers like Gary Snyder have written at length about it; for thousands of years Native American people have centered their lives on it; and ancient writers have expressed it in many ways. As Hakuin Zenji muses, in "Song of Zen":

> *How sad that people ignore the near*
> *and search for truth afar:*
> *like someone in the midst of water*
> *crying out in thirst,*
> *like a child of a wealthy home*
> *wandering among the poor.*

■ ■ ■

Richard Nelson

92

Instead of heading for camp I cut through the woods and come out on the island's highest, steepest shore, near the murre colony in the sea cave. I've scarcely reached the edge when a burst of sound comes from below. A lone humpback whale rolls up through a necklace of froth, the curve of its back glistening beneath a cloud of breath. Then comes the long, hollow intonation of its breathing in, a sound like the inhaling of Kanaashi's blowhole. The whale rises again, like an island being born. Watching it, I imagine the beginnings of Kanaashi, a hot fist of stone thrust up from the submerged flank of Kluksa Mountain.

Two islands and a whale, all separate yet conjoined, all sharing in a single birth. Kanaashi is the island's child, as the whale is Kanaashi's child, as Ethan is Nita's child; as we are all one child, spinning through mother sky.

Clark Mishler
Alaska Wildlife #1
Cibachrome
1981
UAP83:041:001

RESPECT GAALEE'YA

Howard Luke

THERE'S A PLACE down on the Yukon River, below Tanana and Ruby, they call Bone Yard. You can see where those tusks are sticking out. Years ago, this place used to be a desert here. We used to have sheep. This used to be just mountains here, not hills. All of the elephants and all of the snakes—some people say giraffes and everything—they had a big cave. The animals knew when the world was coming into the end there. They knew the world was coming in together. The world was going to change. That's what is going to happen right here, because we don't take care of our land. And that's what happened at that time. All of the animals got together, and they buried themselves. The animals told people not to go up there, not to go into that cave.

They had that big cave, and today, some places, you can find those tusks out there. When I was working on a boat, we used to go right by that hill and see those tusks sticking out. By the side of that hill, you can see them sticking about three inches out—just white. All of the animals said it was the end of the world, so they just buried themselves. This is why I say it's going to come yet. It's going to come because we're mistreating everything. We don't take care of it. People don't want to listen. They want to make that shortcut. That's why I say we've got to respect our land.

The animals told people not to go to the Bone Yard, otherwise something's

Written in collaboration with Ann Oury Lefavor.

95

going to happen. There are a lot of different places that people tell you not to go. People are not listening. They want to see for themselves. Someone told me a story just the other day. There was a fellow down by Ruby selling that ivory. He was picking it up, and he made a lot of money with that ivory, getting those tusks down there. He keeled over. So you see, there's something to it. When you're told not to do those things and you still do it, it's bound to catch up with you. This is why we're supposed to respect our animals. The animals used to be human at one time.

We've got these airboats, and the airboats are going out on the rivers and the flats in springtime, and they run over the eggs. Ducks have their eggs out there, and the airboats go anywhere—over the grass. They run over the eggs. That's why our animals are not coming back again. They've been mistreated. Those are the things I talk about, because they're really ruining our country.

Years ago, when there were birds' nests, they told us, "You can go look at the young ones, but when you go to the young ones, you close your mouth. You don't breathe on the young ones, or else their mother won't come back." This is what we were told, and those are the things I want to put out.

We need to protect our animals, and protect our fish, and our ducks. I'm raising heck about the airboats. I've been doing that for the last year now. I wrote letters to the editor twice, and one lady gave an awful write-up about me. She said that the airboats don't make as much noise as the outboard motor. I sit in my cabin on the riverbank, and I can hear them twenty miles out there. What do they have those earplugs on for? Let them take those earplugs off, then they'll know what the hell the noise is. The airboats go out in springtime and they can run all over the grass, and they're running over the eggs. Ducks have eggs, and the airboats don't know where they're going. They just run anywhere it's wet. So they just kill all the young ones off. This one lady wrote a letter back to me. It's about time I wrote another letter and backtalk her again. Our animals are disappearing.

Every year we're getting less and less. Every year we're getting less water. We don't get that much water now. They predicted that years ago, that if we don't respect these things, they're not going to come to us. I mean they're going to disappear. As I was growing up, I heard people talking about it, and I'm still talking about these things yet. I believe what my elders told me. I'm an elder now, but I believe in what they told me at one time. And it's happening right today. We don't respect our animals and our trees.

Everything is alive. The trees are alive, the moss, the sand, the gravel. Everything is alive. The birch, we use all that. Years ago when my mother and them used to take birch bark off a tree to make baskets, they used to talk to the tree and leave something there. They said, "Always take some and leave some," and we are not doing it.

Just like the animals. The animals, it's the same thing. We have all kinds of animals. We used to have a lot of them. I remember way back in the 1930s, animals just started showing up. Before that we had to go hundreds of miles for moose. If we saw one track we just kept following it and following it. And we shared with one another. I don't care who it was, they got a little chunk. That's respect. And if that person says, "Thank you," that means he is giving you his wisdom. But now it's not that way. My own people are not doing it. I get moose, and I get fish, and I put it in the freezer. Beaver meat too, I got a freezer full of it, and I cook it up, and I give it to the people at Denali Center. It helps you when you do this, respect the animal. If you respect the animals, they will give themselves to you. I believe strongly in that, and I believe strongly about our trees. They're cutting our trees, and they're not using it all. They're just wasting the stuff. They're not taking every bit of it. They're not scaling the logs right. They're finally finding out that we're losing money on the trees. If they got someone that knows how to scale logs, it would be different, but now they're just clean-cutting everything. It's not right, because everything lives on each other. There's our whole problem right today, that we're not living up to what we were told.

There's a story way back there: There was a caribou, and there was a bear, a grizzly bear, and he was hungry. He was hungry, so he took after this caribou. The caribou got away from him. The caribou looked back, and there was no bear. The bear was gone. So the caribou stopped and thought. He thought, "We're supposed to share with one another. That bear needs. He's hungry. I'm going to give myself to him." So he turned around and went back. He went to that bear and gave himself.

What I like about today is over at Denali Center, they got a place for the elders to go. My mother was eighty-some years old, and there was no place for her to go. I think they feel good about themselves. It's awful that they take people away from us, but I mean they should let the people run it like they want to run it. A lot of our people up there really like our Indian food—like dry fish and beaver meat. They get tired of this other stuff. What I'm saying is they should get with these villages and these people that trap. There are some white people who are trapping. They don't know what to do with the beaver meat. They could take it up to Denali and cook it for the people. I think people would be much healthier, because they miss their food. That's their livelihood.

What I do is cook up a bunch. Right now I got nobody to take me up there. But I got one more beaver I want to cook, and I'll take it up there and pass it around. That's what I usually do.

I think they should let the people have their traditional stuff. For someone to cook, they don't have to be "qualified." All you have to do is use some common sense. Working with kids, you know, like a counselor, you don't have to be "qualified." Just use some common sense, and I think the young people will really understand these things. It's the same way with our food. Just get some cook—anybody—you could just get them off the street. Ask them, "Do you want to help the elders? Make them feel good that you're going to be cooking our Native food?" I think that will go a long way. It'll make the elders feel good. I bet you'll see a lot of smiles, and that's what we need.

They're taking our livelihood away from us. A lot of people ask me, "What are you going to do when you get old? Who is going to take care of you here?" I say, "Don't worry about that. Time will tell." I got to be pretty bad off before I go to Denali. I like Denali. I like the people there, but I want to live my traditional life. If I live my traditional life, I think I'll live longer. Every morning I go out and take a good walk. If I get crippled, I can wheel around my yard. You go out and smell the old balsam, and it's just like you're floating in the air.

Use some common sense. They got people from the States running these things, and they don't know how to cook our Native food. It's just like eating pizza. When I go to town I get sick. When I come back, I feel weak from it. It's not my food, see.

It's just like the moose. The moose were starving one winter, and people started throwing them hay. They can't eat that food because they're not used to it. And it's the same thing. They're just like humans.

I like Denali Center, but they've got to change their ways. Some Alaskans got to step in there and take it into their hands. I think we could save a lot of our people. They'd live longer, and they'd feel happy about themselves.

When people come out to my camp, I try to teach them about these things, how to respect our elders, our animals, and our land. I believe if we sit down together and we talk, we can solve all the problems with our animals and our land. Our land is the main thing. But there's something that people are doing wrong. They go back to the city and do the same thing. They don't respect anything. They don't respect the animals, the water, nothing. Money talks. There's too dang much money involved. Money is nothing. Friendship is friendship. Money never dies. He's there all the time. But your friend, you talk to him now, and the minute you walk out he may drop. So that's why we want to share with one another and respect each other. There's a story about a woman, and her husband was blind. She'd go out every day, and she finally snared a moose, I guess. They used to snare moose at that time. So she used to go out every day, and her husband would stay home. He was getting weak and hungry, and here she told him nothing, and she got a moose.

One day he heard a loon down by the lake. So he crawled down by the lake, and the loon came over to him. "What's the matter?" Loon said. "You look like you're weak and you're sick to me."

"I'm hungry, and I'm blind," he said. "My wife . . ." (I don't know, in those days they never said "wife"—"my woman," they said) "my woman just left me. She goes out every day. I don't know where she's at, and I'm getting hungry."

He had a necklace on his neck. In those days they used bone to make necklaces—like a fishhook—and big people were the only ones that used those things.

"So, you've got a necklace," the loon said. "If you give me your necklace, I'll try to make your eyes come back, so you can see again."

"Anything," the man said. (In those days they didn't say "God." They just said "Our father.") "*Denaxwto' basi*," the man said, "Father, thank you."

The loon said, "You get on top of me, and I'm going to dive with you. You hang on."

The little giant got on top of the loon. The loon dove down with him and came up on the other side. He asked the man, "How's that?"

The man could see a little bit. It got a little bright to him, but he told the loon, "No, not yet."

The loon went down with him again. He came up on the other side and asked, "How's that? Can you see good?" (He didn't say it just like this. They talked in their native tongue, you know.)

So, OK, he went down with him again. He came out on the other side, and gee, he could see really plain.

The man said, "Thank you." He said, "*Basi' chwx denaxwto'. Selo' uniniyh, se'al ghiyol*," he said, "Our father, take my hand. Thank you very much."

"Dah," he said, and he gave Loon his *guho*, his necklace.

There's a little mark on the loon's chest. It looks like a hook. That's the one that the blind man gave to that loon. So if you get a loon you look right on his chest, and you can see that fish hook mark.

The man thanked the loon and took off, started walking fast. He saw smoke down at his camp, so he started walking fast. He saw his woman. She had her back towards him. He came closer. When he got closer, he pretended he was blind, and he used his stick.

She turned around and looked. "What are you doing?" he asked. "I'm hungry. I'm getting weak. I smell something. It's just like I smell meat," he said.

She was roasting meat, and she had a lot of dry meat hanging up. "I got nothing," she said. "I scorched my parka is what you smell."

"No, I smell meat," he said, and he kept saying that. He could see that she had a lot of meat.

She turned her meat over and looked the other way. While she wasn't looking, he took his cane and hit her on the back. He hit her on the back, and she crawled away. It broke her back. He said, "*Noduya ghwla'. Noduya ghwla'.*"

Right there, that woman turned into an ant. You see where that ant is connected together? Well, that's that woman. That's that woman, and that's how cruel they are. That's when they say, "You don't listen."

Glen Simpson

Thule Bird

Copper and sterling silver

1982

UA82-3-35

So that's the end of that one.

Right now, moose season is open. I just come back from town, I saw moose horns on a pickup right ahead of me coming down Airport Road, and no meat or nothing, just horns. And they're going down to send it out. That's awful. People got to look into these things. What the hell do we have leaders for? We don't have leaders. People say they're our leaders, but they're nothing. They're just for themselves. I'm sick and tired of that. I hope that someone will listen to me and people will hear what I say and think twice.

But people got to work together. I get disgusted. Some people are just starving for meat. My own friends kill a moose, and they don't bring everything out of there. They bone everything out. Look at the head. We cook that up and use it for the potlatch. We have a big potlatch, and we never waste anything.

We've got to really work together to save our land. People used to say, way back when I was growing up, to really treat your land right—and your animals. If you respect those things, they'll pay you back in a lot of ways, but it's terrible how it is right now. It makes me sick once in a while when I see it. A couple of years ago, my nephew and I went out and saw a bunch of crows. I told my nephew, "There's something over there." So we went over, and there was a big moose. They had just cut the head off and taken that. We turned that in to the Game Commission, and they never did anything about it. Every time we turned something in they asked, "Did you see it happen? Who did it?" That's a hell of a law we got. One of these days, though, they shall see. The city is getting too big for itself, and people are getting too big for themselves. They are just for themselves. I got relations here in town. They got a moose, and do you think they cut me off a steak?—no. I'm not going to tell them I need a chunk of meat. That's them. They got to decide that themselves. That's how it is right today.

Things are tight right now. I can't even get a moose. But I know it'll come, because I've been forgiven. So it'll come sooner or later.

The reason that I say I was forgiven was that some time ago I really helped someone out, some old lady or some old man. Maybe I packed water for them or something like that. And she gave me her wisdom, or he gave me his wisdom. And I know I was forgiven for a lot of things I did, because I had a heart attack, and I shot my finger off, and I went through the ice, but I'm still here yet.

When I went through the ice a lot of my friends were here. I made it across the river, but one fellow here wanted to come back across with me. I said, "No. The ice is too thin." It just froze overnight. I slid over on a sled, and I slid fast, and that's what helped me out. He said, "No, I want to come over and help you, stay with you." I couldn't talk him out of it, so I told him, "Go ahead." We got on each side, and we started pushing over. We got in the middle of the river, and the ice went down with us. It was too much weight. We went down. And you know how fast that current is going out? Five miles an hour. We went down, and that sled went straight up. That current could have taken that sled right down, and could have taken us right down. That's why I say I know I was forgiven right then. Because the current went right around us. Otherwise it could have sucked us right down there. I knew right there that I was forgiven for things I did.

I did a lot of things in my young days. I was forgiven for those things, because right now I'm trying to help people. I know a lot of people. Friends of mine—there's two of them—are traveling all around the world now and telling people how they destroyed alcohol. What I mean is I don't think they did it on their own. They were forgiven. And that old man or that old lady gave them wisdom to do these things, and now they're doing it. They came up here two or three times for the spirit camp. That's what I say: I know I was forgiven. This is how I learned things. I'm not going to quit. I'm going to continue and talk more. By talking and sharing my wisdom, I can help people.

Animals share and help each other by giving themselves to each other. They give themselves to us, too. Weasel is the leader. He's so fast, and he tells the animals, "Don't go there." That's the reason they call him Gaalee'ya, that's "luck." If we take care of things and respect them, the weasel gives us luck, and he tells the animals to give themselves to us. I think about those things. Right now it is just so disgraceful. We're just ruining the country. We are doing it ourselves.

They blame the wolf for killing all the moose off. They live on each other. They don't kill each other just for nothing. What are wolves going to live on if they don't kill moose?

I've said the same thing time and time again. They blame the wolf for killing the moose. I think we got more two-legged wolves running around here in this country than we got four-legged wolves. A wolf will just get so much, that's all. If you had your belly full, you wouldn't go back for seconds would you? I wouldn't. I'd get sick. So that's what I say; if they want to keep the law real straight down like they used to do, they never blame the wolf. The wolves always take what's given to them, and then that's it. 'Cause there were wolves ever since I was a kid, and they share with each other. Animals all share with each other. And the coyotes all share with one another.

Right now they're hiring a helicopter to go out and shoot wolves. You know how much it costs to shoot a wolf? How much does it cost an hour for a helicopter, a couple thousand dollars an hour? Besides the cost, it's cruel to kill a wolf like that. The wolf who is hunted from the air is just like a man. He has no place to go, and that's just cruel.

We would have more respect if we went out and found the wolves ourselves. If they opened the bounty, like a hundred dollars or two hundred dollars, people would go out. And like they used to do years ago, they used to dig the pups out. And they'd keep them down. That's what would keep them down. But people are too bull-headed. We got a lot of bull-headed people in this country. Some bull-headed people we should get rid of, and start on our new generation, give them a test. They can do it. We got some qualified people right here, in this country here. We don't need to send for people in the States. All we got to do is use some common sense, and use it in the right way. I think we will all get along fine and learn to love each other, but it's not like that right now. Even relations are not like that now.

They don't think about the young generation or what the young generation is going to be like. They're going to be paying for all these things that are happening right today. We talked about a lot of this stuff when I went down to Colorado. We had a big meeting. A lot of people from all over the States came there for it. They have the same problems, but they say down there that they work together. They say they don't have all the big-time operators sitting on the bench, like being on the Fish and Game Board. They got their Native people on the board, and that's the way it should be. Right here, we have people that are business people that are on the board. I went to the Fish and Game Board twice. I never did get to speak.

People that they have on the Fish and Game Board—like lawyers—what the hell do they know about our livelihood? I'd like to take one of them out there, take him out a couple of hundred miles into the bush and let him see what it's like. I bet he'll change his mind. I just get so disgusted. I intend to do that too. Just take them out for a boat ride and tell them, "OK, you get the hell out here. You go on your own." This is the way I'm thinking right now. I'm so darn disgusted with these things. People talk and say, "We've got to go the white man's way." But they've got to respect our ways—respect our animals, birds, trees, and land, because these things are not going to be here forever. I don't think they'll be here forever.

A lot of people don't understand what "respect" means. Why do they get an education if they don't learn about respect? Respect is how we share with each other. Respect is "don't destroy that thing." People want to leave their mark there. That's not respect. Respect is leaving it just like you've never been there. If you blaze a tree, blaze a big tree, you kill that tree right there. It's going to have a scar. It's the same thing as your finger or something like that.

Like the animals. People just take chain saws and table saws and cut them up. That's not respect. That's what these hands are for. When I cut a fish, my right hand never gets bloody. This left hand does the work. If you let go of the knife, it gets all slimy and bloody. That's how people cut their hands. I never let go of the knife. That's what they call "respect." And that way people will see you, and they will say, "Oh man, that fellow really works hard to respect the animals and respect his hand." You see, you don't get blood on your right-hand side.

Respect and sharing are the same thing. They're related—and our subsistence—they're all related. We've got to respect these things, because if I was mistreated, I'm not going to go back to the same place again. If a fellow is eating, and he doesn't share his Pilot Bread, or whatever, and I'm sitting there watching him, I'm not going to go back there. I'm going to go some other place. It's the same thing.

My mother used to tell me stories at night. I told Mom, "You told me that story last night." She said, "I don't care. You're going to have to pass this on." At that time, there never used to be cotton, just a piece of rag. She'd put that rag in my ear and leave it there until she'd get done. Then she'd say, "How's that? Any difference?" So that's what I tell kids right today.

I want to tell you a story about a girl becoming a woman. I don't know how old those girls are—twelve or thirteen years old. Their people really look after them. I've seen them out in Arizona. This girl became a woman out there, and I'll tell you she had to go through a lot of things when she became a woman. They do it a little different here. What we do here is the mother looks after the girl. Nobody talks to her. The brothers don't look at her or anything. They put a blanket up, and she has a little can to go to the bathroom. Her mother looks after her. That's our traditional way. That's why I say a lot of things are not going our way. When a girl becomes a woman, she's got to be clean. She's got to take care of those things. You don't know; you might be standing next to your brother or something like that. It's bad. This is our traditional way. We should carry that on. People say we got to take care of our culture. Well, this is part of it.

This girl—her mother went out to do something. The girl was in the corner. That time they were staying at camp. It was before my time. Like I say, this used to be desert. We've got to respect our land. So, this girl threw the blanket off her, and she went outside. There were no trees. It was just like desert here at one time. She saw a bunch of sheep over there on the hill. She said, "Mom, look at those sheep."

Right there, her mother just cried and she said, "*Eshuya, eshuya.*" What she said was it was, "Terrible, terrible." She prayed right there. (Those days they never said, "God" or "Jesus." They just said, "Our Father" and "the devil").

When that girl said, "Look at those sheep," they just turned to rocks right there. You know those white rocks you see sometimes up on the hill there? That's those sheep. They turned to rocks.

That's why I say we have to look after our things. Even if we live in town, we should have respect for that. I think if we respect, a lot of things will go our way.

There are a few things I want to leave behind. No one has talked about this lately. There were a lot of sacred places years ago, when I was a kid. They got a place down there at Denali; down there at the mountain used to be a sacred place. Just the big people—that's all—could go in there, like the chief—were the only ones that could go in there. They had to go through certain people, counselors or something like that. They had counselors in those days, like second chief and first chief. They had to talk to these people before they could go over to Denali. That was a sacred place. Nobody could go in there. This is why a lot of things are not working, because they tell you not to go in there, and no one listens. They just go in there. This is why the whole world is not working right for us. I know I do a lot of that too. I just say, "Oh the heck with it. I'm going to go over there." That is why we have got a problem right today.

Over there, on the side of Denali, is a little hill, and there's a tunnel. The crow was the one that found that place. And he was the one that named all these birds, like the mallard ducks and teal ducks, all the birds. He named the cranes—the Canadian crane, the honkers, the swallows, the robins, and all that. They're all different. And just like clay, up there on the wall, are all the colors of all the birds.

People used to talk about it. I remember when I was a kid, that they said that they didn't want anyone to go into that tunnel. Because if you go in there, the things you want to do are not going to turn out right for you, or something's going to happen to you in years to come.

This is what I say right now—there's too much money talking. People are just not listening, and they're just going into that tunnel by Denali. Back years ago when I was a kid, they talked about that. We tried to keep it quiet and not say anything about it, but someone around Nenana started to talk about it. Now it's all over. They say—I don't know if it's true or not, but they say—Tanana Chiefs is going to put in a road, and that's going to be for tourists, just like Denali—right now, what they are doing to Denali. That's too bad. It's just that money talks right now.

I don't believe that—I don't believe only money is important. Money is not the only thing. It's there all the time, but your brother or sister . . . the minute you walk out the door—you don't know what's going to happen—they could keel over. I say money is nothing. You take care of your friends and your neighbors because you only see them once. Money, it's there all the time. So, I don't know. It's so bad now. Everything is money. There are a lot of sacred places around here, and people are going in.

I know there's one near Stevens Village. Me and a friend of mine, Dave Roberts, went by there one time, and, I'll tell you, it just got a white-out. There's a stick-man that's living there. They used to call them Stickman. Now they call them Bigfoot. He lives in there, you know, and they don't want you to go in there. They scare you.

When we went by there on our snowmachines, it got a white-out. It was up on a mountain, and you couldn't see two feet in front of you. You couldn't see any-thing. It was night on a mountain, both sides. We were running out of gas, so we'd run our motor just so long. We'd holler, and we'd go a few feet. We kept doing that, and finally we got away from that place where that animal was living. It started clearing up. We never even thought about it.

I thought about it afterward. I said, "Man, I think there's something that we did wrong some time ago." So, that night we were having supper, and Dave Roberts said, "You know something?" I told him, "No." He said, "There's a cave over there. They say there's a stickman living in there."

We went too close to it. That's the reason that we had a white-out.

So those are the things that we shouldn't be bothering with. But we just go ahead and do it. It's happening right today. It's too bad that people are doing it. They don't believe you or something, and they want to find out for themselves, for sure. Years ago, they used to have a lot of stories about how people used to be little people at the time, and this place used to be desert at that time. Those are the things I try to tell people about. Our leaders are not telling the people that right now. It's too much money that's involved, you know. Years ago, they used to be awful particular and superstitious. I'm superstitious about a lot of things too.

I've said that for years, and they predicted years ago, that if we don't listen and we don't pay attention, if we just go where we are told not to go—that outlook, or something like that—we just go there. We don't listen. We're just like kids. And the kids right now know what is going to happen in years to come. There will be nothing left for them. Right now, we're running out of water. It's going to be all drained out, because the glacier is going to be all melted out. You see how some years we have a dry season? We have no rain. We're bound to get punished for some of this stuff, because they predicted years ago, "Be sure and take care of your

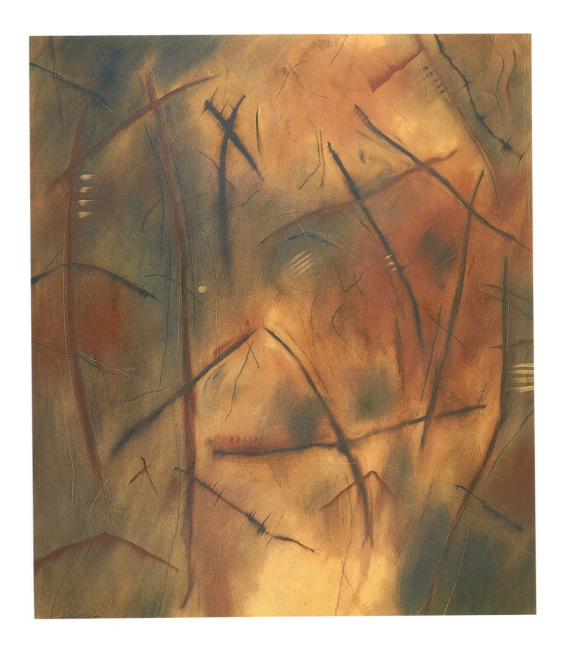

Robby Mohatt

Traces VI

Oil and alkyd on canvas

1993

Gift of the Friends of
the University of
Alaska Museum, 1995

UA95:060:001

land. Take care of the trees. Take care of everything that is alive. Be sure and respect those things." And we don't respect that.

We got to change our law in a lot of ways. Just like our children. All of these things are related. People are having problems because their children are running away. It's the same thing. A lot of people say, "No, it's different," but it's not. And that's what I mean. Hunters go out who are just after the horns, and a lot of people just hunger for meat today. Sharing. This is what I say: Nowadays we don't share with one another, and we don't respect. That's our biggest problem today. That's why our kids are going the other way. I got fish and stuff like that in the freezer, but that's for the potlatches. I share it with different people. But people are not looking at it that way.

We talk about kids, you know, and the main thing we have to do right now is change the law. The government is telling us we can't do this, we can't do that. The government says we can't put the names of kids who break laws in the paper. If kids do something wrong, and we have their names printed in the newspaper, I think the kids will straighten out, because they'd be kind of bashful. They'd be ashamed that they did that. This is what I'm saying; that's the first thing we have to do, because a kid might do something, and we don't know who he is, and he's standing right along side of us and just laughing, and we don't know. We've got to change the law, because if we continue like this, the kids are going to just continue. I believe that right today, that kids are not dumb. They know. They know what's coming ahead.

A lot of people say, "It's a free country." Sure, it's a free country, but we got to take care of it. That's what I'm saying, and the kids right now today, they're looking at it. They know that by and by, it's going to come to them. Just like I say, they're going to run out of water, and stuff like that. I believe they know what's coming up ahead, so they just don't care. I talked to a lady that's working with some kids. They said they don't care if they die right today. And, you see, that's awful. I think they're just like the old people who used to predict all this stuff.

We've got to respect them, and we've got to learn to love them. That's the main thing. I think what they should do—you know, they have all these survival camps—what they should do at a camp like that is have a circle talk every night. Every evening, have a circle talk, and let the kids tell their problems and get it out of them. They'll feel sorry for themselves and start crying. The other kids will go over and put their hands on them. It'll draw it out of them.

I know they did that to me, here, years ago, in a spirit camp here. I didn't like this one person, and I talked about that. They took it out of me. Those are the things they've got to look into. I get disgusted with these things—what they are doing. The kids know that too, but they got nobody to explain that they got to be proud of what they do. They've got to work with their hands. They've got to make something. And they've got to listen . . . and use their lips. Everything is there to use. You use your eye, your ear, your hand, and your foot. That way, they'll feel good about themselves.

Right today, all they say is, "You got to get your education." Sure, I like the kids to have their education, but there's something else we're leaving out. I think that the part we're leaving out is that we are not respecting the kids. I've been thinking about it. I sit down here alone at night, and I think about it. I wonder, "How can I do this?" There's some way we can do it. It's there. It's there, but we got to reach out and grab it. Not only one person can do it. All the people here got to get together, and they'll find that word—they'll find that thing we're looking for. A lot of people say it's too late. I know a lot of elders say, "It's too late. We've got to go the white man's way. They've got to get their education." But they're not thinking about all this alcohol and drugs and stuff. That's what ruins our kids. I know. I've been through it. I know what it is. I was just so lucky that I did the right thing when I did it.

I am particular in ways, superstitious in a lot of ways. I believe it too, because I learned it down the trail. When I fell in the water, and we were right in the middle of the river with no one to get us out, we got out on our own. The current just went right around us. So, you see, there was something. So I've been forgiven for what I did. And I believe a lot of kids will realize that. Something happens like that, and they realize that, if you keep telling them these things.

So I talk to the kids a lot of times, and I put it this way. I believe our stories come first, if we want to teach kids and start working with kids. We've got to start with stories, two, three stories, anyway—about how people survive and how they heal each other. If kids listen to that, they'll say, "Oh yeah, that's the way I got to go." And they'll turn the other way—not all of them, but, like I say, "If I help one,

I help a thousand." I tell the kids all the time, "I'm here to give you my wisdom, and I want you to pass these things on."

That's what these things are all about. I know, the last two, three years, it's getting worse. It's getting filthy. People don't respect. They don't share with one another. There are mothers and daughters that don't get along. They predicted years ago that would happen, and it is happening right now. This is why I say we have to listen.

Stories, stories come first when you talk to people. You're going to leave something, your wisdom, with them. 'Cause years ago the animals used to be human at one time. That's why they say to respect the animals.

David Dapogny
Projections for a Forest in Three Dimensions #5
Electrostatic photograph and
stitching
Undated
UAP84:124:001

THE VIEW HELPS ME
KNOW WHERE I AM

*Marybeth
Holleman*

"WE'VE GOT too much weight for this bucket of garbage," the pilot said to the ticket agent, as he looked at the mail sacks, pile of boxes, and my lone duffel bag. They loaded them all into the rear of the two-seater plane anyhow, and I climbed into the passenger seat. After a run down the short airstrip, we left the tiny Bethel airport behind.

It was a long flight, the pilot was silent, the bucket of garbage warm. Behind a thin line of blue clouds the sun rose, set like a minimalist painting, sharp and brilliant on the endlessly flat white land of the Yukon-Kuskokwim Delta.

I'd read about this place, seen pictures of it in summer. I knew I was flying across the largest wildlife refuge in the United States—at 19.6 million acres, the Yukon Delta Wildlife Refuge in western Alaska is equal in size to the state of Maine. I knew that in summer millions of swans, geese, ducks, and other water birds congregated here to raise their young. And I knew that, even now, underneath several feet of ice, there was life. Blackfish, one of the mainstays of the villagers' diets, ball up together in winter and survive under ice until breakup in May.

From the plane, though, all I could see was snow and ice, frozen ponds and streams. The streams looked like roads at first, perhaps made by snowmachines.

I tried to follow them and wondered why someone would be driving around out there. Where would they be going? What would they be looking for? But the paths they traced were so dense with soft curves, so inescapably random, they could only have been made by wind. Roads for wind. I tried to imagine life out there, maybe a lone wolf padding down a frozen wind road. I saw nothing.

At the Bethel airport that morning, I was surrounded by the bustle of a small community, but I was aware only of my own anxiety. I had hoped the storms that frequently roll in from the Bering Sea and blanket the coast of western Alaska would keep me from leaving Bethel. The prospect of being dropped off, by myself, in a small village I'd never seen within a native culture I'd never experienced filled me with apprehension.

My conversation with Stephen Stephens, the person I planned to meet in Napaskiak, had not stilled my fear of being an unwelcome visitor. Instead, it had left me wondering if he would be there to pick me up—or if he would, as had happened to my co-worker, Russ, not even be in town. And I would be left waiting at a remote airstrip, on the edge of a tiny Yup'ik Eskimo settlement, in temperatures hovering at thirty below.

When I had finished my monologue to Stephen about needing to review his records on juvenile detention, I wondered if his silence meant he didn't understand the purpose of my visit, or if he understood but thought it trivial. Thinking it trivial myself, I would understand if he didn't bother to show. I recognized my mission as all taking and no giving—I was just some government stranger coming in to take up his time and leave nothing behind, just one in a long line of city dwellers skimming the surface of their lives.

Russ and I were working on a project for the University of Alaska's Justice Center. Our task was to decide whether jails in Alaska's rural communities were following the prescribed guidelines for handling "juvenile offenders." The rules were different for younger criminals, and so we were traveling to villages, reviewing the files kept by the Village Public Safety Officer (known as a VPSO; these places are too small to have a "police force"), recording what we found, and then reporting back to the Justice Center. So far, Russ had made two trips; this was my first.

A few weeks earlier, Russ had flown into Aniak, just up the Kuskokwim River from Bethel, only to find that the person he was to meet had left on a caribou hunting trip. Russ considered that, between the static-heavy phone reception and the halting English of people for whom Yup'ik is their first language, they had somehow miscommunicated. Perhaps the VPSO just didn't understand that Russ needed to see him. All Russ could do was wait for the next plane back to Bethel.

When he told me about this trip, Russ attempted to quell my fears. "Yup'ik Eskimos are pretty quiet and reserved," he said, "but they're helpful when you need it."

I stirred from my trance as a tiny settlement suddenly appeared. The Yup'ik village of Quinhagak sat on the coast, where a faint line delineated land from sea. It was low tide, and the beaches were tinged with green, as if they harbored the seeds of spring. Spring, when the delta resounded with the songs of whistling swans, emperor geese, sandpipers, arctic terns, spectacled eiders.

This time of year, all was quiet and white, a still life. I was relieved that we were stopping here and at another village before reaching my destination, Napaskiak. I needed to shake this feeling of invisibility.

After we landed, the pilot unloaded eight boxes, all full of frozen turkeys to help the 350 residents of Quinhagak celebrate Thanksgiving. I wondered what the Yupiit, who had inhabited this terrain for thousands of years before white people arrived, thought of our holiday celebrating abundance in the middle of their season of scarcity. It must be in the spring, when the birds and salmon return, and the blackfish unfurl in fast-moving water, that they feel thankful.

The pilot pulled out a cigarette and started talking planes to a white man in a beaver-skin hat who had come for the turkeys. This man owned the village's only store and the turkeys.

"Should be out checking my lines today," said the man in the beaver hat. "Got a couple of foxes and a wolf this week."

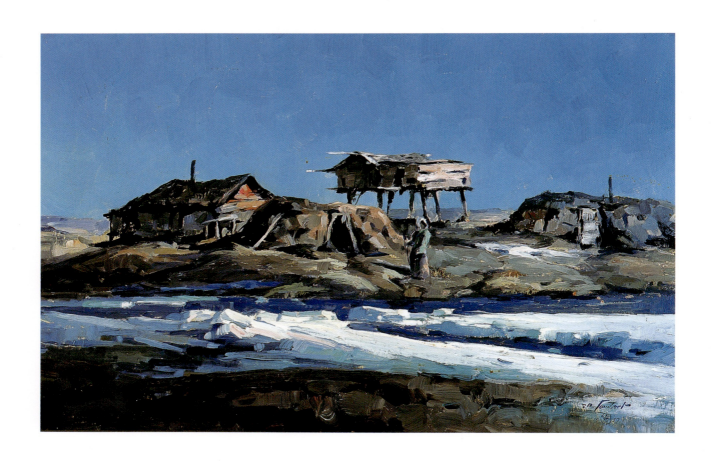

Theodore Roosevelt Lambert

A Tundra Town at Breakup

Oil on board

1937

Gift of Charles M. Binkley

UA81-27-4

"Wolves come down this far?" asked the pilot.

"Oh, yeah," he replied, pushing the fur hat back on his head to reveal eyes as blue as ice. "But I'm getting less of them every year, and every year they get more scrawny. I might just get out of this God-forsaken place real soon."

The pilot finished his cigarette, crushed it against a box of turkeys, and dropped it on the ground. He climbed back into his seat and the engines sputtered and roared. Our plane's two tiny tires spun and sprayed ice and gravel in a crystal plume as we became airborne again.

As Quinhagak slipped quietly behind a snowbank, I shook off images of a starving wolf searching for food only to be lured into a trap. I gave in to the flying. I love small planes, love the bumpy runways, the dipping and rocking of takeoff, the view of a village as it grows smaller and smaller. Most settlements of any size look best from a distance, as if they had been designed from the air. But most of all I like to see the landscape, the patterns of life revealed with distance. The view helps me know where I am.

The sun was higher, dawn had passed and thin clouds had vanished. With the sun a brilliant globe, the land sharpened. The blinking eye of the world was fully open. I saw no forests, no mountains, not even a hill—nothing to stop the wind. The only relief was created by the wind itself, sculpted snow hills and snow valleys and snow ridges.

Within minutes, the plane landed at Eek. As we waited for someone to meet us, the pilot warmed to conversation. He had been a pilot for Camai Air in Bethel for two years. From Texas, originally Arkansas, he was up here for the money: he made, he said, what a first-class pilot makes with Delta Airlines. He was saving to move back to Arkansas and buy land. The trapper in Quinhagak, he said, was from Mobile, Alabama. I told him I was from North Carolina. A bunch of southerners, what were the three of us doing up here?

A four-wheeler with a trailer bounced toward us. I could barely see the driver's broad brown face in his bundle of clothes. He smiled and nodded a quick hello, his deep brown eyes catching mine for a moment. We filled his trailer with bags of mail and a few boxes, and he sped back down the frozen path to his warm home. "Yeah, Eskimos, they're pretty friendly I guess," said the pilot. "But they got this saying, 'God damn Gussacks.' It means white man. It's not a bad word though," he added quickly, looking at me sideways.

Gussack—the term comes from Cossack, the word for the Russian fur traders who first encountered the Yupiit several hundred years ago. Was I any different from those Russians, or from this pilot and his trapper friend, dropping in to take what I wanted and then return to my home, which was as foreign as another language here?

Sun now exposed every twig, rock, snowdrift to its harsh bright light. I searched the ground for a moving form, a dark spot signifying life, but saw only the same sharp snowscape like the cold, empty stare of a stranger.

All too soon, the village of Napaskiak came into view. A tiny cluster of brown buildings, it sat on the banks of the Kuskokwim River. The Kuskokwim—the roaring eight-hundred-mile-long river that brings life to this place in summer, that brings food to all the settlements on the delta and farther inland—now in winter was a solid sheet of ice, quiet and still. But smoke curled from a few chimneys in this village, and a dog howled into the wind. I took a deep breath and climbed out of the plane.

Two men on four-wheelers met our plane. One loaded up the remaining mailbags and boxes and sped off without saying a word. The other grabbed my duffel bag and threw it on the rack of his three-wheeler.

"Hop on," he gestured to the space behind him on his seat. I could only assume he was Stephen Stephens, so I climbed up behind him on the seat and hung on to his thick coat.

We drove upon snow-covered boardwalks, so cold no ice had formed. We passed a yard full of dogs tethered to doghouses made of old fuel drums. They howled at our passing, jerking on their short chains so hard their houses shook. Buildings slid by my eyes, a jumble of multicolored pieces of wood, plyboard, aluminum, tarp, plastic. The wind bit my face, and after a few minutes it was numb.

"I can't feel my nose. Is it still there?" I asked Stephen.

"Yes," he answered quietly, missing or ignoring my attempt at humor.

The police station stood in the center of the village, a small building, bright blue with yellow trim and a hand-painted sign. Stephen showed me into the small, chilly office and pulled out three file folders stuffed with papers. With our hats and overcoats removed, I noticed his boyish, smooth face and wiry body, and thought that he seemed rather young to be a village public safety officer.

Now that we were inside, he spoke easily. He joked with me about the ludicrousness of paperwork, his and mine, as I poured over the tumble of records. Juvenile detention regulations seemed as remote here as did the rush-hour traffic of the city where these laws were created. How can you keep young troublemakers seperate from older offenders when you barely have one room to hold them in? And since everybody knows everybody here, how could an adult be more likely to corrupt or endanger kids in the town jail?

I smiled and chattered to Stephen, clinging to this common frustration with bureaucracy as I would a fingerhold on a smooth rock face. For the next hour, I looked at his scant records, took notes, and my business in his village was done.

The plane, however, wouldn't return for four more hours. Stephen took me to the village store, where I left my bag until my flight arrived. Then he pointed down the boardwalk to their new school, as if of course I'd want to go see it. He left, saying he'd be back in his office later if I needed anything else. I didn't see him again.

I walked down the boardwalk, the cold snow squeaking beneath my boots like the only sound in the world. I felt conspicuous, wandering their streets, looking at their lives. Surely I must stand out in this village like a wolf in a herd of caribou. A young woman wearing seal mukluks and no hat passed me. She smiled, said hello. That was all.

I was surprised, thinking that the presense of a stranger in a small town would create interest. But later, back in Anchorage, a friend who had been a teacher in Western Alaska for many years said this lack of curiosity was now common.

"So many white people come and go through those villages now," Dennis said, "that it's no longer surprising to them. It doesn't interest them or bother them, as far as I can tell. It just doesn't have much effect."

The school, big and bright and brand-new, sat like a monument of change in this tiny weathered village. Inside, the lobby was full of trophies and pictures and a large tank filled with fish from the Kuskokwim River. The principal, originally from Oklahoma, came out of his office and talked with me for nearly an hour, telling me all about how the school was run and what state-of-the-art facilities it contained. I asked a few questions to keep the conversation going.

School children came and went, the hallways periodically filling with voices in the same way they did when I was in school. But here, I couldn't understand the words echoing in the halls. As they passed me, some children glanced at me briefly, and others made no visible note of my presence. A few younger ones stopped and eagerly named the fish in the tank for me: whitefish, blackfish, dolly varden.

I walked back into the cold and down to the river. Time passed as quietly as the water flowing beneath the ice. I stared at the monochromatic scene of frozen river, snow-covered land, and crystallized willows, broken only by a lone red three-wheeler on the edge of the ice. Waiting, I guessed, for the trip to Oscarville. Stephen had told me that they could drive to the small community across the river when the ice became a little thicker.

Back at the store, I bought a bag of almonds and waited for my flight. A young girl, hanging on her mother's skirts, peered at me shyly. I offered her an almond, and she took it, giving me a small, quick smile. I gave her a handful more and she disappeared behind a counter. The Camai ticket agent and mailman, James Jameson, ran outside, then back in.

"The plane's coming," he said to me. But it was only 3:15, not 3:45. I hadn't expected it to be early. "I'll give you a ride over there."

Outside, we hopped onto James's three-wheeler. We raced down the bumpy snow-packed trail, past hand-painted signs saying, "Slow Going." Two boxes sat on the snow by the runway.

"It's already been here. Yes, that's the flight number. We'll go back and call," said James. Before I comprehended what was happening, we were on our way back to the store.

James H. Barker

Carrying River Water

in Kwethluk

Gelatin silver photograph

1973

UAP90:019:001

I followed his lead and didn't get agitated, even internally, about a plane show-ing up thirty minutes early and then not waiting for me. I thought about my first conversation with Stephen, when I had called to set up my visit. "OK," he'd said, no why, no wondering. Just, OK. Everything was taken in as if there was no un-expected—or no expectations.

At the store James dialed a number for me, said, "Ask for dispatch," then began unloading his mail. Customers lined up at his window. Dispatch said they would send the plane back for me in fifteen minutes or so. I waited, but James was busy passing out the mail.

"The plane's coming back. I'll just walk down there," I told James. He nodded his head and smiled.

Once more down the boardwalk. In the summer, when the ground stays wet and soggy, these wooden pathways serve them better than dirt or pavement. Even in winter they helped define some pathway through the cluster of homes.

I stopped to pet a dog tied up outside one house. He did not bark, but wagged his tail and licked my gloved hand, his warm breath penetrating the wool. An old Russian church, one I must have passed three times now but hadn't noticed, stood like a sentinel in a field of frost and crosses. Wind had weathered it to a fine patina of white, blue, and gold.

I smiled as I passed the sign "Slow Going," thinking about how it might sound when Stephen said those words. Stephen's voice, James's voice, the children's cho-rus in the school hallway—they echoed a river's flow.

At the airstrip, I wandered back down to the river, drawn to its silence. I watched the geometry of ice, felt my lashes freeze, and listened to absolute still-ness. I breathed deeply, wanting to fill my lungs with the sharp air that seemed newer, more elemental, than any I had ever breathed. Not until I heard the plane's buzzing overhead did I realize my feet were numb. I walked slowly, silently, to-ward the airstrip.

As Napaskiak faded from sight, the sun's rays slanted across the frozen land-scape, cast in a golden hue. Ground and brush, awaiting spring, lay exposed by wind, then faded under drifts of soft snow. Wind's undulating roads linked pond to pond. Thin stands of golden trees lined the river bank. Waves of ice glimmered, stretches of diamond snow sparkled.

As we approached Bethel, I looked back from where I had come. I imagined I saw a wolf trotting down one of the winding roads, picking up diamonds in his paws.

■ ■ ■

Nelson Gingerich
Bore Tide
Gelatin silver photograph
1978
UAP83:051:001

UNDER THE TIDES,
UNDER THE MOON

Nancy Lord

AT THE FAR END of our beach, more than two miles from our camp on the shore of Alaska's Cook Inlet, I have one last eyebolt and buoy to put in. I had to wait for the minus tide to hit bottom before I could wade from the beach to a rock pile where I replaced a plug with an eyebolt in a drilled rock and attached two lines and buoys—one I'll pull in and attach to a setline, one I'll leave as the inside anchor to an outside set. Now I rush across the rocky beach to the base of a long curved reef, barely exposed, that reaches out and around a sort of water-filled trench it shelters. On the far end of it, there's another plugged rock, the last place I need to ready for fishing.

The inlet is rough today, which means the water didn't suck out as far as it normally would on a minus-two-and-a-half-foot tide, and with the tide's turn the waves are hammering the reef, tossing up spray and surging through the breaks. I hesitate for a second to think about whether I have enough time to get to the end and back. Then, clutching my totebag and the buoy attached to a coiled line, I scramble out the path of sea-rounded and mud-slicked rocks. It's like walking on the backs of turtles, and I never lift one foot until the other is firmly in place.

At the end, water's already flooding around the rock. I brace a knee high against it, grab the pliers and loosen the plug, then unscrew it with my fingers and drop it into my bag. I squirt grease into the hole, screw in an eyebolt, bang it tight with a hammer, grab the end of the line, tie it tight to the eye and finish it with a bow-line. I throw the buoy out into the water to pull the line straight, and I'm done. My leg is vibrating like a sewing machine, and the reef behind me is getting spottier.

Returning, I feel like Harriet Beecher Stowe's poor Eliza crossing a river by jumping from ice floe to ice floe.

I exaggerate. No slave trader is chasing me, for one thing, and my feet are always firmly on rock. The surging water never even comes halfway up my boots. I'm in no danger of stranding or being swept away, but still, the power of the cold, pounding ocean is cautionary. The tides here are among the most extreme in the world, second only to Canada's Bay of Fundy.

Low tides here mean long stretches of exposed beach and a huge volume of water that first pours out and then floods back. Every few years someone will get stuck in the goopy mudflats near Anchorage, and the tide will sweep in before help arrives. I don't mean someone's vehicle; I mean someone's *person*, legs stuck in the mud, water rising. From lowest low to highest high, the tides here move thirty vertical feet. Our smallest tides still rise and fall seven feet.

Whenever I walk back home from doing low-water work, I always like to walk low on the beach and look at things, all things, whatever's there. For a place with a large intertidal zone, there's amazingly scant intertidal life. Here we have no tidepools teeming with crabs, darting fishes, the festooned sea slugs known as nudibranchs; no rock walls paneled with colorful sea stars; no beds of mussels or layers of barnacles; no mats of algae and seaweed; no swarms of feeding gulls; no fecund low-tide smells; no sounds of things popping, spurting, digging, or swishing. There's only the slick gray mud and, here, in one low spot rapidly filling with water, the tips of army-green plants that look something like horsetails and are as rubbery as Gumby.

The inlet's mud and the tidal currents that keep it moving are the major reasons there are so few critters here. The waters carry such a load of roiling sediments anything that needs to see to eat will have a problem, and anything that would live on the bottom would have to survive the ground alternately being washed away from under it and piled back on in suffocating layers. The migrating salmon that we catch have already stopped eating; they have empty, atrophying stomachs, and are packed instead with skeins of eggs and slabs of white milt. The inlet's prodigious clam beds leave off about twenty-five miles to our south.

The strength of the currents, even absent mud, is inhospitable to intertidal populations. Whatever wants to stay here must have a good anchorhold or else end up far down the inlet, like anything we accidentally lose overboard. Cold temperatures and ice, likewise, place limits on what can live here. In the warming trend of the past few years we've noticed more seaweed and jellyfish, as though both are on a northward march. Ice brutalizes the coast in winter; it scrapes clean the tops of rocks and imprisons if not crushes organisms that would share its space.

I pass a boulder and tear loose a clump of rockweed to eat. *Fucus*, bladderwrack, popweed, paddy tang, old man's firecrackers—it has many names, but its key to hanging on is a holdfast of tiny tenacious roots that seem to work their way right into rock. The plant's bladderlike ends are like the filled fingers of gloves, swollen with a juicy liquid that contains its eggs and sperm. These tips have a good, green vegetable taste, slightly salted. Rockweed is the plant that got so badly hammered in Prince William Sound by the *Exxon Valdez* oil spill and cleanup, but it's also a plant that colonizes easily and quickly.

Here, out from the base of that boulder, where water's now flooding, Ken and I once found a pale sea anemone clutching a fish several inches long. The fish appeared to be a small cod, and was held sideways, belly-to, in the anemone's tentacled mouth.

Anemones—animals that look like flowering plants—were described by Rachel Carson as resembling chrysanthemums, their underwater tentacles waving like petals. They capture their food by shooting stinging darts from their tentacles, but I'd never pictured quarry as large as a cod. I'd tugged gently on the fish and it came away easily; it showed no sign of being eaten, no digestive juice attack. I pushed it back up against the anemone, which seemed unresponsive, lethargic, and left the two of them alone, to eat and be eaten, or not.

Another time, on a minus-five-foot tide, one of those rare occasions when the sea rolls so far back I can walk a long way offshore and still be onshore, I discovered a large colony of anemones adhered low on the sides of the farthest reef rocks. Fleshy and cylindrical, when they're out of water anemones look more than anything else I can think of like the saggy breasts of buxom old women, even to the point of having nipple-like ends. Some of the ends were simply knobby, while others were opened up, extending clusters of stamen-like tentacles. It was the colors, though, that wowed me. Some were only the flesh-tones of unwashed skin, but others fairly pulsed with fluorescent shades of pink, red, green, yellow—solid and in combinations. I'd wandered among them as in a flower garden, leaning sometimes to touch them, to pat their rubbery sides. They shrank from me, slowly, as though it took a while for the stimulus to connect with whatever passes for their brains. In a sea of gray mud, I'd never expected to find such extravagantly decked-out creatures.

Mostly though, this beach of ours is spare, sparse, some would say empty, even boring. For me, the limits are part of the attraction: we get to know a few things well. What's here is simple enough and few enough to have some kind of relationship with. The tide goes in and out in a predictable pattern, the rocks stay—for the most part—in their places, the kingfisher that lives up the creek rattles past. The rules of the beach are few and clear: stay out of the water, avoid going nose to nose with a bear, don't burn down the cabin. A boat or a plane passes, and we look to see who it is. We note shifts in the wind for what they mean about weather and the movement of fish. We know salmon because we don't also need to know cod, pollock, herring, mackerel, tuna, halibut, crab, shrimp, pigs, and beef cattle. There's nothing to be filtered out, and we don't. If we come upon a rubbery green shoot or an anemone or catch the occasional odd fish—a halibut or sculpin—in our nets, we stop to look it over. We pay attention to what we think we know, and then to anything that's new or different.

Instead of being beach fishermen, Ken and I could be boat fishermen. We could chase salmon, visit another coastline or section of the inlet every opening, anchor in various bays, comb fresh beaches. We could know a little bit—maybe even a lot—about many different places. We could, but I frequently recall a Zen-like line of writer Richard Nelson's, something he'd synthesized for his own life after living among the Koyukon Athabaskans: "There may be more to learn by climbing the same mountain a hundred times than by climbing a hundred different mountains." Even after seventeen summers, I'm still learning from this couple of miles of spare beach, still need to walk it many more times before I'll begin to understand even a fraction of its mysteries.

This low-tide walk, I'm content to look at rocks. Boulders and rocks and stones we do have, in glorious multiplicity—granite and slate and jadeite, conglomerate and volcanic, as red as brick, as shiny as metal, as flat as coffee tables and as round as cannon balls. They have holes worn right through them and big hunks of quartz stuck in their sides. They look sometimes like adze heads or stone lamps, though they're not and, in fact, in all our years of looking we've never found any such artifacts—not so much as a stone sinker or a projectile point. The one time we thought we found something—not even a worked rock but a bone handle to a knife—it turned out to be our neighbor's, something he'd lost twenty years earlier. The prehistoric culture here was thin and frugal, and the place itself casts everything to the sea, to be ground to pieces and washed away.

Partway back to camp I come upon a real find, my rock-of-the-day. It's deep-red, shiny and smooth with a very light pitting. It looks, in fact, like a museum piece, a cast metal sculpture. As high as my knee, it resembles a seal—or at least an artist's interpretation of the muscle of a seal's back when its head is turned. There's no doubt in my mind that this rock-metal-sculpture has been through fire—out the top of a volcano or through the atmosphere, a shelling from a far star. I've never seen anything like it, and it stands alone in a field of rocks to which it bears no resemblance, as though it must surely have fallen from the sky.

A little farther on I stop to study the gray lines that divide black rocks into mosaics, dozens and dozens of windy curves and crossings and intersectings, designs at once random and perfectly pleasing in their balance. They are surely the trails of some variety of a small, fleet-footed snail, but there are few snails on our beach and none in sight at the moment. Surely there are not enough to make all these lines? I can only guess that the snail tracks are extremely durable; the snails lay them down over time, perhaps mainly when they and the rocks both are

Gary L. Freeburg
Marine Growth
Gelatin silver photograph
with selenium toner
1982
UAP82:037:001

under water, and the tides fail to erase them. They are, in fact, of varying shades of gray.

Just as I'm thinking how few snails there are, I come upon a largish cream-colored one with a turreted shell. It's lying on its back in the mud, and I can see where it took a tumble from the side of a rock. It's hanging out of its shell, reaching for the ground and exuding a copious amount of snail-slime, but it doesn't look to me as though it's close to being able to right itself. I pick it up, look at it closely all around, and then set it back down on rock, correctly oriented, and I think of something Annie Dillard wrote. "We have not yet encountered any god who is as merciful as a man who flicks a beetle over on its feet." There's no right and wrong in nature, she says. We people are moral creatures in an amoral world.

As I keep coming along the beach, my eyes settle upon rust spots, circular patches that bleed over the tops and sides of certain boulders and rocks. These are the human artifacts such as we have, our historical monuments, the marks of fishermen past, present, and—I suppose—future. Each rust patch, like those that helped me spot the two all-important rocks I just readied for fishing, surrounds a hardened steel casing drilled by hand into granite. The ones we use I know with a particular intimacy, and I see them with an eye that habitually checks buoys, lines, eyebolts, knots.

It's these others, the record of unused rock anchors along the low-tide line, that interest me in a different way. I like to simply look at them and remember where they are, to look at the particular stretch of beach they address and guess how someone fished there, or why, or whether we might again. Some of the old casings are nearly gone, bled out into the gritty granite. The plugs in others are rusted to a welded solidity, worn to hardened nubs. Some we know well. Some we drilled ourselves. Some we abandoned. Some abandoned us. Some of the smaller rocks, the ones that weigh only as much as compact cars, are ones our neighbor, when he fished this beach, used to winch up and move out to be outside anchors, then winch up again at season's end and move back in.

I step onto a rectangular drilled rock I've never seen before. Every bit of casing and rust is gone; all that remains is a perfect, fat-finger-size hole an inch and a half deep. I imagine a future archeologist trying to make sense of this remnant of an earlier culture. A hole in a rock: if I didn't know fishing, didn't have the whole picture, it would be hard to guess what for. It's hard enough to imagine a person drilling a hole in a rock with two hands and a hammer, a pointy-teethed metal tube and a driving pin. Strike and turn, strike and turn. The collision sings out like a bell. The teeth grind granite to dust. The beach has rung with all this pounding. I've rung it myself.

Then there are the stakes, one more set of artifacts, generally older than the drilled rocks. Pounded deep into the mud and clay low on the beach, they were another way of anchoring lines and buoys. In their old age they're worn and stubby, a mix of dark, water-soaked wooden posts and corroded steel pipes. They tend to disappear and appear as the beach shifts around them, sometimes seeming to lift out of nowhere after years or decades. We used one of these found wooden stakes until just a few years ago, when it truly disappeared during a winter. Others we've struggled to dig out when they've been in our way, catching and tearing nets.

I'm looking at rocks and stretches of sand and mud, the geography that underlies the tides, the places where nets go and get hung up and turn in eddies, the places we steer our skiff in and out of and around. I see the lay of this beach land, and it's also a mapped history of the place, the chart of so many people trying so hard. There were times when this whole long beach of ours was crowded with fishermen, their nets as close to one another as the law allowed and often closer. Years ago, when a cannery sent men after the early king salmon, the flats thronged with two hundred or more fishermen; after the kings moved through—or were all caught—the skiff fleet left to fish runs on the other side of the inlet.

The tide's racing in now, and by the time I reach the old line of pilings, only the uppermost of them still shows. I know how they lie under the water, though—a line of posts that march out under the surf. They're much thicker than stakes, six or more inches across, and they extend no more than a few inches above the sand. Their tops are polished smooth and ingrained with sand that's been beaten in among the wood fibers. The fish trap that belonged to these truncated pilings was one of hundreds that operated in state waters between the arrival of American salmon canneries in 1878 and the abolition of traps with Alaska's 1959 statehood. This one—judging from the hefty size of the pilings and the fact that they're still here—would have been pile-driven; that is, the logs would have been driven into the mud and clay mechanically, in contrast to hand traps, in which smaller poles were set in place by hand each year, then removed and reset in following years. Salmon coming along the beach here would hit the fence of wire web that extended from one piling to the next and would follow it into deeper water, through a cone-shaped weir, into the box part of the trap. This net enclosure was rigged with numerous lines that lifted and lowered the bottom and sides with the tides and to "dry up" the fish so they could be pitched into boats and carried away to a cannery.

As a rule fish traps were extremely efficient, catching every fish that came their way with a minimum of effort. They overharvested salmon to a frightening degree, plummeting stocks rapidly toward depletion. They were, moreover, controlled largely by Seattle-based packing companies, which cared little about Alaskans or the long-term health of Alaska's fisheries and environment. An English visitor to a cannery across the inlet in 1902 noted that one trap could catch twenty thousand salmon in a day, and that all those fish were killed and hauled to the cannery to be sorted. There, only the choice kings and reds were canned, and all the others—the silver, pink, and chum salmon, the halibut and other fish mixed into the catch—were simply thrown into the river to rot. In 1948, of the four hundred thirty-four traps licensed in the state, more than half were owned and operated by eight large canning companies, only thirty-eight by Alaskans.

More than anything, it was the greed and waste of the fish traps and their owners that led Alaskans to choose statehood. Throughout the 1940s and '50s Alaskans voted repeatedly and overwhelmingly for referendums that would either abolish the traps completely or transfer management over the depleting fisheries from the federal to the territorial government. In each case the power of the canned salmon industry thwarted any change, and Alaskans were finally forced into pressing for statehood in order to gain control over their resources. To this day distrust of the federal government and outside influences dominates both the Alaskan psyche and the state's politics.

The trap on our beach, according to our neighbor, didn't operate very long. The current was simply too strong here, and the trap was abandoned long before he came along in the 1940s.

In front of me the highest piling disappears under stone-rattling water, and I think of the men who sank it so long ago. For a brief moment I imagine the beach as a construction site: men and barges, pile-driving equipment, some system of holding back—driving back—the water while they set the outer-most pilings in place, everyone working a furious pace to beat the tides. I see nets draped along the pilings, herding salmon into the trap, and men with rolled-up sleeves and toughened hands in the trap, pitching salmon with pugh forks into dories. It's at once a semi-romantic vision of a hard-working past and a nightmare of exploitation and destruction. Then, with a crack of wave on rock, it's gone, and I'm alone again on deserted beach, rough water rising.

By the third week in August, the nights get dark. From bed Ken and I watch a full moon rise over the eastern shore. We can only gape at its enormous beauty; it floats up over the land like itself magnified—huge and golden and sharply relieved. It looks so close, I can easily imagine how the people of Europe—not all that long ago—believed that geese and swans flew there to winter on its tranquil seas.

In my mind the moon and tides are inescapably connected, and I can't help wondering what the first people to come to these shores—Dena'ina Athabaskans—made of the two. Although I'm unaware of any specifically Dena'ina beliefs about either the moon or tides, certainly anyone living here would have readily observed the relationship—the biggest tidal ranges coming with the full and new moons, the smallest in between. The prescientific explanations I do know of, belonging to the Chinese and the Tahitians, are lovely to contemplate, for their logic as well as their poetry.

For the ancient Chinese, the moon was the spirit of water and the tides rose and fell with its moods.

In Tahitian mythology, a pair of gods created everything in the world but then became unhappy with the way things went from there. They cursed the stars, and

Virginia K. (Kathy)
Marchlinski
Carpet II
Acrylic and mixed media on paper
1983
UA84-3-25

the stars blinked. They cursed the moon, and it went out. They cursed the sea, and that was the cause of low tide. However, the earth's first woman, half-goddess and half-mortal, worked opposite those gods to try to save what they cursed. She brought back the stars so that they blinked *and* twinkled, rescued the moon a little at a time until it was full again, pulled for the tides until they reclimbed the beach. Ever since, the stars, moon, tides, rain, trees, and all the other things in the world that come and go or cycle through different stages continue in those same patterns, balancing between the curses and the kindnesses.

Other "ancients," according to Rachel Carson, attributed the tides to the breathing of an earth monster. Leonardo da Vinci tried to calculate the lung capacity of such a creature.

Big inhalation, big exhalation, regular and forever. I can imagine my predecessors on this beach assuming that the moon, with a will of its own, was simply following those breaths, signaling the tides. This signaling was surely helpful to them, as it is to us. "Uh-oh, the moon's getting bigger. We better move our stuff higher on the beach."

I have to look beyond Dena'ina territory, but not too far, to find a regional story to explain the origin of the low tide. Not surprisingly, it stars Raven, that mythical creature of the Pacific Northwest and much of Alaska. In a cycle of Raven stories belonging to the Eyak people of Prince William Sound, "Raven and the Owners of the Tides" tells that in the beginning the tide was always high. Raven was hungry because he couldn't get at the food hidden by the water, so one day he took a prickly sea urchin to the house of the old lady who owned the tides, and he stabbed her bottom with the urchin's spines until she cried out and made the tide go down. After that the tide always went up and down, and Raven could find enough to eat. In another version from the same region, Raven acted more kindly. He visited the home of the old lady who kept the tides and asked her if she could make them go down so he could get some clams to eat, and he promised to fix her sore eyes if she would. She tried hard and eventually got the tide down, and Raven made her eyes better. In fact, the old lady even got younger after that.

We modern folks know, of course, that the tides are a response of the earth's oceans to the gravitational pull of the moon, sun, and, in theory, every other planet and star out there. Before there was water, the earth's molten liquids were pulled back and forth; in fact, it's thought that the moon was formed when big sun tides and the earth's own oscillation combined with such force that a great wave was torn loose from the earth and spun into its own orbit.

These days it's the moon, because it's closest, that exerts the most pull on the earth's waters. When the earth, moon, and sun are lined up together we get the greatest pull, and when they form a triangle, the least. The exact workings of the tides are enormously complicated, depending on such things as the distance from the earth of the sun and moon and of their positioning north or south of the equator. Most significant, though, is that every body of water has its own period of oscillation; that is, although the force of the moon sets a particular basin of water in motion, the exact motion is determined by the shape and depth of the basin, and varies within it—less in the middle, more extreme at the ends.

Cook Inlet is a long, skinny, shallow basin—thus its extreme tides. A lot of water moves through the narrow entrance where it opens to the Gulf of Alaska and has only six hours to fill all the way to its northern end. It's no accident that the Dena'ina name for the inlet is Big-Water River and that Captain Cook, in his inlet explorations, thought he was sailing up a river. A disoriented visitor to our camp, just flown in from Massachusetts, took one look at the inlet and asked, "What river is this?" The tidal current moves like a river—six to eight knots at our camp—and, curiously, mostly runs *out*.

There is, of course, the water pouring out of rivers to add to the outgoing tide, but that alone can't explain why the outgoing tide at our camp runs much longer and harder than the incoming tide. Although the tide rises on our beach for roughly six hours and then falls for roughly six hours, at the same time that it's rising on the beach, it runs out just offshore. Out of every twelve hours, the boat on the mooring pulls up the inlet for about four and down for about eight, and when it's pulling down a wake forms behind it. Similarly, nets on most of our beach fish well for only four hours of flood, and the other eight hours they flag out in the current, their lead lines yanked right to the surface. There is no slack tide, only the moment when the tide turns from flood to ebb or vice versa. A net fishing in the shape of a crescent turns cork by cork, from its outside to its inside end, into the curve of an S then into the opposite crescent.

The tides are full of mysteries, and one I have yet to understand very well is how it can be that some places in the world have only one high and one low tide each day, while we have two of each. In places as diverse as the Gulf of Mexico and Saint Michael, on Alaska's west coast, local rhythms somehow even out the motions into a pattern of one long, slow rise and one long slow fall during the lunar day, that period of roughly twenty-four hours plus fifty minutes. Most places have in a day neither two evenly matched tide cycles nor one long slow one but something in between — one set of more extreme tides and one set of less. That's the situation for us.

The people who make tide books calculate this all out, fortunate for me. I just look in the book and add two and a half hours to the chart we use, to adjust for our location. I don't bother to adjust for height; we adjust ourselves instead, knowing what the book height means for our particular place.

When I go out later that full-moon night, the moon hangs high, shrunken to a coin. Its cool white light bathes the hillside, the ribbon of beach, the wide water. The skiff on the mooring is all sharp edges and glint. My shadow lays itself across the porch, so defined I can see every kink in my hair. I slept on my hair wet after a tub, and I look like medusa, or at least as that snaky-locked one might have looked if she'd sat for an old-timey cut-paper portrait and been snipped into a black silhouette. I extend my hand and cup light in its palm; the light has a quality like mercury — silver, rounded, both solid and liable to slip away. I spread five fingers, turn my hand and watch its shadow thin to a blade.

In the inlet, salmon circle in bays or stall in current with wagging fins while they engage in fish-sleep, or they move along the coast under the moonlight. We know that the movements of salmon are affected by the moon — or by the amount of its reflected light. The largest movements of salmon fry and smolt from freshwater into the sea correspond to the time of the new moon, when the moon floats invisibly between the earth and the sun. We say they're moving under the cover of darkness to avoid predation, but in truth they're driven by the growth hormone that readies them for saltwater, a hormone triggered by the lack of light. Migrating adult salmon, meanwhile, tend to move less at night than during the day. Fishermen know this from monitoring their nets, and know, too, that among the salmon species, silvers are most likely to travel in the dark. This may be because silvers are largely a "fall" fish, migrating late in the season when the days are shorter, and so have adapted to needing less light.

I take a last look at the moon, the very same one that shone on the first Dena'ina, the pile drivers and fish pughers, generations of salmon. It shone, too, and still shines, on Europeans and Chinese and Tahitians, on the Eyak who know about Raven. In our separate times and places, there isn't much else we've witnessed together—only our single sun, the scatter of stars, that round or sliced or darkened orb moving through its phases, the overarching vault of heaven. Tonight the moon tugging quiet water down the inlet has me in its hold. Millions of years after the ancestor of all us land-dwellers first crawled ashore, my blood remains as salty as the sea. I am 80 percent water, and my cells bulge toward the moon.

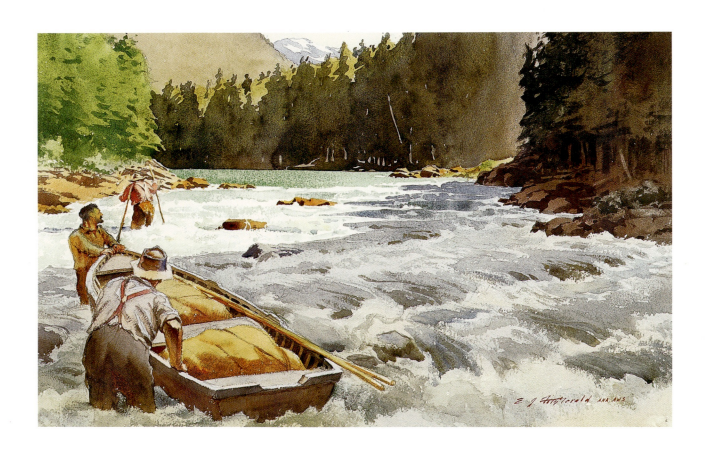

Edmond James FitzGerald

Lining through the Riffle

Watercolor

Undated

Gift of Gerald FitzGerald

UA77-5-3

IN PURSUIT OF VABMS

Clarice Dickess

OUR EARS BLOCKED by the headsets, the four of us and the pilot of the orange DeHavilland Beaver either hollered to be heard or pantomimed our messages. Seated next to me, Mark held the topo maps. He kept an index finger on our progress through the air.

"You can guesstimate the distance we've flown if you know the airspeed," he shouted to me, while I nodded. "A Beaver flies about ninety miles per hour, so we're covering about five miles every three minutes or so." He tapped the map and pointed out my window. "We should get to the Happy River in about half an hour."

He was right. In about half an hour, a ribbon of silver movement flowed far below us, flecked in white. All heads bent, seeking sight around the wings and body of the plane. None of us, Joran, Buckwheat, Mark, or I, had kayaked this river before, so we were hungry for first-hand knowledge. How high was it running? How hard would the rapids be at this level? Would we meet bears? What landmarks could we use to guide us to the take-out, where we would meet the pilot again in four days?

Mark and Buckwheat gesticulated at the same time, eager to show us the grizzly sow and her two cubs crossing the river almost directly under our position. Well, that answered one of our questions.

In a peripheral way, I sensed Mark's movements as he alternately searched the landscape and surveyed the map, using his pointer finger as a constant YOU ARE HERE indicator. Running the glaciated mountains, the river, the drainages through the language of the map—elevation in feet, contour intervals, very accurate benchmarks (VABMs), miles per square inch—offered an interpretation that promised a better chance of survival out there. Since we didn't live a subsistence lifestyle, we needed a buffer layer between us and the wildness rushing along under the belly of the Beaver. The same features that pulled us toward this trip—lack of people and things associated with people—made it threatening. I appreciated Mark's attention to the details, something I always find challenging.

The terrain rolling beneath us offered relief from the signs of premature winter hounding us further north. At this time, early August, snow had crept down to the three-thousand-foot mark near Denali National Park, and we had driven the distance south to the air service in a chilly forty-degree dampness. Even the fireweed had already danced to the head of its stalk, a sure sign of waning summer. Here, though, in southcentral Alaska, off the southern edge of the Alaska Range, the land held its fresh green of summer. As usual, the scale of the land from the air awed me; it refused to allow me to soak it all up. As we flew upstream, following the river's cut through the earth, I felt us moving *up* into the surrounding green hills.

Where are we? How hard will the rapids be? Where will we camp tonight? How many bears will we have to avoid? These questions helped distract me from the ones nagging me at home, ones that had been gnawing on the edges of my consciousness for many months now, even years. During my three years in graduate school I took home less than eight hundred dollars per month. Most of that time I paid three hundred dollars per month in rent. Stretching the remainder over food, fuel, phone, car repairs and maintenance, electricity, and all the unexpected expenses that crop up each month left no margin of safety. Not that I can complain—I managed to leave school debt-free.

But I also left school without a plan and without having paid much attention to marketable skills. I successfully avoided facing a full-on job search for two months during which I rode my bicycle from Fairbanks to Hayden, Idaho, with my boyfriend of three years. When I returned in October, on the cusp of a dark winter, I faced that fact that I needed to leave Randy, that I was out of money, and that I had no job or prospects. My own proverbial hole.

Our smooth landing on Sheep Lake set us at the foot of the Rainy Pass valley. In fact, much of our river trip would trace part of the Iditarod Trail. We chattered happily as we untied our boats from the plane's floats and hauled our gear to the lake's shore. Good luck granted us a warm day and nearly clear skies. Mark and Joran took pictures of us as we stuffed our gear into our kayaks and broke open our food bags—it was early afternoon and past lunchtime. We would have to drag our boats to the headwaters of the Happy to start our trip. We hoped there would be enough water to support the boats. On our trip a few weeks before, Mark, Joran, and I had to drag our boats across uneven tundra, through thickets of alders and devil's club and clouds of mosquitoes on a sticky hot day. We hoped today's drag would be less painful.

We weren't entirely clueless. Good friends of Mark's and mine had kayaked this river the previous summer, coming back with glowing accounts. One evening after kayaking the Nenana River near Denali National Park, Mark and I heard that Joran and Buckwheat had planned a Happy trip for the following week and that they needed two more boaters to share the flight costs. We jumped on it. Buckwheat was one of four owners and teachers of a kayaking and rafting school in the park. We knew him to be fun and talented in a boat. Joran we had already done that one fly-in kayak trip with. We hadn't known either of them very long or very well, but well enough. As for Mark and me, we'd known one another for years, but had only in the last three months become a couple.

This trip, and the others I'd been so lucky to do this summer, were the only bright spots to my then-current unemployment. I had taught a summer program in June and July, as I had done the prior three summers, and was once again dragging the current of my life for direction. What could I do to earn a decent living, to provide myself with the benefits I'd been doing without, to give my life a sense of purpose, a structure—and how could I do all this and still live in Fairbanks, my home, the only place where I'd ever put down roots? A few new texts on my bookshelf became well-thumbed: *From College to Career*, *Jobs for English Majors and Other Smart People*, *What Color Is Your Parachute?* I created a teaching resume and a writing one. I inventoried my skills and experience. I listed potential employers and contacted old ones. I started a credential file at the school placement center. I spent too many hours sitting, job-hunting paraphenalia strewn about me, staring at the walls of my cabin, asking myself how I came to make the decisions in my life that led me to this place.

The easy flight and good weather boded well. We finalized our packing, pulled on our drysuits and, bear pepper spray in one hand, boat and paddle in the other, we dragged our boats with welcome ease over flat tundra to the headwaters of the Happy River.

There was enough water to float a boat, but not much more than that. The level was low, for sure. We started out above treeline and floated through Ptarmigan Valley without seeing any ptarmigan. The green tundra stretched out in what looked a lot like rolling farm hills, as if wheat fields had just sprouted soft green shoots. At the edges of the fields, big hills rolled up and away toward mountain peaks partly hidden behind clouds. Looking up and out at the landscape, I felt sunken—inside my boat, inside the river, inside the cut of the banks. Here the scale was much milder than that of the canyon walls we would encounter in the next couple of days. Kayaking in deep canyons shows the kayaker in graphic terms that she is *in* rather than *on* the earth.

As kayakers who frequent the silt-laden, big-water canyon of the Nenana River, we reveled in the clearness of this small stream. One could look down into the riverbed and savor the shapes and colors of the rocks. I spotted a couple of aging, red king salmon still trying to push their way upstream. We all spotted the first bear almost simultaneously. The big brown boulder on top of a nearby bench attracted our attention when it moved; then it quickly ambled over the hill and out of sight.

A few miles downstream from the put-in, the river began to pick up speed and volume. We started weaving our way through rock gardens, arcing our boats

Charles Ott

Nenana River with

Sugar Loaf Mountain

Gelatin silver photograph, selenium

toned

Undated

UAP84:097:001

around into the calm spots behind rocks where we could pause the downstream ride and look around before proceeding to turn into the next calm spot: eddy-hopping.

Making an eddy turn is like an about-face in the boat. The faster the water runs, the sharper the line between the current flowing downstream and the calm, interrupted flow behind an obstruction (like a boulder) in the stream. The trick to eddying out gracefully is knowing when to switch from leaning downstream to leaning back upstream. It's like throwing your hip around in a dance move, and very much like carving a turn in the snow on a pair of skis. When turning left, you lean the boat up on its left edge and carve it around with your right hip and knee. If your timing is good and you're working with the current, it's just lean, lean, and there you are, facing upstream and in control.

From the air we had seen a distinctive-looking bench at a bend in the river and had pointed it out to one another as possibly a good spot to camp. Now, after a few hours on the river, we began to look for it. Climbing a couple of hundred feet above the river and camping on the tundra would provide good vistas and easier bear avoidance. The weekend before, Mark and I had climbed up to a tundra camp on a different river trip and been rewarded by watching, from across the river, a sow grizzly and her two cubs playing in a meadow and feeding on blueberries.

Buckwheat and I eyed a certain bench on river right. At its terminus on the river, a trail led off into the brush. We decided to get out and scout. After slopping through mushy footing, we abandoned our idea of camping there. The trail, however, gave us a solid landmark on the map. Mark pointed out to us where the old Iditarod Trail crossed the Happy River, right where we were.

We slid back into our boats and continued on. The day began to grow later, nearing six or seven o'clock. Mark paddled next to my boat and said he was getting hungry. He pulled his boat over onto a gravel bar and pointed up the hill to the left, saying he wanted to check it out for a possible first campsite.

We took it. On top of the hill, a two-hundred-yard scramble, the tundra stretched out in a relatively flat table. A clear lake reflected the valley headed northeast, at the head of which a rocky ridge put Mark in mind of a dinosaur. After dinner we glassed the hillsides. Mark took out the maps and we discussed where we thought we might be, based on the number and type of creeks we'd seen join the river that day.

To the east, across the river, there was a bench, a kind of bluff. Then another fold of land rising higher behind it, then a dark peak behind that, partly covered in white snow. Giant terraces. It was all that soft-looking tundra, green, studded with occasional boulders and patches of darker green brush. The land rose up from the river, up and back. That's the motion of the earth, up from the rivers. Rivers are the bottom of the earth. The mountains tip the moisture up and roll it downhill. Down, down, down, until it reaches the ocean. The water carves new paths into the earth as it travels.

Mark had turned quiet during the evening in camp. I worried to myself about what might be wrong. Was it something I said or did? Was it his sore shoulder bothering him again? Was he thinking about his life? Mark was also essentially unemployed. Unlike mine, his career was decided early on and followed a linear trajectory: Air Force Academy, then training, flying A-10s, making the transition to flying for a commercial airline, a job he held for three years. He had been furloughed for a little over a year, a mixed blessing. The break allowed him to return to Alaska to live and to recreate. But we shared similar anxieties about what to do next, when we might start earning regular pay again, and hoped hard to remain healthy and accident-free in the face of not having insurance. Though we both loved long trips in the wilderness, we also suffered a sense of uselessness without work. I didn't have an easy answer when meeting someone new who asked, "What do you do?"

On the second day the sun remained partly obscured, but we didn't get rain or wind. According to our sources, we should camp tonight before entering the deep canyon of day 3, which would connect us with the Skwentna River. The tight, technical nature of yesterday's water held today, at moderate difficulty. After putting in and running the first couple of rapids, everyone was smiling and laughing. Buckwheat teased me about doing "tricks," meaning having to roll back upright after tipping over during play.

I remember first learning to kayak at the age of twenty-three, ten years ago. My first river day in the boat was on the Snoqualmie in Washington State, a mild class-two stretch. The boat felt unstable. Any little movement I made reflected back to me, magnified, in tipping the boat. So preoccupied with what was happening a few feet in front of me, I completely missed the approach of a large boulder in the middle of the river, surrounded by enough space that even an attentive beginner could maneuver around it without trouble. When the rock at last loomed large enough for me to notice, it was almost too late to correct my route. It was a shock and a lesson. I had to look ahead and plan my route beyond the immediate end of my boat. The only person I had to depend on to do this was myself.

After lunch we found an excellent play spot. It was a nice-sized hole, big enough to hold a kayaker but not big enough or deep enough to get "stuck" in. I'd been shy of surfing in holes ever since I got stuck in one on the Nenana River about six years before. My companion on that trip said I rolled in the hole nine times before I finally washed out downstream. I made my way to shore and sat gasping and shaking for several minutes before moving back onto the river.

Sometimes kayakers hold competitive events called "rodeos," in which they compete for the best hole "ride." The analogy is apt—a boat bouncing inside a hole, moving neither upstream nor down, looks and feels much like a bucking bronc. Buckwheat, Joran, and I entered the hole one by one, time after time, going for that ride. We turned 360s by toying with leaning and prying our paddles in the water. We yelled at one another's great performances and enjoyed showing off for one another. Unfortunately, Mark had to observe only, his shoulder too sore for play.

After more than an hour, we finally tore ourselves from that magical spot. It was time to search for tonight's camp. The terrain had already begun to feel canyonlike. We stopped about four times to climb up onto flatter-looking possibilities, only to be turned away by bear sign or thick brush. Our vistas were mostly obscured by the walls of shores now, forested in alders and mosquitoes. Buckwheat began to suffer from a chill—we had discovered during our lunch break that his drysuit had begun to leak heavily.

Mark was again searching for a high spot, for bear protection, but we had a hard time finding anything workable. Finally we settled on a gravel bar where we could cook, and we found two tiny patches of ground among the woods for our compact tents. On landing and scouting, we traced the source of a rotting odor to four king salmon carcasses lining the shore. Holding our breath, we picked the things up with sticks and threw them into the river.

"Maybe we should camp out there," Mark suggested to me, pointing to a small gravel bar in the middle of the river. "This is probably as good as we're going to get for tonight," I said, feeling as apprehensive as he about the bears. He agreed. Somehow I felt a little better after he admitted his fear. We built a big fire at this camp and tried to dry Buckwheat's gear and toast the chill out of each of our bones. We discussed the relative merits of Gore-Tex fabric and drank a fruity juice spiced with rum. I think we all slept well in spite of our bear phobia.

I wasn't sure why my work life had always been so dissatisfying. Maybe I was spoiled by not having to work as a kid. Even during undergraduate school my social security benefits covered my expenses. I suppose it has taken me longer than the average bear to mature to a realistic expectation of work life's difficulty.

My employers seem to have liked my work. Others perceive me as being a good teacher. I had always assumed that satisfaction would follow on the heels of competence, but it didn't work that way, especially with teaching. But if not teaching, then what? Most of my friends, in their generous desire to help, to see me happy and, I suppose, to shut me up, suggested making a career out of my recreational activities. Teach kids in an outdoor school. Teach for Outward Bound or a similar program. Become a mountain or river guide. I wouldn't consider it. I couldn't face having to entertain, to prod and coax, to *interact* with people in an intense setting. The fact is, I had become cranky after delivering ten years of direct service to people in one capacity or another. I wanted to make my living without pursuing a people-centered profession. But what?

The whitewater began to wane after lunch on our third day. The canyon walls opened out once again as the river flow slowed. Soon we would reach the confluence with the Skwentna River, wide and slow. Tired and chilled when we reached it, Buckwheat suggested camping there. Mark, map in hand, shook his head vigorously. "We'll never make it to the take-out in time tomorrow if we camp here," he said, showing us how much further we had to paddle to reach Red Salmon Lake. "We can't risk missing our flight out."

If we did miss the flight, we would have to pay for the extra trip. Of course, the ever-present possibility of getting weathered in concerned us, too. Not showing up at the take-out at the assigned time would also worry people. If the pilot couldn't spot us from the air, he might assume that we needed a rescue. More mundane reasons made the flight out important—I had a job interview scheduled for the day following the trip, a fact that had almost kept me home. Mark was working part-time for a flight-seeing service in the park and was expected back to work.

In retrospect, I can see that my fears kept me from recognizing some important benchmarks in my history that would've helped point the way. I call it the Bag Lady Syndrome: part of me is certain that I'll end up on the streets, homeless, carrying my every possession in a backpack. A similar subsurface fear has me convinced that I will never sustain a long-term partnership. Air these fears and they sound silly—surely I had seemed silly to my friends, who never really worried about me. Most of them assumed I would be fine, because they looked at me and saw value to the work world and to the world of love.

They were right, of course. I nearly lost a second chance at a job I really wanted, due to being overqualified. For the first time, I knew in no uncertain terms that I wanted this full-time, permanent position with benefits. Before my post-graduate semi- and unemployed experience, I probably would've balked at the hours and pay and job duties. But I had promised myself that this time, if I got a job, I would not complain about it and I would not take it for granted. My new boss later told me that it was my persistence that got me hired over someone with more experience. She said, "I just got the feeling that you wanted it more."

■ ■ ■

I felt the same pressure Mark did to keep going, and I was glad he was willing to be firm about moving on. We needed a margin of error for finding the take-out,

James Thompson

Untitled collagraph

1984

UA84-10-1

too, as it involved spotting and paddling up a slough off the big river to access the lake. It was hard to predict how much time it would take us.

Buckwheat and Joran seemed less concerned. I think the pairs of us were separated by a fundamental approach to life this way. Both Buckwheat and Joran had more of that laissez-faire attitude. Twenty years ago they would have been labeled hippies. Both Mark and I were more conservative. I've heard him refer to himself as "high-strung," while I see myself as "intense."

We did slide into the Skwentna and move on downstream. Buckwheat paddled hard to generate body heat, and we tried to keep up. This river braided. Though no rapids challenged us, we had to choose a route through the channels that wouldn't peter out. A few yards downstream from the confluence we were treated to the sight of a sow and three cubs on the shore, a couple of channels away. Even though they were grizzlies, the cubs looked cheerful enough to romp with.

Landmarks here were rare. To make matters worse, for this part of the trip we had a map whose scale was too big to tell us much of the details. Mark had taken to storing the map inside its plastic pouch between his life jacket and chest. I watched him draw it out and study it while his boat turned random circles in the current. He shook his head. "This thing is worthless," he said when I paddled near. Even so, I saw him consult the paper with the squiggly lines on it at regular intervals.

Our last camp, found after we had all become hungry, chilled, tired, and irritable, renewed our spirits. The sandy shoreline was one of the few nongravel spots we'd seen. Further investigation revealed a freshwater spring, sparing us clogging our water filters with silt. A stock of driftwood was readily found. The search also revealed a set of wolf tracks clearly indenting the damp sand.

We did make the take-out, with an hour to spare. The sun shone clear on the fourth day, warming us. Just after we put in, a huge bald eagle peered down at us from the top of a cliff. We all eddied out and craned our necks to get a good look at him.

The river took on a new character farther downstream. The braids grew thinner and more numerous. Deadwood appeared in snarled stacks on the gravel bars.

I felt less of a descent here, more of a stagnation. A sense of decay became so strong that I almost expected stench. If I stopped paddling, maybe I would never get anywhere. Guessing at our position in relation to the key slough, we worked our way to the right shore, searching for the break in the bank. Mosquitoes from the brush-infested land swarmed us. The slough, when we found it, resembled a choked tunnel. We had to make our way upstream, often getting out of the boats, bent double under the dense canopy of willows, to drag around deadfall in the tiny stream.

Did it take an hour from river to lake? Something like that. At a slack pool we surprised a large school of healthy red salmon. The aptly named Red Salmon Lake is one of those places in Alaska that's too good to be true, more like the perfect photos than the photos themselves. The water reflected a group of glaciated peaks; trumpeter swans called. Summer colors bloomed in vibrant greens and soft browns. On time, the big orange Beaver noisily but gracefully set down, scattering the birds. Our ride home would be as safe as it gets in the skies of Alaska: an experienced and cautious pilot, a craft in good repair, and clear and calm weather.

When my friends ask me how I like my job, I cheerfully respond that I don't hate it, and for me that's saying a mouthful. Most of the time I actually like my position in the grant-writing department of a Native organization. My co-workers are cordial and compatible, though I miss the closeness I've had with others in different jobs.

A woman five years my junior works the next level of job above mine. I watch her maturity in action, compare it with where I was at her age, and I marvel. How does she do it? She's married; they own more than one house. At times I feel like I'm running hard to catch up, and those questions about my decision-making since high school crop up again.

But, then, that's not taking in the full landscape of my life. Yesterday I had to send several faxes at work. An Alascom mural calendar is posted above the fax machine, depicting the mountains on the north side of Denali. The tallest, most impressive mountain in the photo is one on which I've climbed a new route. I can't say, in all honesty, that I would trade that experience and others like it for the life that my younger co-worker is living now. What she is doing seems right for her, now, and perhaps what I did at her age was right for me.

As we roared out and lifted off the lake, the big white birds scattered and flapped in confusion. I felt bad for disturbing their idyllic setting this way. On the flight out, we could relax and let the now more familiar land roll out without worry. We laughed at ourselves and made a mental note for the next trip when we saw a clear and easy strip of water flow into the lake from the Skwentna just downstream of our hellish route. Buckwheat tapped my shoulders from his seat behind me to point out a couple of running bears. When I turned to him we shared a grin. The pilot remarked that he wanted to learn how to kayak, that it looked like a heck of a lot of fun, that he felt like he was missing out when he dropped off groups like us and flew away while we started our trips. DO IT, I thought to myself. Even though he must earn most of his money during the summer flying season, and he has mentioned having a young son, still, I hope he finds a way to learn the sport and someday kayak the Happy River. Some other pilot can fly the Beaver that day.

■ ■ ■

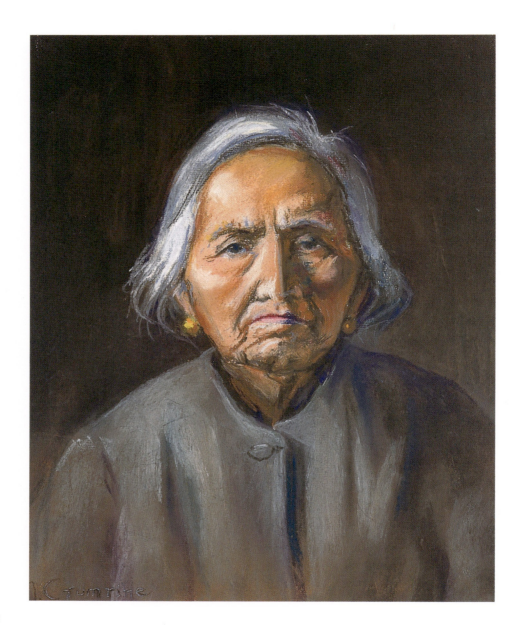

Nina Crumrine

Chief Johnson's Wife

Oil pastel

Undated

UA733-1

SEEING THE RIVER

Mary Odden

All the rivers run into the sea;

yet the sea is not full; unto the

place from whence the rivers

come, thither they return again.

Ecclesiastes 1:7

MY MORTGAGE says I'll never die, just pay four hundred dollars a month forever. Television advertising suggests that if we just solve the bladder and joint and bowel problems of this generation of old people, there aren't going to be any more old people. Especially not me. But as soon as I open a history book on the level of nations or movements that span more than one generation, I have to face the knowledge my ego won't allow—I'm just a passing thing.

Looking at history from the standpoint of messy generation after messy generation made the writer of Ecclesiastes a pessimist, and the A.D. 90 canon-makers nearly kicked him out of the Bible for it: "The thing that hath been is that which shall be; and that which is done is that which shall be done: and there is no new thing under the sun." Weariness and vanity. But the rumor persisted that Solomon himself had written the piece, so the Bible-builders put it in, thus preserving some of the loveliest thought owned by our culture. Much of the beauty comes from the overview itself, the way rivers are beautiful from the air, the way earth is beautiful from space.

Human activity viewed from such a distant platform is a swiftly revolving door, birth and death over and over again, a perspective without detail and without voice but with its own discouraging poetic: "A time to be born, and a time to die" and "The race is not to the swift nor the battle to the strong." But I forgive this

159

writer who finds women even "more bitter than death" because he admits he's not sure that dogs won't go to heaven. "They are all one breath," he says, men and beasts.

I think I understand why he's in such a bad mood. I feel this way every morning from about 3:00 to 4:30 A.M. That's the time of generalities, when sleep has removed me to an outer space from which nothing is visible but aging and loss, far from the particular joys of hugging my kid or eating a sandwich. Between 3:00 and 4:30, if I get up to pee, that's particular enough and I'm OK again. Another way I enter the doldrums is when my mom sends me one of those big epic historical novels with the man and woman embracing in torn-up clothes on the cover, the kind of book that covers four generations and buries three of them—reading *that* puts me in a dust-to-dust mood for days. Characters drop like flies. It is a crazy-making virtual reality of hard closure where all loose ends are tacked down before the final page and lives are spent like nickels. This kind of long view is breathtaking in two senses: it is vast, and it is a thief of detail.

I prefer a particular kind of history whose very unimportance is profound, which examines even a day or a conversation and is not consumed by its flowing backdrop. Dorothy Stone, an old woman in McGrath, uses a ski pole for a cane. Winter and summer she walks the road, and when you meet her she starts right in the middle of the story: "We had foxes. Way up the river. My son and daughter-in-law are up there now." She doesn't remember me, though each summer we have coffee and cake a few times. I see her walking by and go out to get her. She says, "I had a good husband. Politician. I used to know the people who lived in this house." She is looking at my house. "They had a little girl." My daughter, the then-little girl, will come out to see what rocks Dorothy has in her pockets today, because Dorothy picks up tiny stones that look like they have noses and eyes and mouths and shows them to anyone who stops to talk with her. After three or four rocks, Kari loses interest and wanders off, but Dorothy shows me several more. "Look, here's a cute little fellow. See him? He's laughing at us! I used to be a school teacher. You have to show children, or they won't learn." I say yes. And I offer her coffee because one time she told me that everyone thinks old people drink only tea. She accepts, and I put out canned milk, even though she told me the miners drink it because they ran away from their mothers too soon. She pours a little milk in her coffee today and takes a teaspoon of sugar.

Dorothy doesn't remember who we are, but she likes us. If I bring out one of the local historical calendars, she'll page through it and tell me stories about the people in the pictures, half of whom she is related to. Her step-father, Charles Koenig, drove a mail team through Ophir to Flat, the end of the line from Fairbanks. Her mother, Helen, came from a family of reindeer herders near Bethel. Dorothy was schooled at the Catholic mission at Holy Cross and went to Chicago for the Eucharistic Convention of 1926. "It was a biiiiiiig town. I held on to Father's skirt. I was so scared he would leave me!"

There is little continuity in what I know about Dorothy, only pictures and pieces, and I am a stranger each time I greet her. But the frame itself provides continuity: the stories she tells to introduce herself, the familiar offering of coffee, the river town where we like to talk to each other. People pass by on the river and we invite them in, one by one, detail by detail.

Alaskan rivers provide a point of view on history, one that does not deaden and discourage the watcher. In Alaska, rivers are still a serviceable metaphor for history because there are few roads, and despite the all-important coming of airplanes and airstrips, the river serves as road, stage, human journey. Especially before the advent of bush television in 1980, river villagers pulled out couches and chairs and left them on the bank for years. It was all the news: Who's on the river? Who's coming to visit? And it was and is an attention to the river itself. Is it rising and getting dirty, or failing and clearing up? Did the ice move? Is the channel open?

For those looking for a quintessential Alaskan thing, my vote is not for the little face made from the caribou anus, but for the couches that sit up above the now-freeway at Eklutna. I saw them twenty years ago, with people on them, and the people were just sitting there watching the cars go by. Last Thursday the couches were still there, maybe the same ones, without the people. Twenty below and several inches of snow on the cushions could explain the absence of life. But those couches are prima facie evidence that rivers and travelers on rivers have been of singular importance to Alaskans, such importance that a road's mere similarity to a river is enough to make a person drag out a couch and sit down to examine the wayfarers. God knows if the sparrow falls, but the folks at Eklutna know that I've been to the dentist, to the grocery store, to pick up my mother at the airport. The fact that eighty bazillion people Eklutnians don't know are going back and forth on the road hasn't discouraged their attention in at least twenty years. So I hope it was the cold and the snow that emptied the couches and not that looking down at car after car full of stranger after stranger on errand after errand made them feel their observations were futile and in vain.

For many towns in the Alaskan bush, the river is a road to be tended to winter and summer, with short, dangerous interruptions at freeze-up and break-up time. When you live with maintained roads that connect all across the country, it seems that rivers are untrustworthy and full of danger, if they are anything at all to us, but in the interior of Alaska the rivers stretch further, join more communities, carry more freight, still. They are as reliably treacherous and changeable as the weather. People live with them, on them, with knowledges and skills gone from roaded landscapes. The barge captains who make their way up from Kotzebue on the Kobuk, from St. Mary's on the Yukon, from Bethel on the Kuskokwim, all know what each riffle hides, what each cut bank tells about the location of the channel, what the wind will do to the boat when they come around the next finger of silt and spruce. This is not just one river, but rivers within rivers, rich with episodes and dangers and prescriptions.

There was a Yukon River pilot who could not read to pass his Coast Guard examination, but he drew the officials a map of the entire route he would run, every cut bank, every sand bar and eddy in such detail that they gave him his license. The story is surprising to me: the kindness of the officials and the confident will of the pilot. It is difficult, without listening to their voices, indeed without living their lives, to imagine what a former generation of Alaskans hoped the rivers would bring.

Spending time where rivers, not roads, are primary, you are dragged into the texture of history. The roads around McGrath are bad, dusty, and rough, and many people use all-terrain "wheelers" instead of passenger vehicles, which shifts the concept of traveling in a car or truck to novelty, even luxury. After a summer of bicycles and wheelers and boats, my five-year-old daughter begged to ride in her father's work truck. A few weeks later, she glowed with pride when our friend Barb toured us around town in the old Chevy she had Northern Air Cargo fly out from Kenai. It is a pleasure when our habits are rearranged so that they come into view. One laughing moment in my job as a forest-fire dispatcher was toppling an Anchorage dispatcher's belief that he would be trucking fire supplies out to Mc-Grath. His refusal to understand that there were no roads through the Alaska Range prolonged and sweetened the discussion for several minutes. Not being able to get here by road is an exotic idea for an American in the latter part of the twentieth century. And the exotic is charming, which hides its importance.

I do not know more than five bends of the river at McGrath, but this small knowledge helps to pry open the primacy of river, which is new to me and old to the world, to make me aware of the barges and the older steamboats, parts and pieces of which stick up through the surface at low water. The aging practitioners of the river life are seldom visible in this small town, walking slowly with sticks, quiet in their houses. When the river comes up in the spring, plugged with ice downstream or swelled to the top of the bank with August rains, then I see Einer or Tex for the first time, hobbling down to the bank or riding a wheeler. A government program built them a line of houses, which they themselves have named "death row," but I've heard this rumor only third-hand or so.

In fact, everything I haven't heard the old people say about themselves separates me from them: how many miles one traveled on a dog sled to dance all night in Ophir, the clunky old troop carrier another sailed single-handedly from Seattle to Bethel, the kids another taught to read in a shack on a willow bank. Mostly, they don't spare a glance for the townspeople who haven't sought them out; their attention is for the river. What will it do? Over the banks or not?

This attention to the river is compelling and can teach us younger ones to look, too. Even the very young. In a world of Nintendo and malls and motorcycles, eleven-year-old Aaron took a look at the big McGrath flood of 1991 and announced gravely, "Now I've seen everything."

Ethnographers everywhere are noticing a curious phenomenon: after dutifully announcing year after year that a particular generation of old people are the last to hold on to a story, a song, a point of view, another generation of old people suddenly pops up that knows the words. To everything there is a season: "a time to keep silence, and a time to speak."

River-watching is preserved here as attitude, long after the particularity of river travel and the knowledge of old travelers is gone. Bush airports gather storefronts and houses as rivers used to, but rivers and rivers' functions are not yet completely gone, and houses and store buildings do not just turn themselves around. When we were in the village of Kobuk and an airplane came in, we'd follow the crowd down to the strip to see who it was. If it was us coming in, there'd be a crowd to greet us, and we'd carry our bags through town, walking up behind the school and through dog lots and caches to the postmaster's house. I always had a sense that I was sneaking up the back way, as if the town's attention was turned in another direction.

There's a lot of scorn from some visitors about the way Alaska villages and towns look, all spread out and "junky," disorganized. But when you come in from the airstrip, the way most visitors come, you're coming from the dog-lot side. Unless it's a town built around an airstrip, such as a mining town up in the mountains or an Air Force station, the buildings aren't looking at you when you come in on an airplane. They are tending the water, where the boats and fish and visitors came from historically. The water is the direction of Kotzebue, of Seattle, of San Francisco, of the rest of the world. The barge will land here with gas, fuel oil, Sheetrock and metal roofing. "When will my new truck get here?" "I'm gonna run out of gas if the barge doesn't get here by Tuesday." To build your house away from the water is like sitting in a room with your back to the light.

Alaskans are reluctant to leave their homes on the side of the river even when the river threatens them with flood each spring and in many rainy Augusts. The Bureau of Indian Affairs built Galena a "new town" in the seventies, but for years, people would move back to the bank of the Yukon, to the little line of cabins and shacks outside the big nine-mile circle of dike that held the Air Force station and

Charles Crosman

Abandoned Dreams

Cibachrome photograph

1986

UAP88:027:001

runway. There were three towns in town: the Air Force, the "old town," and the neat little BIA subdivisions with the houses looking at each other in rows. In 1977 six feet of water and ice flowed through old-town houses for a week. Many of their owners camped out on the dike, played cards, built campfires, and waited patiently for the river to leave their living rooms. No wonder the river towns need to watch the river. It's like waiting for the mail: bad news, good news.

And when I come back to a river town at the end of a day of eddies and cut banks and gravel bars and moose in the willows, I feel like the town has been watching for me, watching from storefronts or the chair on the bank. A neighbor may see me come in, walk down and grab the line at the bow of the boat and pull it up the bank, tie it up in its place: my place. The people on the couches above the freeway, even with a chain-link fence between them and the seventy-mile-an-hour traffic below, hold a kind of vestigial voyeurism and faithfulness to neighbors.

Many twentieth-century Americans from roaded areas can grasp some universal concept of river but not specific ones, just as to a city person a wild caribou becomes abstract, standing for nature but without the specific qualities of the caribou you hunt and eat—without the round circles chiseled on top of each other in the beaten snow of the trail, or the hollow popping sound of caribou ankles moving through the brush in front of you, like a handful of sixth-graders popping their index fingers in their cheeks.

Where I grew up, the river is beautiful and dirty and in the way. It is the famous Snake River, and it divides the landscape like a wall. I have felt drawn to the riverside as to a blank thing ready for meaning—a void left over from an old usefulness of rivers. When I'm standing by the Snake, I often have the curious experience of not being able to recognize whose house is on the other side unless I am close to where the bridge crosses. I will look across at Joe Witte's square fields, not recognizing them. His farm could be the moon, that far removed from the possibility of going there. I can't recognize the place across the river because I can't go across the river at that place.

Or down in "The Bend," that little chunk of Oregon nestled in the inside curve of Snake's elbow, standing in Joe Witte's cornfield, I can look up at the other side of the river, that picturesque but foreign place, and recognize, with surprise, that I am looking at my friend Carol's house. No one I know thinks of crossing the Snake River with a boat to get to the other side, though it is a broad, smooth river. There are no boats tied up along the bank. So not being able to get there from here becomes not being able to think about that from here. The white house with its fence and flowers, a stone's throw away if you have an arm like George Washington, is to my mind's map about seventeen miles away, all on roads.

Other than interdictions like "Don't go near it," nobody paid the Snake River much attention. Even now the new houses built along the river in the town where I grew up face away from it, toward Main Street and the highway a half-mile away. If you were a traveler on the river (and you wouldn't be) you'd climb up the bank and be greeted by all the backyards of town, the junk cars and weed patches, and you'd think, "What a neglected, scraggly little town." All the new little trees along mainstreet and the recently constructed outhouse city hall, which is a joke, would be lost on you.

There were different ideas about the Snake River at Adrian when people traveled on it, before bridges, when you had to come across on the ferry. There's one building left on the Snake across from Adrian that looks at the river. It was a store and ferry boat station, and it is very old, nothing left of it but a silvery gray shell of planks. But it is obvious from the opposite bank, where the town sits, that the building tended the river and not the road. It looks too close, unwisely close to the bank. From its own side of the river, coming up to it on the highway, you see its back like the back of a man standing off to the side, turning away from you so he can take a leak.

There are few square fields in Alaska to draw attention away from the sweep and suck of rivers, their dangerous utility. Here, you are never far from the knowledge that the valley was made by the river, serves the river, and the river can take it back. The evidence is carved out in sloughs and the meadows left by old sloughs, like the tracks left by some monstrous procession of caribou at the beginning of time, sloughs like the front curves of hooves separated by trees like stacks of eyebrows. The old Yup'ik people say "yes," raising their eyebrows. The land raises its eyebrows in the old bends of rivers, says "yes" to river, winter, ice, change.

Heraclitus is at home here, telling us we cannot dip into the same river twice, that "we" itself is a convention, whether vanity or bravery. The river cannot flow around the same "us" twice, still we wish to hang a name on ourselves that will hide our movement, limit and contain the daily and seasonal changes and the shifting of channels over a continuum. There are the changes of weather: rise and fall and "better check the boat—it'll take four of us to get it down the bank and in the river again," or "better go bail it out and tie it up high." And there are seasons: rainy season or low water or the ice coming, bringing the river to a stop, boats long stored away for the winter and then the whole land filling up like a sponge in springtime until even the river comes up, up, nearly over the bank, thousands of square miles saturated with melting snow coming down and the rivers still plugged up, oatmeal in the drain, clotted with rotten ice.

And there are the kinds of changes that deeds and appraisals and surveys deny: we drive out on the one road to look at the place where the river wants to come through above the town, trying to make us an island, trying to make the river in front of us a slough. A woman in California writes the city of McGrath a letter, asking about her property, but her property is gone, the last of it sifting into the Kuskokwim five years ago. We cannot administer properties that dissolve, literally, and so we joke that we all will have riverfront houses if we can only wait a few years. Still, we call it the same river, and we call ourselves the same people.

You have to go fishing, gather plants, look closely at the sides of rivers to see that what seems static is only moving a little slower than the river itself. Berry-picking is good around the old horseshoe sloughs left by rivers. We found most of our blueberries around the margins of old sloughs this summer, on the old riverbanks and not so much back in the woods. I think it was too rainy for the tree-sheltered bushes to produce fruit—maybe that's what happened, or it was something else? Too many variables make the overview difficult, so many details that there are only details, wonderful in profusion. Only when I've been out a few times does the shape of where the berries are this year come to me, that they are looking for sun, clinging to the drier ground, hanging out over the open grass of ancient rivers.

Often when I am looking for berries I can't see them. I walk around in the berry patch for minutes, unsatisfied with the berries I see, unwilling to stop walking for just a few berries, then all of a sudden I can see enough berries, and I know they've been there all the time. It's putting my back to the sun so the colors of bush and berries pull apart, but it's something else, too, something secretive about berries that won't let you see them until you deserve it, until you've settled down out of the future or past you've been thinking of to the present moment where the berries are.

And when I close my eyes for a moment at the end of a day of picking berries, I see berries on bushes, lots of them and big. I never close my eyes and see berries in buckets or bags, ready for the freezer. It's always berries still on bushes, etched with desire on my eye, and I relive finding and wanting them. They are like story cycles—their details fade with time, eventually leaving only forms and frames: emptiness and vanity, if you will. Berries are a gift of a moment when detail is allowed to halt abstraction. In their moment I am privileged to be among them, the promise of their small dark roundness in the hand one at a time, or a lucky handful in the right season.

Stories are hidden in the river, as in history, yet the parts are greater than the sum. They do not deaden, discourage, despair. They come into view and pass out of view, and their details offer a vertical dimension to the flow. If I don't look for names, search out the memory of particular people who have lived where I live, the forward movement of time erases definition specifics, all evidence of the deep vertical axis of my life. To avoid despair in the strong current of generations, I must uncover names, old jokes I don't understand. We have always been new things under the sun, each of us.

McGrath has been built at least three times. The first time it was called Mc-Grath was after Peter McGrath, a U.S. marshall, and it was up at the Forks, so called because that's where the Nixon Fork runs into the Takotna, and that's the farthest distance boats from downriver could reliably travel toward the mining districts on the upper Takotna and the track to Ophir, on the Innoko side. There was a warehouse at the Forks, owned by Archie Higgins from Takotna, and he had a gas boat that shoved a little barge up the Takotna, but he had to wait until it rained so that he could get his boat up over the riffles.

After a few years, though, the boats that came upriver got bigger and the town had to move down to deeper water where the Takotna runs into the Kuskokwim. That's where it was in 1917, when David Alvinza Ray, the wireless operator, fell off the tall wireless pole where he'd been repairing something and was killed. My friend Margaret, who has been in one McGrath or another since 1929, has told me about this wireless operator several times. When she arrived in McGrath, the story was polished but still fresh, told by many, connected in many directions across Alaska. Now she is its only teller, and when I heard it from her the wireless operator had no name, only "the wireless operator who got killed." The life of that story is nearly over, an empty frame.

But I know the wireless operator's name because the water was high enough this spring for us to get our riverboat over into Old Town Slough. The cabins have mostly been eaten up by mushrooms and rot and roses, but there's an outhouse made from half of a round-hulled boat, green paint still clinging to it in patches, and David Alvinza Ray's grave, with a small granite headstone. The grave has a neat picket fence, still, though the white paint is all gone. This is about the only thing left of the second McGrath.

What would have been obvious about McGrath in the twenties and thirties would not have been David Ray or the outhouse made from half a boat, but the big Northern Commercial Company warehouse and shipyard, right on the upstream side of where the Takotna ran into the Kusko. Margaret says there was a dog barn for travelers and mail carriers, big enough that you could drive your sled right through the middle of it. If you were the mail carrier, for example Carl

Tony Rubey

On the Porch, In the Store

Color lithograph

1984

UA84-3-133D

Seseui coming in from Telida, you'd leave your sled there in the barn all night and bed your twenty or so dogs down in the stalls on either side of the sled run. Every mail stop had a dog barn. You drove right up off the river and into it.

Old man Dan Sprague was a buffalo hunter from Montana. He had a homestead across the river, where our town is now, and he'd come over to what was then McGrath in the daytime with an unlit lantern so he could light his way home in the dark after an evening of poker. But the game would stretch into night and back into the short winter day before he'd whiskey-weave the snow back across the river to his side, lantern still unlit. In the summer his farm was literally a one-horse operation. He'd borrow Vanderpool's old white horse so he'd have a team to plow his field. Vanderpool, the magistrate, lived one bend up the Kuskokwim, a mile and a half away, so they'd bring the horse up and down in a boat. When Margaret tells me about Dan Sprague, she often points to where his cabin used to be, a square of absent land off the end of the crosswind runway, long washed away by the shifting Kuskokwim. She said he was "a nice old man with long white whiskers" when she knew him in 1929.

The NC Company had to move their warehouse and store across to Sprague's homestead in 1935, after the Takotna ate through its bank and into the Kuskokwim one bend above its old mouth, which silted in the very same summer and became too shallow for the steamboats. The rest of the town followed gradually, buying up lots from the NC Company. Now what you see when you look across the Kuskokwim from the boat slip is cut bank all the same height, but where the Takotna used to come out the willows are a touch shorter, maybe thirty feet instead of thirty-five, and that's how you know the river has hidden the channel and the town where it used to go. Rivers shift, and then towns drag their heels to new banks and wait to be washed away again.

Margaret has lived on both sides of the river because she came up to McGrath on the steamboat *Tana* in 1929. She saw the second town go down and the third one rise up, and people and events flow through her talk so that you can watch them, coming and going. We drink tea, couch and chair angled toward each other, surrounded by the hardware and mementos of a wilderness life, a river life.

Nameplates from steamships, log tongs, lanterns. I am amazed by Margaret's varied enterprises—her trapping, her freighting, her cooking for mining crews—and by her stories of her father the steamship captain. She knows a trick that turns canned milk into a caramel-tasting flavoring, but you have to use a stove with plates, not burners. I like the big garden she still grows in the deep river dirt of Dan Sprague's old homestead, and the delphiniums as big as blue trees above us when we sit outside in the summer. Margaret can't remember if she or Dorothy Stone brought the first delphiniums to McGrath, but now they're in every yard, and sometimes a stalk or two leans up out of the wild grasses and bedstraw along the road, invisible until it blooms.

Margaret helps me to resist the temptation to view my own life as a solid thing, just one kind of thing, or to get too far away from it, trying to see it. My mother would say, "It's an angry river," because in the experiences of her life, rivers don't have any specific dimension but danger. If it is a flat, shiny river like the Snake, it's hiding something. If it is swift and silty like the Kuskokwim, it's angry. Its character, like its mood, seems to her an immutable fact. It's easier to think about rivers and even whole people and whole lives in this way, never looking any closer, as if we all are just one thing, one kind of person, one kind of life. This kind of looking is shorthand for being conscious, and I practice it incessantly. Although people are kind or cruel or smart or dumb one right after another, it seems like I know each of them, and myself, to be just one thing. When I think this way, there is no "give" to the way I treat others, no idea that we all could break through into another channel anytime, out the other end of even this moment, leaving expectations behind like a vestigial circle of slough.

I met Ted and Margaret in 1991 when an ice jam downriver brought the Kuskokwim out of its banks and through the town. We were renting one of the few houses that didn't flood, though we had water over our top step, and we sat with our feet in it and handed out coffee and cake to people who were driving up and down the streets in their motorboats. Across the street, Margaret and Ted brought everything they could up out of their cellar and off the floor of their house, stored it in old barge containers that looked to me like railroad cars, up on blocks, then waded around in rising water, tying empty barrels together as a breakwater to keep all of the lumber and boxes and boats in their own yard—fifty years of stuff to keep from floating away. We hadn't collected anything to have to save, so I watched them and the other neighbors struggle, wanting to help but not knowing how to grab ahold of anything.

All day, kids got canoes stuck in willow thickets. There was a breakup party at the Alaska Company boat slip in the afternoon. The ice was gone, even if the river wasn't. We cooked hot dogs and hamburgers and drank beer and pop, standing in icy water and trying not to make waves that would wash over the top of our breakup boots. In the morning, when the water was going down, I took some hot biscuit cake out to the barge container where Ted and Margaret had slept. So the flood introduced us, and I've been thankful, as I love them, as their lives open in stories I hope will last the winter.

After the water went down, people went into their houses and scraped out the inches of mud, peeled the carpets off the floors so the boards wouldn't rot, and moved back in. Most of the kids were disappointed the water went down so fast. They looked at their old town in a new way for a while, as if it had done something surprising.

Sometimes when you come down to McGrath, across the Kuskokwim from the Takotna mouth, it is a smooth mirror and you see the little pointed tops of the AC store and warehouse reflected in the water. At the moment, the storefronts are dark green, with big white signs and red letters. They peer at you across the runway, because there were already airplanes landing at McGrath in 1935, when the town moved, so the old NC Company built a runway in front of its store, and Main Street runs alongside this old runway. The buildings along Main Street— the stores, the electric company, the cafe, the radio station, the FAA—all have to squint to see the river, but they do it. They are still curious to see who is coming across.

Our bravery, not vanity, crosses the flowing length everywhere. Each lived moment divides the current and makes the river new; each story ties us up for a moment to another life and opens, briefly and out of time, a view of what we are to each other and to the earth. When I look across the glassy mouths of rivers, seams invisible, I want to go close to the bank so I can see who's coming and who's passing.

Draw up a chair with me on a nice day.

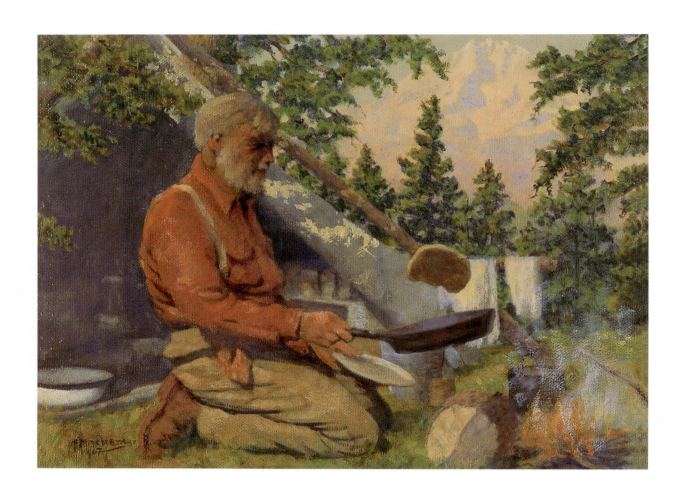

Fred Machetanz

Sourdough Hotcakes

Oil on masonite

1967

Gift of Grace Berg Schaible

UA95:059:001

COMING OUT OF THE COUNTRY

Dan O'Neill

I may have liked places that

are wild and been quickened

all my days just by the sound of

the word, but I see now that I

never knew what it could mean.

I can see why people who come

to Alaska are unprepared. In

four decades being beyond some

sort of road, I never set foot in

a place like this.

John McPhee, Coming into the

Country, 1977

IT WAS a great steaming pile of bear dung, in the wild country along the Yukon, downriver from the village of Eagle, that so spooked and inspired John McPhee. If he were left on his own here, he wrote, "I would have to change in a hurry, and learn in a hurry, or I'd never last a year."

That night my wife and small son and I would be camping very near the lonely place where McPhee recorded these observations some twenty years earlier. The next day we would continue on down the Yukon River for the next week to Circle, the first village we would encounter, one hundred sixty miles away.

This was more than a canoe trip. I was in search of some of the river people memorialized by McPhee in a series of articles for *The New Yorker* magazine in 1977 and in his masterpiece *Coming into the Country*. McPhee had written a sympathetic portrait of a new breed of young voyageurs who, when they decided to leave their counterculture enclaves in urban America and head "back to nature," made it farther than the Berkshires or the Sonoma coast. They drove their pickups over the thousand miles of gravel that led north to Alaska, stopping when they reached the literal end of the road: the Alaska villages of Eagle and Circle, two of the most remote points on the American road system. From there they headed off into the immense wilderness of the Yukon basin, recapitulating (to the consternation of federal land managers) the historic migrations of trappers, prospectors and homesteaders.

But a lot of Yukon River water had passed by Eagle in the years since McPhee had rented a cabin there, and I wondered what had become of the young river people. Whither this tribe of stalwart idealists, these woods-wise and well-spoken renegades, now entering middle age?

We shoved the bow out to where the current could catch it and turn us down-river, called a final good-bye to our friends at the boat landing, and stowed our paddles. I lowered the kicker, pulled on the starter rope, and set the throttle to a quiet putt. A minute later, we could hardly make out the shapes of human figures standing on shore by the vehicles. Shrinking by the second was the village of Eagle, a couple of dozen tin roofs glittering in a five o'clock sun shower.

The first camp to check would have been Steve Ulvi's, up near the Canadian border. But I was not going there. I knew that Ulvi had moved off the river and now worked for the National Park Service in Fairbanks. And I knew his story, which was not unlike that of many of the riverfolk. In the mid-1970s McPhee had found Ulvi to be an articulate embodiment of the new-age pioneer. He had grown up in the San Francisco Bay Area and attended college in Oregon. There he'd read and pondered several classics of wilderness lore, hiked, backpacked, and camped. He established himself in a tepee in the coast range and commuted to school. But, inevitably, he craved escape ftom the consumptive and wasteful culture that surrounded him. He wanted a larger and more elemental and primitive space into which his emerging philosophy (which was tending toward Buddhism) and aesthetics (which was distinctly agrarian) might expand. And he was ready to embrace the hard work, isolation, and even danger that might come with it. So, in the summer of 1974, before he quite had completed college, Steve Ulvi headed north to see about living in the deep Alaskan woods. He was joined by his girl-friend, his brother, and a couple of like-minded California buddies. They all piled into a rebuilt '51 Dodge pickup with two canoes strapped on top and the back crammed with tools, gear, and eight or nine hundred pounds of food.

Eagle was an unusual Alaskan village in those days. Almost no one was out on the land. There were those who had come to Eagle because it was a jump-off point for heading into the wilderness. But, for one reason or another, these folks hadn't jumped. Instead, they picked up seasonal work or, in a few cases, started small businesses. Eagle also attracted a number of comfortably well-off retirees drawing government pensions. Like the first group, they sometimes kept a canoe tied up at the riverbank and occasionally checked their gill net for a salmon for dinner, but they rarely ventured farther into the country. They were the frontier equivalent of gentlemen farmers, and the value of their harvest was best measured in psychological, rather than economic, terms. The occasional fish had less to do with providing sustenance for the body than with sustaining an identity. It was the slender thread that connected the townsfolk to the wilderness and permitted their deeply valued self-image as frontiersmen and -women. And, finally, there was a village of Han Indians just outside Eagle. But these folks, too, had largely given up trapping and fishing and dog teams in favor of paying jobs, government assistance, and store food. Not a single one of the Han in 1974 was living out in the country. A few still did some trapping, cut wood for sale, or operated a fish wheel in front of the village. But gone were the days of training good teams of working dogs and of spending a large part of the winter out at a trap camp and most of the summer at a fish camp.

In short, the traditional skills of the old-timers of this region were about to be lost when a kind of salvation came rolling down the hill into Eagle. It emerged long-haired and smelling of unfamiliar herbs from pickups and vans with license plates from California, Oregon, and New Hampshire. It was the white, urban, typically middle-class hippie kids like Steve Ulvi and his friends.

Ulvi and his pals set up their tents at the Eagle campground and strolled downtown to look things over. Perhaps predictably, the inhabitants of Eagle tended to discourage newcomers. Did they have any idea what seventy degrees below zero felt like? Had they ever lived in a small cabin with no electricity? no running water? Hell, the darkness alone drove people crazy, with the sun not up for much more than the lunch hour. Who'd they think they were, Sergeant Preston? But, as Ulvi would learn later, the most naysaying of the townsfolk tended to be those who had not themselves lived out in the country.

The group found a more sympathetic reception at the Native village. At least they met a man there who would let them move onto land that he claimed just this side of the Canadian border, on the Yukon's opposite bank. It was nine miles above the Han village, twelve miles above Eagle proper. An old cabin stood on the site, which two of the party could fix up and live in, while the other three (Ulvi, his girlfriend, and his brother) could build a new cabin. The man probably doubted that they would last the winter, Ulvi thought, and was figuring that he shortly would acquire, without cost, one new and one rehabilitated cabin. They concluded the deal with a handshake, never putting a time limit on the occupancy.

Like old-time sourdoughs, the partners "lined" their outfit upriver. That is, they loaded their gear into the two canoes and, walking on shore, hauled the canoe upstream with a loop of rope, the ends of which were tied to the bow and stern. By holding the rope at just the right point on the loop, they could make the bow point slightly into the current and thereby stand off from shore in deeper water instead of tracking right behind the hauler, where it would run aground in the shallows. If they came to a steep, eroded bank or a rock outcrop, they would have to paddle across the great river—which could be two-thirds of a mile wide in places—perhaps losing a half mile or more to the current, then resume lining. If the group's approach to transportation seemed overly labor intensive, it fit their collective notions of right living. They did not care to use outboard motors. And they had decided that in constructing their cabins, they would employ only hand tools: axes, augers, and an old-fashioned crosscut saw. Ulvi had owned a chain saw in Oregon, but sold it before heading north. The racket and fumes seemed almost an impiety in the deep silences of the Alaskan wilderness. And he didn't want to be dependent on gas, oil, and parts. They would cut their house logs, roof poles, and floor poles by hand. And by hand they would rip saw what lumber they required. No plywood would taint their camp with a prefab look. Once, when a sheet of the stuff drifted down the river and fetched up nearby, they poked it back into the current.

Nor would Ulvi, in siting the cabin, allow himself the pleasure of a view of the passing river, but set it a hundred yards back in the trees, that way not to violate the river or impose his settlement on travelers. When the fifteen-by-fifteen-foot structure was finished, the occupants settled into a style of housekeeping that suggested the relative opulence of a monastery. As near-vegetarians, and frugal ones, they would parcel out their lentils, rice, beans, and pancake mix from fifty-pound sacks. Of course they baked their own bread, grinding bulgur by hand. As a special indulgence, they would permit themselves one can of fruit per week, split three ways. Candles would provide the only light during the months of dark winter. And they would forgo that inessential artifact of a profligate era: toilet paper. Moss would suffice.

But ascetic purity, even on this impressive scale, had limits. For one thing, there was a six-mil sheet of polyethylene under the roof sod, which was practically the only way to prevent such a roof from leaking. Squares of plastic film served as windows; nylon sleeping bags lay on the bunks; a high-powered rifle hung by the door. Even the mail-order importation of bulk dried fruit and powdered milk implied the sort of industrial infrastructure that the group seemed to spurn. Secondly, the philosophy of self-denial, while sincere, seemed tinged with sanctimony: weren't these plaid-shirted pioneers cultivating their image as assiduously as the blow-dried kids contemporaneously making the scene at America's shopping malls? And lastly, Ulvi and his friends modified their canon as the country demanded (or as advancing maturity permitted). They hunted for meat, took up trapping, and bought kerosene lanterns, eventually an outboard motor, and even a chain saw.

To a remarkable degree, however, Ulvi and his friends, as well as the other young people living out along the Yukon River in the mid-1970s, approximated the frontier life of the previous century. Like their sourdough antecedents, they lived a life closely connected to the land and one in which simplicity and hard work were both the prerequisites of survival and values in themselves.

As it turned out, the Native man in Eagle village did not fall heir to two abandoned cabins in the spring of 1975. Though the three other young men moved off the site, Steve Ulvi, then twenty-three years old, stayed on until he was a middle-aged man. He and his girlfriend, Lynette Roberts, married and started a family there. During the warm summer months, while Steve and Lynette cut and hung fish to dry or hauled buckets of river water to the garden, the two kids played with the sled dog pups on the beach. When the leaves yellowed and the rank smell of cranberries filled the woods, the kids dug potatoes in the wet earth, or headed out with their pails to help harvest lip-staining blueberries, rose hips packed with seeds and vitamins, and the highbush cranberries that burst in your mouth with a small explosion of sour juice. In winter they sometimes rode in the sled over the trapline trails, spending the night in a wall tent miles from the sight or sound of another human being outside of the family. When the children became school-aged, Lynette sent away for correspondence-school materials and taught them at home.

If Steve Ulvi had jumped headlong into a wilderness life, he would return from it in stages. As the kids grew, Steve and Lynette wanted them to be able to play more with other children. Lynette, too, was beginning to crave more of a social life, and she wanted the opportunity to work. And Steve, who had begun to reach a point where a declining enthusiasm for trapping had been overtaken by an ascending interest in a steady paycheck, was offered a permanent position with the Park Service in Eagle. The family moved from their snug cabin upriver to an ancient, sagging, and drafty one in town. The kids enrolled in the Eagle school; Lynette served on the school board and Steve worked a steady job.

A few years later, when the kids reached junior-high-school age, Fairbanks beckoned. As the hub of Alaska's vast Interior and home of the state university's main campus, Fairbanks (area population 80,000) could offer libraries and swimming pools, ballet and drama classes, gymnastics, soccer and track. Eagle (population 168) could not. And both Steve and Lynette wanted to "exercise the mind," as Steve said, to finish college, for a start. Now, for the first time, they were ready—eager—to turn their energies and intellect toward some traditional career progress. So, for all the reasons that generally make more sense to people approaching forty than to people barely out of their teens, the family moved out of the upper Yukon country in 1990.

It should be ice, not paper, that covers the rock that breaks the scissors. In the mountains far upstream from where we have stopped, millions of tons of moving glacier ice reduce bedrock to specks of grit as fine as flour. The gray, powdery stuff roils the glacial outwash, clouding to a pearly translucence every creek and river downstream all the way to the sea. This suspended silt hisses now against our beached canoe, the aluminum hull magnifying the sound tympanically, like brush strokes on a snare drum. A quiet drumroll. Enter Dick Cook, McPhee's most notable river character.

We are eating lunch on a cobbly beach when a canoe pulls out from shore just a quarter mile below us and glides across the wide, sparkling river. We can see the two people aboard checking a salmon net on the opposite bank, gathering lunch, perhaps. In a few minutes they motor back. But the outboard quits. A half mile or more of silence between us, we can hear their voices over the water as the river sweeps them away downstream, the man pulling on the cord repeatedly. Finally, the motor fires and they point into the current. But in a minute, it quits again. He pulls and fiddles as they drift, pulls until the motor catches and runs long enough for them to make it back to shore.

We pack up and drift down to where Cook's boat is tied, and I give my son Kyle a bag of grapefruit to carry up the trail. If we are to disturb this famous denizen of the wilds at meal time, I figure to do so a couple of paces behind a cute kid bearing gifts. But Cook is already at the head of the trail before we start up. In seconds his eyes have taken in the three of us, scanned the canoe, registered that I am running a fifteen-horse Evinrude on a nineteen-foot square-stem Grumman with a lift, computed the volume and weight of our gear, and followed the bag of grapefruit until it is in his hands. He receives it with thanks, introduces us to his friend, a woman from Texas named Pat, and invites us up to his camp.

Cook is as McPhee found him: thin and balding with longish, gray-streaked black hair and beard, alert as a mink. He wears a generic T-shirt and old pants with a busted zipper, but he is shod in the latest sandals. He looks like some kind of marooned pirate in Birkenstocks, a castaway scavenger of goods swept overboard from passing freighters out in the shipping lanes.

It is the time of gardens, and once up the bank we inspect Cook's well-managed plot, discuss fish guts as fertilizer, cauliflower that will not head, and subsistence living, generally. I mention seeing some fish heads on the beach where we had

Sam Kimura
Homage to Henry
Gelatin silver photograph,
selenium toned
1985
UAP85:091:001

stopped for lunch and ask if he fishes with rod and reel. No, it was the work of some floaters. For him to fish with a rod would make about as much sense, he says, as taking his rifle and shooting into the woods, then taking off walking after the bullet to see if it had hit anything. I laugh, but remark that old timers in this country sometimes fed their dog teams by jigging for pike. I'd read accounts of holes so productive that a person with a spoon and a length of twine could stack up fifteen-pounders like cord wood. But Cook isn't buying it. He delivers a short lecture on the need in a subsistence economy for maximum return on invested effort. It puts me in mind of a bit of McPhee's scathing tact. He described Cook's voice as soft and gentle, except "when he is being pedagogical. . . . He is not infrequently pedagogical. "

But neither is he ungenerous with the fruits of his wisdom. As we move to leave, Cook plucks from the garden a perfect, deep green cucumber and hands it to Kyle.

With the breeze in our faces again, and the wide river bearing us deeper into the country, I think about Cook's staying power and his influences on the younger river people. Having moved out of Eagle and onto the Yukon in the 1960s, Cook was the old man of the river twenty years ago. To some extent, as McPhee implies, he was mentor to the young people who arrived in the '70s. But because they were, by definition, tough and adventurous, I doubt they were the sort to spend lots of time sitting at Cook's feet. The mentees would have been wise, though, to have followed Cook's lead in one respect. Because he had taken over a woodcutter's homestead that dated to the sternwheeler days, he was on private, not federal, land. Ulvi had been lucky. The land on which he had built was claimed by, and eventually transferred to, his Han landlord under the Alaska Native Claims Settlement Act. He was able to stay in the country until he had gotten his fill of it. Cook likewise avoided extensive federal intrusion into his life and remains in the country. Most of the river people, however, were not so lucky.

When McPhee was among the river people, the bête noire of the woods was not the bear, but the Bureau of Land Management. At that time BLM officials had begun patrolling the country in search of trespass cabins to post with vacate notices or maybe, they threatened, to burn. Because the cabins were often tiny and made from the natural materials at hand—unpeeled logs with sod roofs—they weren't easy to spot. And though they blended into their surroundings, though they were sometimes fifty miles from the nearest town and then more canoe-dragging miles up a side creek, the BLM had its orders. And it had helicopters. When the woodsfolk cut a tree for firewood or for some construction purpose, they took to placing a chunk of moss on the fresh-cut stump to make it less visible from the air. In town they were cagey about where, exactly, they lived.

From prehistory forward, anyone who took a notion to move here could do so. And the U.S. government seemed to give tacit approval to the occupation. Basically, it ignored the land for a century. And why not? The few people who were tough enough and savvy enough to take the extreme climate, the months of darkness, and the maddening mosquitoes and wrestle a living from such a place had certainly lived up to the spirit of the homesteading programs. But things began to change in the early 1970s. A new logic took hold that said no old fashioned, dues-paying residency amounted to a "right" to live on public land.

Part of the reason for this turn of events had to do with the discovery of the nation's largest oil field at Prudhoe Bay on Alaska's Arctic Ocean coast in the late 1960s. Alaska Natives and environmentalists stopped the rush to oil development until aboriginal land claims were resolved and provisions made for establishing parks. In short order, land issues dominated Alaska politics. Out of this controversy emerged the Alaska Native Claims Settlement Act in 1971, an unprecedented legislative victory for Alaska's Athabaskan, Aleut, and Inuit people. Along with a tidy cash settlement (about a billion dollars), the Native people were permitted to select forty million acres of federal land in Alaska (roughly a Wisconsin plus a New Jersey). And tucked away in the legislation, too, was something for the environmentalists: a promise that Alaska lands for refuges, preserves, and parks would be identified and set aside by 1978.

Like players in a board game, federal land managers from the National Park Service, the Fish and Wildlife Service, the Bureau of Outdoor Recreation, the BLM, and the Forest Service sat down together with their maps to see "which lands should go into what system." And at the same time that the conservationists, the oil companies, and the Natives were eyeing Alaska lands, the state government staked its claim. The Statehood Act granted the state of Alaska the right to select 104 million acres of public land, but much of it had yet to be selected or transferred. All this activity amounted to a sort of institutional land rush. And that is how, by the mid 1970s, briefcase-toting bureaucrats came to be jumping out of helicopters in the middle of the wilderness to assert the government's ownership of lands it had long ignored, and of little cabins it had never before bothered about.

But the main event in the skirmishes between the river people and the government took place *after* McPhee left Alaska, after the agencies finished their horse trading and made their final land selections. The result was the 1980 Alaska National Interest Lands Conservation Act (ANILCA), said by its framers to be the most significant land conservation act in the history of the United States. In one stroke, ANILCA more than doubled the size of the country's national parks and wildlife refuge lands and tripled the size of wilderness preserves. It designated twenty-four new wild and scenic rivers and named ten others for possible inclusion, established four new national conservation areas and two national recreation areas, and created one new national forest and added to several existing ones. If the ANILCA real estate in Alaska was declared the fifty-first state, it would rank third in land area. Only the remainder of Alaska and Texas would be larger.

All this had big consequences for the river people. With the passage of ANILCA, most of the land adjacent to the Yukon River between Eagle and Circle was given to the National Park Service. Many of the cabin dwellers found themselves squatting in the middle of a new unit of the National Park system: Yukon-Charlie Rivers National Preserve.

There seemed to be a ray of hope for the river people, however. Congress recognized a difference between back country in the lower states and wilderness in Alaska. For one thing, there were people—both Native and white—who lived in or near these wild places. Their livelihood depended on their freedom to hunt, fish, gather berries, cut trees, and so on. And this way of life in rural Alaska, Congress noted, "may be the last major remnant of the subsistence culture alive today in North America." Accordingly, the "subsistence lifestyle" was declared a "cultural value" and its practice was to be allowed in the newly established park lands.

Furthermore, in the case of Yukon-Charlie Rivers National Preserve, it was precisely the human use of the country that made the area especially unique and deserving of protection. "The history of the upper Yukon River area is rich and still visible," said Congress. "Along the banks of the Yukon, the remains of many old buildings attest to the river's historic use as an artery of trade, travel, and communication." And these old cabins, roadhouses, mining works, trails and equipment—these "historic resources," in Park Service parlance—were said to be among the primary "values" present in the preserve.

In consideration of all of this, the Park Service established regulations that would allow some of the few people living on the land to remain there, at least temporarily. It went like this: those who had built cabins on federal land after 1978 were slated to lose them to the Park Service straight away. Those who built before 1978, but after 1973, could apply for a permit to stay in their cabins for one year.* And those who built cabins prior to 1973 could apply for a permit that could be renewed every five years but not transferred except to an immediate family member residing in the cabin "at the time of the issuance of the original permit." Applicants were required to sign away any interest in the land on which the cabin stood and agree to turn the structure over to the Park Service upon expiration of the permit. The current regulations, therefore, phase out, over the course of one lifetime, the residency of all people living on preserve land. And with them will go the culturally and historically significant activities that, in part, justified the preserve to begin with.

Below Dick Cook's camp the next day, it rains and blows and the gray Yukon kicks up into waves that slap the bow. Kyle hunkers down under the hood of his yellow rain slicker until not even his face shows. I head for a cabin marked on my map at the base of Nation Bluff. After a bit of looking around in the dripping woods just below the mouth of the Nation River, we find a cache and then the tiny

■ ■ ■

Dan O'Neill

188

* With respect to the one-year permits, the Park Service has not enforced the time limit. Preferring to let attrition take its course, the agency has allowed virtually every resident who qualified for a one-year permit to stay on. But that grace period will end in 1999.

cabin, set into the hillside perhaps a hundred yards from the Yukon. Inside, a log book advises us that the cabin is owned by the Park Service but may be used by travelers. A brief historical note says that the place was built in the 1930s by a talkative trapper named Chris Nelson whom folks called "Phonograph." Nelson trapped up the Nation into the 1940s and used the site as one of his camps. He died in his bunk, right here in this cabin. Looking the place over, though, it didn't seem likely that it would be standing now had it been abandoned to the elements for decades. The tin on the roof and the cardboard tacked up on the interior walls looked to be neither fifty years old nor recent improvements by the Park Service.

Though the log book's historical note did not mention him, a young fellow named Dave Evans and his girlfriend, Sage Patton, along with their friends Brad Snow and Lilly Allen, moved to the Nation River in 1974, just two weeks before Steve Ulvi and his friends arrived in Eagle. A gifted woodsman and carpenter, Evans built a cabin a little ways up the Nation. He used only an ax—wouldn't even use a Swede saw to cut the trees down and buck them to length. "In some people's mind it was an unreasonable thing to do," he says, "but in my mind it was the only thing to do, and the only way to do it." It was Evans who rehabilitated Phonograph Nelson's bluff cabin.

Trapping by dog team, Evans confronted the same obstacles as his predecessor had done: the windy places where the trail always drifted in; the spots on the river where the current weakened the ice from below, or where moccasin-wetting overflow tended to pool beneath the snow. Inevitably, confronting those obstacles, he reestablished the routes used by Phonograph Nelson and those before him, dating back perhaps a hundred years. Here and there, he came upon blazes on trees or a bit of wire on a pole cut by an ax. As the years passed he almost felt he knew these men who had died before he was born. When he saw the need for a line cabin at Hard Luck Creek, and built one there, he discovered the ruins of two other cabins within sight of his window.

Nation Dave stayed nine years, until 1983. He left for a variety of reasons. He had split up with Sage; he felt he had reached "a point of diminishing return," where trapping and fishing offered less in the way of exhilaration and discovery than of repetition; the son of a college professor, he wanted more intellectual and social stimulation; and, finally, the federal agencies were zeroing in on him. His friend Brad Snow had been "trespassed" from his cabin by the BLM and forced to leave the country. Now the Park Service owned the land, and Evans didn't like dealing with the agency, its regulations, and its permits.

"I truly thought I was going to spend the rest of my life there, and happily so," says Evans. "And that's OK. I would not go back out there to live. No way. Too much is different—probably more so in me than in the country—though the country has changed—the Park Service being a primary instrument of that change." After a bit, Dave Evans went to work for the Park Service as a carpenter restoring old cabins in Denali National Park.

Talking to Park Service people, one sometimes hears that the would-be pioneers like Evans simply didn't have what it takes over the long pull, that, unlike the old-timers who died in their cabins, the modern-era homesteaders somehow broke faith. But talking to the river people who have come out of the country, one is struck by how their stories resonate with those of more notable—in other words, legitimated—American rustics who re-created themselves in the wilderness. Henry David Thoreau said, "I left the woods for as good a reason as I went there. Perhaps it seemed to me that I had several more lives to live, and could not spare any more time for that one. . . . Perhaps if I had lived there much longer, I might have lived there forever. One would think twice before accepting heaven on such terms." Alaska's great poet, John Haines, who lived on a homestead in Alaska, trapping, hunting, and fishing for about twenty-five years, wrote in a similar vein, "Trapping for me was not the single, lifelong occupation it has been for others. . . . But what I did had its own seriousness, and I learned from it what I wanted. Another lifetime, perhaps, I might have remained and let the wilderness take me."

The Park Service may not recognize Evans's tenure as "history," says Melody Webb with regret, but one day it will. Webb is a Park Service historian and superintendent who, for her doctoral dissertation, wrote a history of the Yukon basin. In the course of her research she hired Evans as a guide to help her find the old sites of gold rush activity. "The Park Service does this all the time," she says.

"They move into an area and they think that its most recent history is no history."
At Ozark Scenic Riverways the Park Service bulldozed all the cabins on the river,
says Webb. "Very characteristic. Very shortsighted." In Big Bend National Park
they knocked down all the ranchers' cabins. "And now we regret it," she says.

The same notion of history reveals itself when one talks to Park Service planners or reads the agency's policy papers on subsistence living in park lands. It is
a view inclined to regard white old-timers (personified by the gold seekers of
1898) as true-blue subsistence users on a near-equal standing with Alaska Natives,
while managing to suggest that the young people heading out into the woods in
the 1970s tended to be greenhorn malcontents from suburbia indulging such
trifling impulses as "social experimentation," "the novelty of the experience," or
"departure from the mores of modern society," as one policy draft said.

Had the Park Service writer familiarized himself, even a little, with the history
of the gold rush, he might have noticed that nearly every account suggests an opposite interpretation—that, of the eighty thousand people rushing north in the
1890s, the average argonaut looked a whole lot more like a bank teller from
Cincinnati or a shoe-store clerk from Des Moines than like Daniel Boone; that
every species of grifter, pimp, con man, and prostitute rushed north along with
the gold seekers; that greed, as contrasted with a wilderness ethic, was a dominant ideology ("Everybody was money mad," as one '98er wrote); that, as Bob
Marshall, a seasoned Alaska outdoorsman who knew many of the stampeders,
said, "Many of them knew nothing about the outdoors, most of them knew nothing about gold mining, and all of them knew nothing about the requirements for
existence in the North."

As for "departure from the mores of modern society" being somehow an ig-
noble rationale for setting out for a new country, one wonders if Park Service
planners suspect the motive was absent from those who boarded the May-
flower, or the prairie schooners, or from every other wave of colonist, settler, pioneer, and mountain man in the history of this or any other country. And what
sense of the history of the American republic can one have who sniffs at social
experimentation?

Lost, also, in this simplistic reduction is the historically interesting proposition that the 70s-era river people may have accomplished greater feats of woodcraft and survival than did their turn-of-the-century forebears. Park Service papers steer clear of this heresy, of course. But it seems at least arguable that, compared to the sourdoughs, the hippies were a tougher breed. For one thing, at various times during the gold rush there were likely to be hundreds, maybe thousands of people living adjacent to this stretch of the Yukon. In the 1970s there were only a couple of handfuls. In the early days the federal government, in the form of the mail carrier, kept open a system of trails between camps. And strung along that trail, never more than a day's travel apart, were the roadhouses. These outposts provided food and beds, trade goods, and company gathered around the stove. By contrast, the latter-day pioneers broke their own trails. There were no road-houses; you built a fire and set your bedding on a caribou hide rolled out on the snow. In summer the sternwheelers kept the same corridor open, a lifeline of transportation and commerce, stocking the roadhouses with bacon and beans, canned goods and hardware, bringing in fresh recruits and hauling out those the country had broken. But there were no sternwheelers to flag down and step aboard in the modern era. If a trapper at the mouth of the Kandik River wanted supplies in 1970, he tied a rope on his canoe and dragged it upriver to Eagle. Eighty miles upriver to Eagle.

But the Park Service has drawn a line across time: on one side lies the sacred, on the other, the profane. The Coal Creek dredge sits across the Yukon from Nation River, and on the favored side of that line. Put into operation in 1936, the diesel-powered floating factory scooped up and processed a hundred cubic yards of gravel an hour. Today the Park Service embraces the dredge and mining camp as tangible history, directing hundreds of thousands of dollars to its restoration, remediation (removing the mercury-contaminated soils) and "interpretation." A display at the dredge offers colorful anecdotes about the heyday of its operations. But nothing at the site, except the still-remaining junk piles of twisted scrap metal and the rusting drums leaching who-knows-what-fluids into the shallow water table, suggests the irony of a parks agency celebrating a machine that ate its way through a pretty creek valley excreting uniform rows of barren rock, while over-looking the historical worth of folks like Dave Evans, whose developments were, as McPhee noted, essentially biodegradable.

"Overlooking" is not fair. Through oral history interviews conducted by University of Alaska researchers, the Park Service is documenting the stories of the people whose lives are connected with this place. And my trip down the Yukon is part of that effort. The voices I tape record will reside in the university archives and in a computer terminal in the Yukon-Charlie visitor center. At a keystroke, they will float up like phantoms, the disembodied remains of the characters who lived here, a digitized substitute for the thing itself.

A fine sun is flashing silver off the wet fireweed and willow leaves when we emerge from the cabin at Nation Bluff the morning after the storm. Peregrine falcons call in high whistles from their aeries in the cliff face above. We poke around in Evans's old garden, many years overgrown, and find where Phonograph Nelson kept his wooden boats, now pinned implacably to the land by trees growing between and through them.

Six miles below Nation River we see a microscopic black dot on an island most of a mile ahead. With the motor cut, we drift silently to within yards of a black bear unwarily exploring the beach. Six miles farther on, a bald eagle, whose great wings may measure eight feet from tip to tip, jumps from a spruce tree and lumbers off to another perch. Twenty-four miles below the Nation, a golden eagle permits us to cruise slowly beneath his lookout on a leaning snag, his coppery head swiveling, his dagger eye never leaving us.

About thirty miles below Nation Dave's operations, we arrive at the mouth of the Kandik River. Willard Grinnell, whose taste for canned milk earned him the name "The Eagle Milk Kid," trapped this country in the 1930s. After some years he moved over to Beaver Creek, then spent his last days running a motel in Berkeley, California. An Athabascan man from Fort Yukon named Paul Solomon also trapped the Kandik in the '30s, as did Chris Nelson, working his way over a pass from his cabins on the Nation. By 1960, however, the country was again empty of trappers. Then, in 1963, Gordon Burtoson built a cabin at the mouth and, for a couple of winters, trapped upriver as far as Johnson Gorge. In the late '60s Morris Gunderson ran a trapline out of that cabin, then he, too, left. The cabin stood empty until 1975, when a fellow named Fred Beech, "Dirty Fred" to his friends, moved in. But from the late 1970s until the early '90s, the Kandik was Randy

Brown country. "Old cabins are here and there and everywhere out here," says Randy Brown. "There are dozens of old trails." In the 1970s Brown hunted for and found those trails—then choked with decades of overgrowth—and cut many of them out.

As a kid, Brown spent a lot of time hiking and camping in New Mexico. By the time he was eighteen, he had one definite career objective: "To be out in the country to such an extent that I would travel by canoe or by foot beyond the mountain range that you see in the distance; to travel by foot there; to go by your own power; to know the country enough to be able to take off and walk up a river valley, over a ridge of mountains, down another valley, beyond the mountain range on the horizon."

In the summer of 1976 Brown, who was then eighteen, and a partner named Little John Gaudio, who had come from California with Steve Ulvi, packed a few supplies into their two canoes and pushed off into the Yukon at Eagle. Their idea was to keep things simple. They had along a twenty-five pound sack of rice, a twenty-five pound sack of beans, and a five-gallon bucket of tallow. That was it for store grub. Brown and Little John planned to be gone for a year. And they were heading so far beyond the horizon that there would be no resupply. Whereas Steve Ulvi had traveled twelve Yukon River miles from Eagle to build his cabin, Brown would travel eighty. Whereas Ulvi set his cabin a hundred yards off the Yukon, Brown would move sixty miles off it, lining his canoe that distance up the Kandik River.

The float down the Yukon was easy enough. Lining the loaded canoe up against the current of the Kandik was slow, heavy, wet work. But they ran into Fred Beech and Jan and Seymore Abel on the river, and the group decided to collaborate on the construction of three cabins, which they all would use in pursuit of their separate trapping plans. They put up a ten-by-twelve-foot cabin at Indian Grave Creek, sixty miles up; then a ten-by-ten-foot cabin above Johnson Gorge, about thirty miles up; and another, just six-by-nine feet, near Judge Creek, about ten miles upriver. When the construction was done, Little John set out a trapline from the Johnson Gorge cabin, while Randy put in trails out of Indian Grave Creek.

With all this lining of boats and building of log cabins, the rice went pretty fast.

Brian Allen

Christmas Lights and Plug In

Gelatin silver photograph

1979

UAP82:017:001

The tallow, too. There were still some beans left when they shot a moose. Eventually they learned where to find, and how to hunt, the winter caribou that came through the upper Kandik in small bands. They learned to render every ounce of fat from every animal. Fat is a crucial nutrient in a lean country, says Randy. "If you just eat lean meat, you'll go downhill."

Besides food, the young men needed tough, warm clothing. Using a sewing awl and caribou skins with the hair left on, they sewed their own clothes: caribou liners in their mukluks, caribou pants, and caribou parkas with hoods and wolf ruffs. Sometimes they attempted a brain-tanning method Little John had learned from the Han people. But other times they just forced their way into the garments, which were as stiff as cardboard boxes, and allowed their sweat and movement to soften them. Like aboriginals of the North, they were dressed completely in skin clothing, eating an all-meat diet and living, literally, from kill to kill. They had some "hungry times," Brown says, but they didn't starve.

For Randy Brown, "starve" is not a figure of speech. "There was a fellow," he says, ". . . he did. He starved. He died. That's the way it was." That's the way it was in Alaska in the early days, and that's the way it was in the fall of 1978 when Randy heard about two fellows who came downriver intending to head out into the woods. They launched their boat at Eagle and floated down the Yukon, stopping and staying with various of the people living along the river and ending up at Sarge Waller's cabin at the mouth of the Kandik. During the night, one of the partners slipped down to the boat and took off with all the gear. The stranded man was left with only the clothes he wore and a double-barrel 20-gauge shotgun. The same day, the man hailed Dirty Fred, who lived on the other side of the Kandik, about a mile away.

Fred was an easy-going sort who loved to show floaters the country around the mouth of the Kandik: the cabins and trails, the lakes where he had stashed canoes, his caches of grub and ammo. The stranger was strange. At various times, he claimed to be one or another biblical character. Eventually, the river people referred to him as "Smeagol," after the two-faced character in J. R. R. Tolkein's *The Hobbit*. But Fred, who liked a bit of company and wasn't too fussy, let the fellow stay with him. He encouraged Smeagol to hitch a ride out of the country, though, with one of the moose hunters who soon would be motoring back to Eagle or Circle. Fred himself left before freeze-up on a two-month trip to the States.

When he returned in November the Yukon was running ice and it was starting to jam up. He had to pull his canoe on shore a few miles above the Kandik and walk home. Arriving cold at his cabin, he found no lamp, no sleeping bag, and no stove pipe. There was a note explaining that the gear had been moved to a cabin three miles up the Kandik. It was signed "John the Baptist."

Fred spent the night in a spare sleeping bag, without a fire in the stove, and walked upriver the next day. He found Smeagol settled in the cabin surrounded by Fred's cache of winter food, as well as ammunition and gear belonging to Fred and Randy Brown. Smeagol had done a pretty good job of eating up Fred's moose meat and jarred salmon, particularly the precious buckets of rendered moose fat. Fred lived "pretty darn marginally," say those who knew him. "He didn't have a whole lot of extra."

Dirty Fred was hopping mad. But the fellow claimed to have shot a moose ten miles up the Kandik near Judge Creek. He said he'd dried the meat and cached the fat in a tree. Well, said Fred, in that case he had better get his butt on up there and bring back some of that moose. Fred meant to get his food replaced and then kick the freeloader out. Because there was no way Smeagol could walk there and back in a day, Fred told him about the small cabin he'd helped to build near Judge Creek. Next morning, Smeagol set off up the Kandik with a few handfuls of split peas and beans, carrying Fred's .22 pistol and wearing a pair of Randy Brown's brand-new, store-bought snowshoes.

Two weeks later, Brown showed up at Fred's cabin at the mouth. He had hiked from his main cabin sixty miles up the Kandik across his overland trail to the Yukon. He was traveling on homemade snowshoes that were now broken, and he was looking forward to strapping on his new pair. When he heard Fred's story about Smeagol and the filched meat, salmon and snowshoes, he decided that he and Fred ought to take a walk upriver to "have a talk with him and get our stuff back."

"Well, there was a lot of snow that year," says Brown. "It snowed and snowed

Coming Out of the Country

197

and snowed." And Fred didn't tend to keep his trails broken out. After a whole day's work, Brown and Fred had covered just three of the ten miles. Faced with the prospect of spending three or four days breaking trail to retrieve his snowshoes, Randy decided that he had better things to do. The two turned around and went back to their respective cabins and traplines.

Smeagol never came out. Because of the deep snow, no one visited the Judge Creek cabin all winter. Whenever Randy or Fred or Dave Evans met over the next six months, they speculated about Smeagol. Maybe he walked out and slipped by Fred. Maybe he flagged down an airplane. He'd said something about walking over into the Black River, and down it to the Gwitchin village of Chalkytsik. But that was a long way. Nobody believed he could do it. He's up there, Randy Brown figured, and he's dead.

As was his custom, Brown spent breakup at the mouth of the Kandik, watching ice from the two rivers go out. Then he and Fred hiked overland to the cabin above Johnson Gorge to bring the canoe down the Kandik for the summer's fishing on the Yukon. When they stopped at the Judge Creek cabin, Randy saw his snowshoes leaning against a tree. He knew Smeagol was in the cabin, and that meant he was dead.

He was lying on the bunk, or what was left of it. It looked like he had frozen his feet, then starved. His body was emaciated, except for his feet, which were gigantically swollen. Apparently no longer able to walk outside to get wood, he had been burning the bunk poles. Its length was down to just four feet. "Oh, it was a pretty tough scene there," says Brown. "He didn't have any light. There were no candles, no lamps. There was no reading material, no writing material." The cabin was only six by nine feet and there wasn't even a window. The only light to enter the dark cell came in through a plastic-covered three-inch gap between two logs—and then for only the few hours that the sun was up that time of year.

Brown carried the man out and laid him on the ground. They thought about burying him, but they had no shovel. Even if they had, the ground was frozen. They could have taken him down the Kandik and then on down the Yukon eighty miles to Circle. But there were several problems with that idea. They had no money with which to buy food while in Circle. They had no motor to use to get back. Nor could they line back upriver—which would have been a week's work—because it was spring and the Yukon would be running high, all the gravel bars under water. And, they felt that Smeagol had been warned to leave; that things shook out about as one would expect; that "that's the way it was." When Randy returned later in the summer, Smeagol's body was gone. No bones. Nothing. Maybe a bear dragged him off. Or a wolverine. More likely, it was the wolves that denned near Judge Creek.

In 1981 Randy Brown married Karen Kallen, a school teacher. They built a new home cabin on the Kandik just above the gorge and very near the cabin Willard Grinnell built in the '30s, now tumbled in. This site lay outside the park lands and would be transferred to Doyon, Ltd., a Native corporation established under the Alaska Native Claims Settlement Act. There they raised two children. But about 1990, Doyon, which was interested in developing the land's oil potential and had permitted an oil company to drill prospect wells, asked the Browns to leave. The family could not live at Randy's other cabins above or below the gorge because those lands were now owned by Doyon, the State of Alaska, or the Park Service.

Talking about his life on the Kandik makes him "homesick," he says. Thinking about the influence of the Park Service and the Native corporations discourages him: "The park itself has resulted in the depopulation of the country, [as has] Doyon, the state, BLM. . . . You can't do it with this administration—with the bureaucracies that manage this area. Nobody new can get in . . . . [In the past] there was a constant circulation of people. People would come in, stay for a year, two years, five years, and then leave."

To listen to Park Service historian Melody Webb, Brown is right: "A large part of the problem with the Park Service is that it still manages scenery. It manages natural resources. It cannot manage people, so they want to get the people off . . . . There is no provision for a continuation, a continuum [of residency within the preserve] to occur, which is the way that the Yukon-Charlie area always existed. That was its historic tradition." In other parts of Alaska, says Webb, a subsistence culture was traditionally passed from father to son, mother to daughter. "You don't have that in Yukon-Charlie. It is a culture that each individual acquires as they go into the area. And it is different. It is an individual culture. And, yes, the Park Service is incompatible with it."

In the 1970s Melody Webb worked on the early data-gathering and planning preliminary to the establishment of new Alaskan park lands under ANILCA. She had great hopes that the Park Service would "recognize the meaning of a white, subsistence lifestyle" and that regulations would reflect "understanding," "perception," and "compassion." And even though that lifestyle was declared in the law to be culturally important, it was ineluctably at odds with the agency's own institutional culture: "They're trying to make parks in Alaska like parks in the Lower 48. And they've done so. That was our greatest fear."

Below the Kandik we leave Eagle's sphere of influence and enter Circle's. From here on down, the river people will use Circle (population seventy-three) for access to the road system, telephone, mail, and some supplies. A few years ago crews from the National Geographic Society were in the Circle area working on a film about bush life in interior and northern Alaska. As people on the river tell the story, they were especially keen to get an interview with a certain trapper who for seventeen years had been living alone on the Charlie River, the next tributary below the Kandik and one of the most remote places in Interior Alaska. He was Charlie Kidd, or, inevitably, Charlie River Charlie. But it was not for nothing that Kidd lived fifty miles up this wild river. The film crew chartered river boats, and even a helicopter, to look for Kidd. But all they accomplished, besides boosting the local economy, was an occasional aerial glimpse of the reclusive trapper as he slipped out of one of his cabins and ducked into the woods.

I had been told to look for his fish camp about a mile and a half below the old Slaven's Road House on the left bank. After floating by the bluff below Slaven's, we saw a canoe pulled up on the beach. Nearby there were a couple of spruce poles set into the ground with a few crossmember sticks tied in place. A sheet or two of corrugated tin leaned against this tiny structure. It looked to me to be too small an operation to fit any definition of the term "fish camp." I started to cruise by, but then thought I had better stop and check it out.

Kyle was the first to see the man coming toward us on the beach. He was perhaps in his mid- to late-thirties, with brown hair trailing down his back, and a long brown beard reaching about as far down his chest. He was shirtless and barefoot, wearing a fur headband and leather-patched jeans that had seen some mud recently. Slim but muscled, he walked purposefully, with his arms hanging loosely at his sides. His eyes were light brown and clear. It was impossible not to see, for a moment, Jesus, or one of his fisherman apostles, walking the shoreline of some Northern Galilee.

Charlie invited us up to his campfire, and we dug out of the canoe some gifts we'd brought for him. By the time we climbed up the bank to his camp, he had stirred the coals of a campfire to life and disappeared into the brush. He was staying at—or perhaps beside—the old McGreggor cabin. It had been built more than half a century earlier, and the roof was partly fallen in. Charlie came back with a few green alder branches, from which he stripped the leaves. Tossed on the fire, these made an aromatic smudge that kept the mosquitoes at bay. That done, he rustled in the willows around the cabin until he'd rounded up three five-gallon gas cans (left over from some previous occupant) and dropped them by the campfire for us to use as seats. He muttered something about tea, grabbed a battered and blackened kettle and headed back into the woods. When he returned, the kettle was stuffed with a green shrub whose common name is Labrador tea. He set a few split sticks of dry spruce on the fire, filled up the kettle with water, and put it on an old grate. He let it boil until it made a good dark brew, then rinsed out for me a discarded can that had been opened with a knife. When it started to sprinkle, Charlie pulled on a very tattered, home-made vest of what I took to be dog fur.

Everybody said Charlie Kidd was the guy who came into the country with practically nothing but the intention to "keep it simple," that he didn't deviate a degree over the course of eighteen years, that he still used the original pot and pan he arrived with, that he was never lured by outboard or chain saw or big dog teams, that he was incredibly tough, snowshoeing 120 miles into Circle maybe once a year. But Charlie didn't see the point in talking about his life in the woods. He seemed uncertain about his future. The U.S. Air Force, which flies combat-training and live bombing missions over vast areas of Alaska, had just started a forest fire in the upper Charlie River drainage. Thirty-five thousand acres were burned, right up to the doorstep of Charlie's home cabin. And, like most of the other river people, he had had to sign over any interest in his cabins to the Park Service. But he was willing to work with the agency, to compromise, and to hope things would work out.

The afternoon of our visit Charlie had been invited to dinner by his neighbors, who were Park Service volunteers at Slaven's Road House, a mile and a half up-river. It was about five o'clock, and we didn't want to hold him up. He tossed a piece of burlap over his few things piled under a tree, fed his two dogs, and pulled on a pair of army boots. He grabbed an old T-shirt but not a life jacket. I offered to tow him up, but he said he'd line. We said good-bye at the beach and he ran into his battered canoe all the way to the bow, stopping short so that his momentum forced the boat into the river. Pointing toward the far shore at an upstream angle, he stroked powerfully against the current, first on one side, then the other. Slaven's was on the same side of the river as Charlie's camp, but there was a bluff in between. He had to cross the river, then line his boat far enough above Slaven's so that when he recrossed he could reach the bank above the road house and not be carried into the swift current at the bluff. We watched him cross until he was a tiny figure jumping out of the canoe in shallow water just off a long gravel bar. Splashes shot up from his feet and flashed in the low-angle sun as he strode up-river. He was moving through the shallows so that the canoe would ride far enough offshore to float. But it looked like he was walking on water.

I was glad not to get Richard Smith's bear story until we were within striking distance of Circle. For most of the last week we had been camping on gravel bars along the Yukon, but, as Richard says, "After you hear a story like that, you don't want to camp on the river for a couple of nights."

When I was sure we would make the forty miles to Circle by evening, I passed up to my wife Sarah in the bow the headphones and tape recorder cued to the recording I'd just made of Richard Smith.

Richard came into the country as a ten-year-old in 1968 when his mother and stepfather converted a school bus to a motor home and drove with their five boys from Grand Rapids, Michigan, to Alaska. Five miles out of Central, on the way to Circle, they pulled the bus off the road to spend the night. In the morning they found that the bus was stuck, so Richard's stepfather set out for Fairbanks, where he filed for a homestead on the land surrounding the bus. They cut logs right on the property and built a twenty-two-by-twenty-four-foot cabin. About half of the 528 square feet was devoted to the kitchen-dining-living room. Of the remaining space, about half was partitioned off as master bedroom, and half accommodated the five boys.

The family had lived on the homestead for three years when Richard's stepfather took a notion to spend a year in the woods. He was friendly with a bachelor sourdough named Gordon Bertoson, who trapped and fished at a grassy spot below a rocky bluff on the Yukon, forty miles above Circle. Bertoson had occupied the site, known locally as "Fortymile," since 1960, but he was getting pretty old for the heavy work of living in the woods. Once he hurt his back while working on his fish wheel and lay in his bed for two weeks before a friend from Fairbanks visited. Then, in 1971, around breakup, the time when the river ice begins to move, Bertoson's cabin mysteriously burned down while he was away in Circle. "I'm all done with it now," said Bertoson, according to Richard's stepfather, Ray Bell. The old trapper allowed Bell to take over the site, together with the trapline trails and the fish wheel spot, which was just upstream of the cabin. Richard, then thirteen, and his brothers helped their stepfather build an eighteen-by-twenty-foot, one-room cabin at the site. It was ready by fall, and the family moved upriver.

The Smiths filled their days with chores: fixing up the cabin; hauling water from Eureka Creek in summer and from the Yukon in the winter, when it runs clear; cutting firewood from driftwood piles on the islands in the Yukon; trapping and skinning fur through the winter; cutting, hanging, or canning salmon in the

■ ■ ■

Coming Out of the Country

203

summer; tending a huge vegetable garden; hunting and putting up meat. Mrs. Smith taught her kids from correspondence materials. In Richard's seventeenth year, his parents moved upriver to work for wages at mining claims, first at Woodchopper, then at Coal Creek. Richard kept the place at Fortymile, though sometimes he'd work a summer "running cat" at the mines.

One day Faye, a pretty, dark-haired girl from Canada, floated down the river and into Richard's life, and they were married. In August of 1981 Richard and Faye took a boat trip two hundred miles upriver to Dawson, Yukon Territory, to visit friends. On the way back, twenty miles below Dawson, they saw at the water's edge a sow grizzly bear and three good-sized cubs. Grizzlies are larger than the more common black bears, and they can be aggressive. A traveler might not even mention having seen a black bear, but spotting four grizzlies is always a notable occurrence. Richard, who had seen a lot of bears over the years, decided the cubs were bigger than any black bear he had ever seen, and that the sow was the biggest grizzly he had ever seen. The cubs ran up the bank, but not the towering sow. "She stood there," says Richard, "and gave me a look in the eye that I've never seen from anything. Like, 'I'll remember you. I'm going to get you.' It was that kind of look, you know."

A mile downriver Richard and Faye stopped to spend the night with some friends at their fish camp at the mouth of Fifteenmile River. There were two couples there, each with two kids and a few dogs. Richard mentioned seeing the bears. Their friends said, yes, they had seen some bears in the area. No one said much more about it, and after a bit of visiting everyone got ready for bed. There were two canvas wall tents housing the families, with a picnic table in between. Richard and Faye, traveling light, had no tent and only one sleeping bag, which they laid out near the picnic table. Everyone fell asleep.

About one or two in the morning, the dogs began to bark. Faye sat up, says Richard, "and right there's that grizzly bear. The sow. And it only took [snaps fingers] like that. I mean Faye tried to turn over on her stomach, you know, hide her face, but before she could do that, that bear jumped around that picnic table and got her by the head. Drug her out of her sleeping bag."

Perhaps because he grew up with six other people in a one-room cabin, Richard has developed the ability to sleep through a fair bit of commotion. While the bear continued to attack Faye, Richard slept on.

One of the women, however, heard the attack and woke her man, who opened the tent flap. The bear at once dropped Faye and charged the tent, says Richard, piecing together the others' recollections. "He's standing there and sees this thing come charging at him and the only thing he can do is close the tent flaps and pray to God that thing didn't get him." With one swipe, the rampaging bear brought down the wall tent, then clamped her jaws on the man's leg and "shook him like a rag doll." There was only one gun in the camp; it was in the other tent, in the custody of the third man, another deep sleeper.

Richard finally roused, but he was disoriented. "When I woke up I was standing up. And I had this really weird feeling, like doomsday, you know. I didn't know what was happening yet, and I look down and I see Faye laying there, just all chewed up and blood everywhere. And my back was to Zeke and the bear. Zeke was the guy getting mauled at the moment. Well, when I stood up, the bear saw me and dropped Zeke and came over and stood up behind me." As Richard turned, he became fully awake. He knew he couldn't run, nor was playing dead an option. "So I start slugging it. . . . I was yelling at it, you know. I was freaked out, you know . . . it let me hit it a few times." Then the bear gave a swat, which Richard reenacts as an effortless forehand, as if he were shooing a fly. "I was airborne. Just flying." As soon as he hit the ground, the bear was on top of him. "Its teeth kind of raked across my skull, split it, tore it wide open, tore my scalp off. Started chewing me up and down the back."

Zeke got up, hoping to crawl under the fallen tent, but now the bear saw him and dropped Richard. Zeke ran once around the picnic table with the bear on his heels, then dove under it. The bear kept running. Straight back to Richard. Meanwhile people were beginning to shout and scream; the chained dogs were going berserk. The grizzly stopped for Richard, clamping her enormous jaws around his midriff, stopped again for Faye, gathering her up under one arm, and ran off into the woods with both of them.

All of this took just a minute or two, Richard thinks.

About thirty feet down the trail out of camp, the bear dropped or lost her grip on Faye, who fell into the bushes, but the bear continued on with Richard. The trail led to a deadfall tree, and as the bear sailed over it, Richard remembers having a clear vision of his fate. "Well, when she jumped, I was hanging there, seeing what all was going on, you know. I was going, 'God, this thing's taking me out to its cubs!'"

But the deadfall saved his life, he thinks. "She probably figured she couldn't make it over with me in her mouth. As we were sailing through the air, she dropped me right on top of it and kept sailing over."

It took a couple of hours for the badly injured friends to reach Dawson by riverboat. There was no hospital there, no doctor. The clinic seemed incapable of doing more than putting in a call to Whitehorse, the territorial capital, 270 miles away, for a chartered plane. Richard tells the story matter-of-factly, as if he really hadn't expected anything anyway. "They didn't do nothing for us, didn't stop the bleeding or put bandages on us or anything." It was ten hours before the plane arrived. And then a long flight to Whitehorse. "I don't know how you guys are alive," Richard remembers the doctor saying, "you ain't got no blood left."

At about the same time that Richard and Faye were being stitched back together, some well-armed Dawson people motored down to the camp at Fifteen-mile River. The bear had returned. The camp was destroyed. She had knocked over the picnic table, staved in the shelves in the cooking area, and sliced to ribbons the tent that had been left standing. The Dawson people found Faye's necklace in the brush behind the camp. It was "a choker-type necklace," Richard said, "that you couldn't slip off your head." When the people found it, the clasp was still fastened.

During breakup one year, when Richard was away at Circle, Yukon River ice jammed below Fortymile and the river rose until Richard's cabin began to float. It floated right out into the river. A pilot friend had flown over the area after the water dropped and reported that the cabin was sitting on ice floes out in the middle of the Yukon's channel. But then the water—and the cabin—rose again. Somehow it floated back to within a few tens of feet of its original spot. And there the river deposited it. Richard was lucky. Or maybe the Park Service was.

The cabin was plenty worse for wear, and by the time we visited Fortymile late that same summer, Richard was about seven rounds up on a new cabin. "It really ain't mine," though, he says. Park Service people had visited Smith after the Yukon-Charlie preserve was created and noted that he had not filed for a homestead during the years when it was possible to do so. According to the law, they said, he had "no possessory interest" in the place. He was a trespasser on public land.

It was true that Richard Smith hadn't done the paperwork necessary to get title to the site. Neither had his stepfather, Ray Bell; nor Gordon Bertoson, who lived there before them; nor Phil Berail, who was there before him; nor Walter Roman before him; nor John Nathaniel before him; and so on, going back half a century, at least. In those days, title to the land might have been easily obtained. The federal government even ran advertisements in stateside newspapers promoting the colonization of Alaska through homesteading and other programs. But the old timers didn't always bother with the legalities. Many say they always thought they'd be left alone, that they didn't need to own the land anyway, they just wanted to use it. Besides, respect for each other's rights to cabin, trapline, and fishing site was an unwritten law here. By any moral standard, they felt, they owned the modest bit of material culture they'd wrestled from a tough country: a cabin, a cache, an outhouse.

The park managers explained the law and told Richard that he could apply for a five-year permit to stay. "But when the permit finally came in the mail, they put in there that I had to sign over all rights to the buildings and the land and everything. And that kind of stumped me there for a while. So, I don't own the cabins. I don't own any of the buildings I built around here or nothing. It's all Park Service. And I don't know what to make of it. It wasn't the way I understood it at first."

A lot of people on the river "get up in arms about it," says Richard, but he himself takes a live-and-let-live view: "Well, I just figure, you know, I'll just live here and do what I've been doing. If they decide to kick me out, well, that's my tough luck. I can't worry about it. . . . I'm building this new house here; I'm not worrying about all the time and effort and money I'm spending on it. I've got to have a house to live in. So, I just do like I would have done back in the old days. Just go ahead and do it and hope that nothing will ever happen where they'll phase me out."

Richard thinks that the Park Service people he's met, the ones who sign his permit, are nice guys. But considering that the permit must be renewed every five years and that the average length of a superintendent's stay at Yukon-Charlie has been three years, Richard has reason to worry about his domestic security. "Maybe the next guy who gets the job there, he might not like me. . . . It's up to them, you know. And that's kind of scary. To me it is. But I been getting along with them. I don't see no reason why I can't get along with them. But there's always that to think about."

Richard Smith is wary—not afraid, not bitter. It's rather like his attitude toward the other large omnivore that claims these woods, the bear. He gets the jitters whenever he talks about either encounter, but he makes his peace with each. "It don't bother me to have bears around. I don't go shooting every one I see."

The Yukon begins to braid out into vast flats just before Circle, and the distances are immense. I keep to the left channels until we see a blue oil drum on the bank and know it as a sign: Welcome to Circle.

On nearly the last page of his book, and in a rare instance where McPhee permits himself to write, in first person, just exactly what he thinks, he says, "If I were writing the ticket, I would say that anyone at all is free to build a cabin on any federal land in the United States that is at least a hundred miles from the nearest town of ten thousand or more—the sole restriction being that you can't carry in materials for walls or roofs or floors."

It didn't work out that way, though it is said that his book, which came out the year before passage of ANILCA had appreciable influence on Congress (portions of it were read into the congressional record). The law did speak of the value of residents' living the old-time subsistence lifestyle. And the law did provide for a subsistence lifestyle within park lands in Alaska. But the agency cannot abide such activities, says one of the Park Service's chief planners in Alaska, Zorro Bradley: "The Park Service as a whole has a 'no subsistence' attitude. I think that's pretty well recognized. They'd like to get rid of it." Bradley, now retired, was a key man in Alaska overseeing subsistence research: I suspect that what we'll do is eventually kill it off entirely. And, as we did in the Southwest, remove the Natives from park land. Today you go to a place like Navajo National Monument where they excluded all Native peoples, now they hire them as people to come in and demonstrate their cultural activities at the visitor center. They are paid actors."

At least one of the Park Service managers at Yukon-Charlie had the same thought. The day is not so distant, he says, when all the river people will be gone and the Park Service will put GS-5 summer hires in the cabins. They'll be drama majors from colleges in the States. They'll wear red flannel shirts and spit snoose. They'll hang a few fish so the floaters can see people living the old-time way. And come the first frost they'll head back to school.

Malcolm
Lockwood
Ester Aspen
Cibachrome
Undated
UAP85:064:001

MOVING TO FAIRBANKS:
SOME NOTES ON POETRY AND PLACE

John Morgan

IT'S 1976. and Pan Am still has direct jet service from New York. We get on the plane at Kennedy, and seven and a half hours later we pass over the zig-zag pipeline snaking across the tundra and land in Fairbanks. It could be anywhere on the globe. We have no feeling of having traveled to a particular place, no sense of a difficult journey, obstacles overcome, a passage, a goal achieved. For a poet this is surely the wrong way to do it, but we're modern people, we're mobile, and we expect the convenience of jet travel when we want to get to anyplace far-off.

Moving to Alaska was easy, being Alaskan harder. Nearly twenty years later, I've seen only a fraction of this vast state, but I've built my house here, learned to ski cross-country, and one winter I changed three flat tires at minus fifty. I have to admit, though, the New York I brought with me still makes me, in a sense, a New York poet. The twentieth century is too far gone in me for any easy nostalgia for Robert Service.

The other day, as I shoveled out the mailboxes along with my neighbor, a German electrician—the one who wired my house—we paused after every few shovelfuls and looked out on the frozen Tanana River, where skiers and snow-machiners cavorted. Occasionally you see dog sleds out there too, and in summer several stern-wheelers ply the river with their cargo of tourists.

Beyond the river: a hundred vacant miles of low spruce and then the Alaska Range, mountains that rise to thirteen, fourteen thousand feet, and—visible on the way out from town, though not here—is Mount McKinley, at twenty thousand feet, the highest point in North America. Though mid-February, it was thirty above, and we shoveled in down vests and shirtsleeves.

I came here vowing to myself not to appropriate too casually what was not, after all, my native material. I had it in mind to hold back and live here a while before writing about anything Alaskan. I stuck to that resolution for about two weeks. I couldn't help myself, so much was new and interesting. Within a month I'd written a poem and an article about my first day in Fairbanks. Though other people have liked the poem, I distrust it because it seemed to come too quickly. But in a way, I suppose I'd been preparing to write that poem for a long time. Seven years earlier I'd written another poem which seems to me now to foreshadow what moving to Alaska means in a sense deeper that geography:

The Twenty-Six Years War

Where is the land beyond landscape?
Slipping across the border
distant herds of snow.

Leaving the map behind, with its
diagrammed cities, four-square
musics, and all that predictable violence,

here clouds become ideas, as black
as headlines, and even less discreet.

I am learning a language
of otters and elk,

of distances
and profound insecurities

Why do we kid ourselves?

Where teeth rot and stars fall, even sex
is a perpetual war with the dying.

Here the stone
seashell is my mother, I do not deny
it, here I am open, alone
advancing into the sky.

From Belle Harbor, where I spent my first four and a half years, you could see in the night sky the reflected glow of Manhattan. It was less than ten miles away as the crow flies, and I remember a dream I had more than once about that glowing place, a city of pleasure and light. It was a fairy-tale city, constructed of children's blocks piled magically high, and it was the first place that impressed me deeply enough to become a subject of writing.

Later, in New Rochelle, a singularly moderate and—to me—uninteresting suburb, I remember another magical place, a railway cut down below street level, with a station that had belonged to the Putnam Line (then defunct) of the New York Central. There were no tracks there anymore, no booths or benches, though the ladies' room—a dark alcove without door, toilets or sink—could still be explored in its damp, crumbling state. The station was an exciting, even daring spot for me in those curious, preadolescent years.

These two examples from my childhood could stand for many others. I'm sure everyone carries these special, magical places around at a deep level. For writers they are a payload, there to be mined for the precious ore they bear.

But what happens when we grow up? Do places lose that special power, that charge they have for us as children?

It's not that the character of places changes, obviously, but that we ourselves change. Our education makes us practical, but in the process we lose something, some capacity to explore ourselves through place. Other things take precedence.

At the most banal level, we choose a house on the basis of what school district it's in and give up the woods or the railway cut that might have had more meaning for us and our kids than the entire curriculum of the fifth grade. In the effort to be sensible, mature adults, we overlook the emotional or spiritual powers that lie about us.

For there is a spiritual component to place, something our less mobile ancestors were more attuned to. But basic human nature hasn't changed, and if you open yourself to it, a certain locale can get into you, can lodge itself deeply in your mental world. Then, if you are a writer, it will become a natural setting for your work.

But this magical connection with a specific place doesn't ensure that the writing will be good. I once drafted a novel based on a summer I'd spent on a fossil-hunting expedition in Wyoming. Great material, I thought. And I found that I could write endlessly about the landscape—the fields and orchards bleeding into badland, the buttes and canyons, the storms brewing high up in the mountains, the mountains themselves, and the sky, hundreds of miles wide. In fact, my draft gave altogether too much of that landscape and not enough of something else—character, tension, drama. Without the landscape there would have been no impulse to write, but that in itself did not make the writing good. Later I went over some of that material and found whole chapters becoming paragraphs as I tried to reduce the novel to what I simply could not leave out. Pushing the process further, I took what seemed the strongest of those paragraphs and worked them into a poem.

This is certainly not the most economical way to write: pages and pages out of which only a few details survive. But there is a benefit. The writing process teaches you what details are really essential. Better to start with the welter of life than with some bloodless abstraction.

Several winters ago my family and I drove a hundred and fifty miles northeast from Fairbanks over frozen tundra through blowing snow to the town of Central. On the way, a flock of winter-white ptarmigan crossed the road. Only their black

Diana Hamar

Skater

Gelatin silver photograph

1981

UAP83:117:001

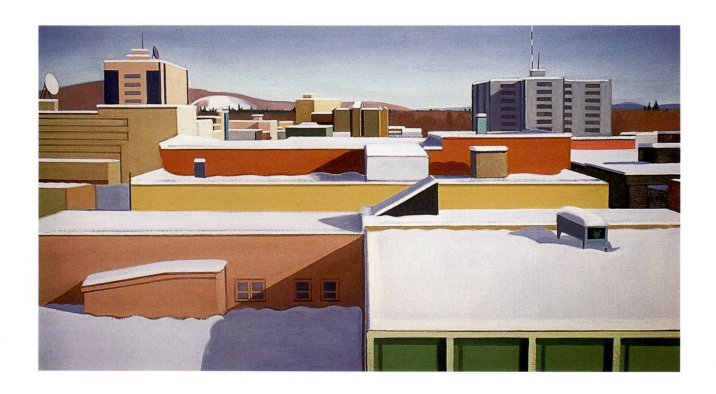

David Mollett

Fairbanks Rooftops

Oil on canvas

Undated

UA85-3-32

eye-spots showed up against the snow, dots blurring and dancing, like watching TV in its early interference-plagued days—like that, but also strange beyond description to see those eye-spots lifting and hovering, vaguely attached to the white-on-white of hundreds of chicken-sized birds.

From Central we made our way to Circle Hot Springs, where a 1930s vintage hotel set among low spruce draws local visitors to its large, open-air swimming pool. Here, in minus-ten-degree cold, we swam comfortably. The hot spring provides water at over one hundred degrees Fahrenheit, too hot, where it enters the pool, for swimmers to linger. Mid-pool, you can loll comfortably on a black inner tube in eighty- to ninety-degree warmth, while evaporating water condenses over your head and falls as tiny flakes of snow.

No writer can fail to be influenced, and many are overpowered, by the beauty and strangeness of this huge state.

More than half the population of Alaska is urban, though you might never guess this from the poetry we produce. Perhaps it's because our cities, like other cities, are hard to love. I suspect it is also because cities by their very nature are difficult to come to grips with, though that is one of the tasks modern poetry—from Whitman to Frank O'Hara—has set itself.

Nature is our nature, always. We are usually alone in it. We are its consciousness. In nature we expand, we become mountains, glaciers, and rivers; we encounter the other in its purest form—bear, moose, hawk, raven, mosquito.

In cities we are only one of many. Tall buildings cramp us, wall us into a narrow grid of possibilities, a grid inhabited by thousands of others like us. Instead of expanding, we are fractured, becoming many. It is like a hall of mirrors giving back oneself in a grotesque multitude. In plateglass storefront windows this reflection is literal.

Nature offers us clear pools where we can gaze at our own image undistracted as we wait for a fish to nibble at our hook, but in cities it is not acceptable; we must glance surreptitiously, as we are hurried along by the crowd, to see that our dress is appropriate, our hair in place. We feel judged, slightly embarrassed, and we can't trust our own natural impulses.

That's one aspect of the city. Another is that it changes all too rapidly. Buildings are torn down and new ones take their places; stores close, move a few blocks, and reopen under new management; whole neighborhoods go to seed. And the city's boundaries keep shifting. Meanwhile, over there the mountains remain the same, stable, enduring only the seasons, and returning always to their former state.

If nature is of God, cities are unquestionably man-made. They are planned, of course, but whatever people plan and execute is full of error and accident. How can poetry deal with the accidental and the botched? Even a dying tree is perfect in its dying. Nothing about a city is perfect. That wonderful little restaurant—you know the one—where they have a few tables out on the sidewalk and usually a jazz group or folk singer, and great food: oh, that was last year. Now they've gone over to hard rock, added a bar, shut down the kitchen; you can probably still get a sandwich.

For some people this flux means, paradoxically, that cities are alive, vital, organic. Nature, by contrast, is static, dull. "If you've seen one mountain or moose, you've seen 'em all." That's what my mother, who lives on Eighth Street in the Village, said on her only visit.

Interestingly, in Alaska, the moose have adapted to the cities. They cross the expressways to invade gardens. Sometimes in winter they bed down under the big spruce in our backyard. Alaska is pipelines across mountain ranges and floatplanes on tundra lakes. It's log cabins with outhouses on downtown city streets. Alaskan cities still display their frontier roots and even the wilderness doesn't always keep its distance: occasionally bears and even caribou—though not residents like the moose—visit their former territories. Last fall my wife saw a moose cow and two yearlings racing traffic along Chena Pump Road as she drove our younger son to school. Last summer we slowed, then stopped, as a huge beaver dragged itself across that same road. Foxes on the bike paths, porcupines in the backyard, eagles circling above the river. Even a fluffed-up chickadee checking out the bird feeder at minus forty can make you feel this place is pretty wild after all. What is special about Alaska is its mix of the urban and the wild without that Death Valley of suburbs in between.

I teach in the graduate writing program at the University of Alaska Fairbanks. Most of our students come from out of state. Many came here for the challenge of it and, as I did, for a sense of something distinctive in their lives. Some are born travelers, having been previously to Africa, India, New Zealand. Others had never been outside their home regions before. A recent letter of application from a southern California woman announced, "I've always dreamt of living in Alaska. I'm sure it's my fate."

When I got out of college over thirty years ago, somebody was doing a survey on the graduating class. They wanted to know what I imaged my life would be like in ten years. Did I plan to live in the city, the suburbs? Did I expect to marry? How many children? I said I planned never to marry but to have dozens of children. I would live in the city—preferably Manhattan—or else way out in the country. The one place I didn't want to settle was where I was living right at that moment—in the suburbs. For me, city and country are complementary, and I'll be delighted if Pan Am goes ahead and reinstitutes direct nonstop service between Fairbanks and Kennedy. Incidentally, six months after answering that questionnaire, I got married.

Although I'd been writing for years, I'd never consciously written about a place I was then living until I bought a house in rural New York State. I'm sure it had as much to do with my inner development as with outer circumstances. Living in that big old farmhouse, I found that writing about the details of my environment was a way of *placing* myself. Perhaps it's that the self seeks its own image in the world: a willed reflection. By the time I moved to Alaska, I'd caught the habit. A few years ago I composed a twelve-poem sequence called "Above the Tanana," one poem a month, each set at the same location, a ledge overlooking the Tanana River with a view south to the Alaska Range—the same one I see from my mailbox. But since I know that landscape by itself can be boring, each poem in the sequence is dedicated to an important person or a group (or, in one case, a dog) in my life; the poems meditate on my relationships with them. The first poem written was "May"—for my wife.

May
(for Nancy)

Here are the pasques, those
purple-arising, yellow-hearted flowers

brave as spring. And far below,
a duck, small bursts of wing-power

motoring along. Perched on a root above
the slough, we watch the melt of ice

flow west, a tent of wood that piles
on a bar, a dark bird looping larklike

down—so artless, unintended
like that kiss to which our lips

were given twenty years ago. There
on the banks of an urban river

I fixed you in my heart and you
were young as tenderness itself.

A raven passing overhead: he chortles,
caws, and sings, coaxing his mate

along. I add them to my list. Birds
to what purpose? Seeds of a garden

rooted in the mind. I knew when I
first saw you, I could outwait the facts.

■ ■ ■

John Morgan

Now, where mountains, sharp and white,
are rimmed with sky, where river ripples

stipple dark and light, here on this
shelf—hushed, we can almost hear

the tune the earth is singing to itself

Of course not everything I write comes in response to my immediate environment, and I'm happy that it doesn't. I want my writing to take in the range of imag-
inative experience, to address the issues of history, of the arts, and of personal
relationships. It would be much poorer if it could not include the place that
is nearest at hand—rural or urban—the most profound use of which is as a
metaphor for the self in its deepest, meditative self-knowing. All places used
in this way are mythological and reach between people, across decades, across
continents.

Sydney
Laurence
*The Lone
Star*
Oil on canvas
Undated
Gift of Dr. and
Mrs. John I.
Weston
UA83-9-3

WALKING ON CARLSON LAKE WITH BILL

Eva Saulitis

IT WAS MID-MARCH and spring would not come, felt like it would never come. The sun glared bright and false in the ten-below air, and the wind blew for days on end. Undaunted, four friends and I planned our trip to Fred's homestead on Carlson Lake, in the Mentasta Range, five hours south of Fairbanks. I hoped for a change. A change of weather, a change of mind-set from the stilled immobility of winter to the motion and softening of spring.

In March in Interior Alaska, it's not the spring of birds returning and snowmelt and balminess, but people do begin to hope for a mellowing of temperatures in the face of the sun's steady ascent in the sky, the lengthening of daylight. When the temperature stays cold like it did last March, that sun is almost harsh in its light. It seems to give back nothing, and we want so much from it; more than anything, we want hope from it, after winter's long and dark and cold.

As a child I felt apologetic in my prayers to God. I imagined millions of beseeching whispers floating heavenward, little hands tugging at the hem of God's robes, the tugging and pleading that I knew annoyed my mother, so why not God? Here in Alaska the sun carries this burden of hope placed upon it, of longing in winter and the weight of gratitude in summer. I find myself receiving the sun like a gift, the cold and darkness as something withheld, a test of endurance or belief.

The funny thing about nature is that it gives in very strange ways. To have expectations of it here in Interior Alaska is foolish. In nature, desire and fulfillment move along vastly different scales of time.

I thought I knew what I wanted from my trip to Carlson Lake. I wanted to take my friend Bill there to meet Fred, and I wanted to listen to the two of them tell stories of long ago together in Fred's log house, and I wanted to hear them speak in their own separate ways; I wanted to memorize that. But the lake got in my way. Looking back, I envision the black ice of the lake lying in wait for me, even as it gleamed its indifference, even as it held the reflection of the mountainsides and sky, day following day, that and only that.

When I imagine stepping out onto the ice of Carlson Lake now, stepping onto it in full knowledge, I feel a flood of grief come at the necessity of it and at the beautiful indifference of its gift. But the moment that Bill stepped onto the ice, and I witnessed the intersection of the stilled life of the lake with Bill's, I was changed, and now the lake is a lens suspended inside me that I see through.

"Someday, I want you to meet my friend Ed Turwilliger," Bill said. "He must be in his nineties now, still living in Tok. My, he can tell a story. I remember one, began something like this. . . ." Bill tilted his head slightly and looked up, as if calling in Ed's voice from the far corner of memory. He knitted his long, silver brows, lowered the pitch of his voice, and, with a gleam of mischief in his eyes and a smile twitching the corners of his mouth, spoke Ed's words: "Well, I woke up the next morning, and the old man was dead." A pause, and then Bill's face collapsed into a laugh, into his own face and voice. "Wouldn't that be the beginning of a great story?"

On the way to Carlson Creek in the car, Bill told my husband John and me stories of the past and played jaunty reels and jigs on his harmonica. A lively beat and the mournful crooning of the harmonica—a sound so like longing that I felt I was watching our history form, a moment I longed for even as I lived in its passing.

I turned and watched Bill's face as he played. On its landscape I imagined I could read the map of his life: seventy-six years, seventy-six winters, and I wondered, could I see that history all whole, etched there, if I looked closely enough? He reminded me of a stream I once passed while driving to Anchorage—Troublesome Creek. I had felt a jolt of recognition and craned my face back to catch a glimpse of the sun-glinting water troubled by the shape of the stony bottom as it moved across.

I watched Bill's eyes, which take on a glazed look when he plays or sings. Silver gray and shiny as ice, they seemed to look off somewhere above me or beyond me, at something far away. Eyes all aglitter with pain, as if the music released a lifetime's memory from them.

The drive to Carlson Creek took us down to Delta and then onto the Alaska Highway to Tok and down the Tok cutoff toward Slana. Though we didn't speak of it, I was aware of the memories for Bill of this drive from Fairbanks to Tok, where he and Nancy used to live. Bill hadn't been to Tok in almost fifteen years. His eighteen-year-old son Billy had killed himself there early one March, seventeen years ago.

I've never asked Bill about Billy's death directly, though it's there between us, in the gentle tread of intimacy around one another's sorrows. That kind of intimacy is built over a long time, I've found. Bill and I reveal our secrets to one another the way the image of the sea floor reveals itself when I watch for bottom from a boat: first there is a whitening, and then, in fragments, the flecks and shadows coalesce into their actual forms: blades of kelp, the fanning bodies of fish, or eelgrass.

Once Bill came to our house for breakfast. Instead of the laughing, singing, yarn-spinning Bill we unconsciously expect, the Bill that sat in the rocking chair by the woodstove wore sorrow in his gray-ice eyes, in the slump of his shoulders, the careless sprawl of his broad, bare feet. I sat beside him, and he told me, plainly, "It's near the anniversary of my brother's death, and it's funny, I've just been thinking of him these last few days and I miss him so. You remind me of him, you know, you would have liked him. Now *he* could tell a story. He had dozens of stories and songs memorized. And sometimes it just hurts so much, missing him."

I held my breath. When someone reveals to me a fragment of sorrow, I feel as if I am wearing a glass coverall, as if we are both held in a delicate shell made of

■ ■ ■

Walking on Carlson

Lake with Bill

225

glass. My slightest fumbling could shatter the fragile hoarfrost thread of trust formed in that moment. When Bill got up to leave he hugged my husband and me, and when I wrapped my arms around him I felt his solidity in the span of my arms across his back, in the feel of his bones beneath my splayed fingers. I felt his holding on and yet the weight of him planted firmly on the ground. I felt the hoarse break in his indrawn breath and then the long exhale.

My own half-spoken losses hover between Bill and me—the suicide of my friend Carol, the way I, like he, struggle with depression. We lap into each other's pain and back away again, and intimacy becomes a silence, and the silence is a trust.

I wait for Bill to tell me things. One day in early winter, he and I drove down the road in his tiny white shell of a car. Our breath iced the windows. I looked at Bill's face as he spoke of the strange grief that welled up in him suddenly, when he remembered his brother, or Billy, or a friend who'd died. He told me how the grief for Billy finally broke loose one day, driving that same car down that same road several years ago. Karl Haas's classical music program was on the public radio station, and he played a slow, sorrowful piece. Bill lifted one hand off the steering wheel and conducted as he sang out the notes: "Bomm, bomm, bomm, bomm . . ." He told me how the tears and sobs shuddered out for the first time, for Billy, like a dam breaking loose, he said. He wrote a letter to Karl Haas, thanking him. I stared at his broad hands gripped around the wheel, and behind his face through the window of the car rose the slope of Esther Dome, the familiar landscape of our road like a grounding wire to the safety of the present. The air vibrated with the vulnerability of grief. I felt in the presence of something fragile and beyond my meager comprehension of pain. I had nothing to offer Bill but my willingness to listen, and that seemed to be enough for him.

We stopped at the general store in Tok for coffee. Bill peered around at the cluster of buildings. There had been a store in the same spot fifteen years ago, but the flat-roofed building that housed this store was new. A family he knew lived nearby. The wind banged signs against the metal siding of the store. A cloud of ice fog billowed in ahead of us as we pushed open the doors. I came back from the bathroom, and Bill was at the counter paying for a bag of tortilla chips and a cup of coffee. "Yeah, she still lives there," I heard the large, tired-looking woman behind the counter answer him. "No, I've never heard of them. I've just been here five years." Bill's face was alight with recollection. He hardly seemed to need the affirmation of her responses or her interest.

Back on the road we turned onto the Tok cutoff. Bill fell silent. The silence hung heavy with the weight of memory. The light was fading and I knew that we wouldn't reach the trailhead until it was dark, with a four-mile ski before us in the cold wind. I felt apprehension at what I'd initiated, somewhat thoughtlessly; what it might be like for Bill to take this familiar drive after fifteen years of leaving it behind.

I stared out the window as the landscape reeled by. "I used to hate that last part of the drive into Fairbanks," Bill said.

Mostly, the tragedies of his life were a silence, a complicity, between us, and a ribbon of something like smoke that seeped from the small, square openings in his harmonica and coiled around us in the car: loss, and memory, and the tree-stippled hills under snow hurtling past.

A half moon rode high in the sky by the time we arrived at Carlson Creek. John backed our car into the parking area. Our friends pulled their truck in beside us. We changed into our ski boots and pushed the car doors open against the shuddered gusts of wind. I packed up my sled quickly in the weak light from the car. It was ten below, and the twenty-mile-an-hour wind sapped the warmth from exposed skin within seconds. By the time Bill had his thin ski boots on, his feet were cold. "My circulation isn't what it used to be," he said, pulling his mukluks back on. I didn't doubt that was true in the bitter wind, though at seventy-six, Bill walks around in bare feet and thongs when there's still snow on the ground, and bikes four miles a day at forty and fifty below to get his mail at the post office. I jammed his ski boots into the top of my pack. John tied Bill's skis to the sides of his pack, and Bill strapped his small knapsack into his sled. I knew that the trail was hard-packed from snow machines, as fine for walking as for skiing. My fingers stung as I tied one end of a thin cord to Bill's sled and the other end to a tab on the back of my pack.

"We'll get a head start," I told the others, as Bill and I set out up the road. "See you down the trail." I felt guilty at leaving them to pack the food onto sleds, but I was more concerned about the cold and about getting Bill moving.

Bill and I crossed the road and walked along the shoulder until we saw the opening in the trees that was the trail to Carlson Lake. I'd been to Fred's cabin on the lake only once before, two years ago, and that time we'd arrived at two in the morning, with Fred waiting up for us with hot chicken soup. The darkness inside the rambling log house had swallowed up almost all of the light from the kerosene lamp over the kitchen table where we sat. As Bill walked beside me, I told him about that other night, hoping to warm him with the vision of the lamplight, the wood fires, the steaming bowls of soup, Fred's wind-reddened cheeks creased into a welcoming smile.

Bill knew of Fred when he lived in Tok, but somehow the movements of their lives never came together. Bill's wife Nancy remembers Fred showing up at a Christmas party in Slana once, laden with candy for the kids. Fred is in his seventies now, living out on the lake alone. Bill had anticipated meeting him for years. I couldn't wait to get those two in a room together, both of them exquisite storytellers and natural musicians. Fred has an antique upright piano in his cabin on the lake. He bangs out Scott Joplin and Al Jolson and Beethoven and his father's own love songs published in the '20s with equal abandon. I like to turn the yellowed sheaves of his sheet music, soft and powdery with age. Bill can play just about anything, whether it was meant to be an instrument or not, but he'd brought along his harmonica, and, to my ear, he is a virtuoso on it.

The light from the moon was just enough, and the mountains seemed to give off their own light, the way they do when they're snow covered. In the trees, we couldn't feel the wind. Bill walked along at a good pace, and I shuffled next to him on my skis. Sometimes he held the line and took the weight of the sled; sometimes he let it go, and I took it. The dark shapes of trees cast vague shadows on the snow.

After a half mile, the trail narrowed, and we entered the forest. Another half mile, and we came alongside the edge of a fifty-foot cliff, a place I recognized even in the dark: that bit of overflow from Carlson Creek. I skittered across the slick curvature of the rippled ice on my skis. When we reached the snow surface again, we stopped and stood quietly and listened for the sounds of our companions back behind us. I looked back at the dark forms of broken-off, dead trees teetering alone in the middle of the overflow. They could have been the forms of two people, one standing, one lying down, perhaps the ghosts of old miners or Athabascan Indians. Who could know what history formed itself alive and recollected itself in the dark absence of the trail at night?

Just ahead of us, the trail forked. I probed my memory, trying to remember if we were to take a turn. "I'll walk on up ahead and see where this one goes," Bill said. I stood on overflow ice, watching Bill's old yellow windbreaker dissolve into the darkness up the trail. All at once it was quiet, quiet enough to hear the wind in the tops of the trees. I listened closely into the stillness of the forest behind me, trying to hear the squeak of ski poles pressing into the hard-pack, the swish of skis. Nothing. I felt the beginning of the fear I feel sometimes in the dark. I didn't want to look back at the human shapes of the trees. And what if I lost Bill to the forest? I realized that, for all of my protectiveness toward Bill, I needed him as much, probably more, than he needed me. It was he who had forged ahead of me into the darkness to find the trail, while I waited behind, feeling the unknown landscape pressing close upon me.

I heard Bill's footsteps coming back, creaking on the dry snow. He stopped at the top of the hill. "The two trails join up just a little ways up here."

I hadn't waxed my skis or put on climbing skins, thinking that the coldness would create enough friction between my skis and the snow. But my skis slid, the snow warmer than the cold air. They slipped out from underneath me as I began to climb the short, steep hill. Bill watched me from above. I splayed my skis and began to herringbone up. But the trail was too narrow to accommodate my gait, and I floundered, the ski tips sinking into deep snow while the backs slipped on the hard-pack. The sled pulled me backwards, throwing me off balance. Bill descended the slope and took the weight of the sled. I turned sideways to the slope and side-stepped to the top.

We stopped at the top of the rise. "I remember the first time I entered a cross-country ski race," Bill said. We passed my water bottle back and forth. Our gradually slowing breaths crystallized and dissolved in the air. "I was a ski jumper, not a skier, then. I didn't have any ski boots. So I just took a pair of hiking boots and screwed them into a pair of wooden skis." Bill demonstrated the movements of turning the screws with his hands, both of us laughing. His words and his laughter swirled up together like currents of water. "The race started at the top of a steep hill, and when I took off, I was just striding as fast as I could, and the screws came loose and my skis went flying out from under me and shot down the hill. I just had to turn around and walk back with the screws sticking out of my boots like cleats."

Another mile up the trail I heard Bill stop behind me. I turned and looked back. He cupped one hand across his mouth, and I heard a sharp, short spray of aerosol. Bill's eyes were closed. I could tell he was holding his breath deep in his lungs. My heart beat heavily in my chest with alarm. In the span of seconds it took for me to ask, "Bill, what is that," a dozen scenarios passed through my mind. Bill having a heart attack there in the cold, hypothermia, an asthma attack. How could I forgive myself if something were to happen to Bill?

"It's just a little something my doctor gave me to take if I get short of breath. I'm just fine, I was just feeling a little tired. I feel great now." Bill danced a few steps on the snow and grinned at me. I felt a tentative relief. "Well, if it's so great, why don't you give me a shot. I'm feeling tired too." We turned and moved once more down the trail.

As we neared the edge of the lake, we felt the wind at our backs. We broke with the trees and slid onto the rumpled ice and snow at the mouth of the creek. To our right the stumps of Fred's wood-lot cast stunted shadows on the snow. The moon crested the snaggled horizon of treetops. Clouds sheared across the surface of the moon, and I couldn't tell for a moment if it was the moon that was being blown or the blacker line of trees or the earth turning. We turned back and looked down the trail, and in the distance we saw the bobbing dots of light from the headlamps of John, Steve, and Gail and heard the screech of their skis on the snow. We howled out to them; when we heard them howl back, we turned and skied toward the lake.

The lake spread out before us like a vast plain, the mountains rising up steeply from its edges. Billows of snow rolled across the moonlit surface like tumbleweeds. We stood for another moment at the edge of the lake.

The trail was narrow, so Bill and I traveled onto the lake single file. He released the sled from his hand for better footing, and I felt its resistance tug against my backpack, and then felt it begin to slide. The wind gusted at our backs. The weight of snowmachines and skis and boots had packed down a slab track of snow that withstood the wind across the lake, but around us the wind had swept patches of the ice clean, and it shone blackly, like shards of obsidian in the waxy moonlight. I didn't expect to see those black spaces in the white surface of the snow. I stopped, feeling the pin-prickling of sudden adrenaline fear in my armpits. I cast about at the glossy black with my ski poles and struck hard ice. And still I had to remind myself as I skied along that the dark almonds of bare ice were solid, that I was skiing on a trail that bore the weight of snowmachines and moose, that the white smoke like wind-riven clouds sheeting across the surface of the lake was the powder of snow and not steam rising up from open water. Fifty yards out onto the lake I stopped to wait for Bill. His breath glittered in the clarity of the cold air.

I set my sights to the small peninsula that poked out into the middle of the lake, where Fred had built his cabin. I pushed the skis forward. The wind pushed at my back. I spread my arms out to make myself a sail, and gusts caught the cloth of my windbreaker. I rode the strength of the wind teeteringly on the snow and ice across the lake.

In the morning I looked out from the window and saw the places where the lake had been whisked smooth; in its glazed surface the reflections of trees on the steep mountainside opposite gleamed. I imagined the steely hardness of the surface of the lake against my face. I closed my eyes and in my imagination I touched it: it was seamless, and against it my own skin felt soft and vulnerable and sewn with seams.

Janel Thompson

Mom's Bed

Monoprint

1982

UA88-3-3

Upstairs in Fred's house the wind rattled the glass panes of the windows upon which frost crept slowly upward. The brittle branches of a birch tree scratched at the glass like something wanting to be let in from the cold. I could hear the voices of my friends downstairs, but I wanted to be alone. I still rode the far edge of a bout of depression that had come on in December, with winter's darkness. It had been harder to pull myself out of it than ever before.

I had so wanted to feel spring at Carlson Lake. I had so wanted to feel social again, to take day-long skis across the string of lakes that beaded through the mountains. But despite the blazing blue sky, the thermometer outside Fred's kitchen window read minus fifteen that morning and the wind shrieked around the corners of the house. I dreaded even the short walk to Fred's sharply tilted outhouse, with its plastic seat so cold I had to sit on my hands.

I stayed upstairs all morning and wrote in my journal, but something about the obsidian, mirrored surface of the lake dragged my eyes compulsively toward it. I found it impossible to look away for long from the gauze spumes of snow blowing across the shining black ice. I wanted to skate across it. There was something that gave the illusion of braveness, to skate across something so deep and so frozen, yet clear and visible to its depths.

Finally, I threw down my journal and resolved to go out onto the ice, despite the cold and wind that kept everyone inside, lingering around the breakfast table, despite my own lethargy, despite Fred's statement that "it's days like these that look best from behind glass."

I layered on all of my warmest clothes, wind pants, and jacket and walked outside. The skin on my fingertips crimped with the instant bite of the cold as I snapped the bindings of my skis into place with bare hands. I careened down the steep trail and onto the surface of the lake. I skied toward the large swaths of exposed ice, in the direction of the wind. Even in the sun's brightness, there was no warmth. The wind pinched my skin until it felt taut and breakable across my face. I pulled my neck gaiter over my nose and bent forward. There was no glide on the skis, just as much sliding as I could muscle against the wind and the snow's carved, hard-packed surface, peaked and uneven, which formed chiseled reefs and depressions—*sastrugi* snow, it's called.

Between wind-scoured drifts, I wobbled across patches of bare ice. The skis were not meant for the ice; they clattered and slipped clumsily over its glassiness. It seemed appropriate that what was necessary to move with grace upon that ice was a thin metal blade, sharp, carving a pencil-thin tracing of one's movements over the mirrored surface.

Ahead of me more dark openings of ice gleamed with the cold, harsh sunlight. I carefully slid my skis onto the ice. I knew that it was several feet thick, and yet I couldn't bring myself to trust that transparency. I tapped ahead of me with my ski pole as if I was blind, and I *was* blinded to the nature of that ice, to what I would see there. The color was black with the hint of green, like the green of black spruce, the color of the air between trees in a spruce forest at dusk. The ice was riven with cracks, the only thing giving it the perspective of depth. The surface of the ice was smooth. There were no openings; rather, the cracks were suspended just below the surface, pinned like long sheets of just-developed photographs drying on a line. The cracks formed a latticework that radiated out through the ice from central points, like the spokes of glass wheels all interconnected. Lines of fracture, stresses, and yet they were something other, something unto them-selves, apart from their physics, apart from their reason for being.

Each fracture was metallic, like a sheet of crinkled aluminum foil hung down into the ice from the surface. I positioned myself so that the sun glittered on the surfaces of the cracks. Intricately etched upon the metallic lenses were scenes of mountains, jagged peaks. Some of the cracks descended six inches, others what looked to be four or five feet. The narrow bands made the ice look thin, though it was not. It was impossible to know its thickness. It could have clasped to the very bottom of the lake, I thought, until I saw the gray shapes of fish—grayling—moving deep under the ice, five feet below my feet.

The whole lake was something other. Something other than a lake. It was a shattered mirror, and between the radiating cracks all I could see within it was blackness. But it was unlike a mirror. A mirror only reflects, and revealed within the black ice was its depth. It showed what was beneath the surface: fish, deep wa-ter, vegetation.

I saw all at once how the lake was as complex as Bill or any person with a long history is, as we all are. So many people will say, when I ask them if they know Bill, "Oh, yeah, that old guy who rides his bike all the time." And yet we are all lakelike, with our distracting surfaces. We are more like unfrozen lakes, and to most people the surface is everything. It is only in moments of grace, built upon trust, that what is below the surface is known. And when we feel we know someone whole, even ourselves, we still catch glimpses of fish swimming below in the darkness, flickering in and out of view, below what is held in place and seems so permanent.

I unclipped my skis and shot them back at the snow. They clattered on the ice, moving unbelievably fast, and within seconds of scraping the snow's cold surface, they stopped. I knelt on my hands and knees and crawled over the ice. I took off my mitten and felt the slick and rippled surface. Here and there bubbles like milk were trapped in the ice, ascending from some deep point below in a series of mirror images and clotted in sprays of perfect circles of white at the surface, like spilled cream. From the shaded side, the cracks actually looked transparent, gauzy, like streamers of wet tissue paper or single-cell strips of dried skin. And all pinned within the ice. Like the world held into place for my consideration. As if I were crawling on the world for an instant. The lake told me all that in the briefest moment of belief like the very beginning of wind.

I looked up, and there was Bill, his arms swinging. He moved toward me in his yellow windbreaker and his mukluks. His face was exposed to the wind. I walked over to meet him, and his eyes watered from the wind, and the cold seemed to intensify the creases in his skin, which was reddened on his cheeks.

"Bill, look at this ice," I cried, and he stepped out onto the quicksilver surface of the ice, looking down.

"My," he exclaimed, his voice breathless. "Isn't that something. I've never seen anything quite like this before." He shuffled over the ice staring down at it.

I lay down on the ice and cupped my hands around my face and peered beneath the surface. Black green depths, smooth and cold as a tooth against my face, as I'd imagined it. We looked at the cracks, and Bill wanted to take pictures of the ice for Nancy. He got in one or two shots, and then his camera battery froze. I could see his square fingertips red and shiny with the cold. He tucked his camera back into his jacket and his hands back into his moose-hide mitts, and I watched him turn and face the wind and walk farther up the lake, looking down. I watched him a long time.

I thought to myself, Bill is seventy-six and I am thirty-one and we are here on Carlson Lake looking at the miracle of this frozen world; we are residing together within its memory. In the wintertime in Cook Inlet one listens to the marine weather forecast, and the announcer gives the gale warnings and storm warnings and the conditions of the sea ice. There is young, brash, and new ice, and there is pancake ice and pack ice and the fragile skin of ice that forms in bays where fresh-water flows in. But here was ice so thick and so solid, and there was a world caught in it, and Bill and I were sliding across its surface as if we were riding above the skin of our own lives, looking down. We gazed below us into its depth and solidity as if it were a past that we'd finally outrun, and we could stand above it, feeling safe, even as it cracked like a shotgun, even as we considered its torturous stresses, seen in the fractures going deep. And seeing the fish reminded me that there was water below, and it was deep, and that we were capable of sinking. I imagined myself on a boat, and the water was water and not ice, and all those things that had anchored me to life were falling away, falling away deeper into the water, trying to find bottom, and I couldn't go after them.

A woman I met once took my palm in her hand and told me the meanings of the lines there. There was a head line and a heart line, a life line and creases for marriages, crosses and vertical slashes for children. She traced possible paths in the line running through the center of my palm with the tip of her finger. Each line veering off the main one led to a different outcome; only one led to long life and the shape of a fish: some kind of spiritual awakening. I ponder that notion that the lines in my palm can, like those on the lake, contain all of the possibilities of my life, as if in some way my life is already complete, a whole, and I am living my way along those possible worlds. As if they are already mine.

I turned from watching Bill and ran in the other direction across the ice and slid as far as I could. I ran and walked and slid over to the edge where the lake

Shelley Schneider

*Frozen Minnow and
Air Bubbles in Ice,
Judd Lake, Alaska*

Cibachrome

1981

UAP84:022:001

struck land. First the world below me turned a greener shade of black. Then it turned a milky shade of green. Finally, I saw the sandy bottom of the lake, and it rose until I saw vegetation, caught mid-sway in the ice, that was welded to the bottom like a barnacle to a rock. Grass and horsetail and the decayed fronds of water plants all caught in the act of buoyancy, frozen in their live forms. On the other side of the lake, two years before, I'd seen the bones of a caribou killed by wolves. I wondered if the animals balked when they came upon the bare strips of ice, at the clear vision of depth beneath them, as I did when I saw that first obsidian shard in the darkness.

Bill came back toward me with the wind at his back. I ran and slid to meet him. My face felt ready to crack from the cold; even the wind-dried surfaces of my eyes felt tight and painful. "I'm ready to go back," Bill said. "How about you? I'd like to come back after I warm up my camera and take some more pictures. This ice really is something." I jogged over and clipped into my skis, and Bill and I shuffled across the slabbed snow to the shore and climbed the hill up to the cabin.

That night Fred put the thermometer down at the lake so we could see the difference that the slight elevation of the house made. We made ice cream with ice from the stream. John turned the crank. In the night we heard the lake crack and groan. And I knew that what looked so solid and of a piece—that whole frozen lake—cried out always from the strain of holding itself together. I imagined it shattering, huge cracks opening up like crevasses in a glacier or the splitting of the earth at faultlines during an earthquake. Fred told us that during the great earthquake of 1964 the lake did shatter, and the ice broke apart, and spouts of water shot into the air like cold geysers.

When hardships come to me or to those close to me, sometimes I imagine that I can't go on. Life is too painful. After my friend Carol killed herself, I carried a bottle of tranquilizers with me for a month, in case my own pain became too great. I believed that Carol's suicide made my own death more accessible to me, and I wanted to go to her, wherever she was. I wasn't sure that I wanted to live in a world that had killed off someone as beautiful and alive as my friend. The promise of the pills felt like my only access to her.

I scattered the bottle of pills onto the asphalt of the road I lived on and rode my bike over and over them on a spring afternoon, three months after Carol's death. That morning her father had called me to tell me that the autopsy results had come through: Carol had died from the loss of blood, not from hypothermia, as we had believed. I listened to her father's voice break to the point where speech was not possible, and I knew that I was hearing the sound of his spirit, of cracks splitting through the center, the widening slits so near to fracture. And yet he did not break. Only then did I believe that I didn't know Carol's mind or the degree of her suffering when she took her life; could not know her mind or her suffering by imitation of her act. Only then did I know what kind of suffering a person could be left to live with.

I rail against God when tragedies strike, and there is no meaning to it but pain. And in the dark of winter I rail sometimes at the darkness and cold, though nature is indifferent and, like the lake, so terrible and beautiful in its indifference. Nature isn't like God, though. I can't hold it responsible or ask it why.

And I can't even ask Bill why, or how, to live on while carrying unbearable pain. I can only watch and wait and listen. Bill has survived seventy-six winters, and he reminds me what it is to live and suffer and live some more. There's a lot of living left to do. Just by watching Bill, without his speaking, I learn that there's sadness out there and losses I haven't begun to imagine, but the world is a good and a sad place to be seventy-six. I see that in his face, which is like the face of the lake, holding everything beneath its surface, the surface only a reflection and its feel the contour of what is beneath. There's nothing to do but to shore up tight into life. I know how to do it on a boat. Before a rough crossing is made I batten things down, tie everything down and make it fast.

Once I looked out of my upstairs window, and a flash of color and movement caught my eye. It was early spring, and I saw Bill walking on the trail between our houses. He was bent slightly at the waist, bare-headed and -handed and wearing his homemade mukluks. His feet looked huge. Beneath the mukluks I knew those feet were horny and callused, flat and broad from going barefoot all summer long: the body's landscape is etched deeply by both joy and sorrow. Bill was walking toward our neighbor's house through the slender poplar saplings. His walk was steady and purposeful, and mostly it was moving toward something, something worth hurrying forward into.

Now I often consider him walking there on the edge of the polished ice, where the *sastrugi* snow surface gave way to its cold sheen. I consider the bravery of a drive down to Tok, where memories paraded like ghosts across the surfaces of snow, collapsed houses, in the spaces where everything had changed except the shape of the land, and that change is cold comfort, is forever, before us and after us and indifferent to us. Memory sweeping by the windows, the road's curves and mileposts, familiar faces behind the counter at the general store in Tok, so many people gone, vanished. The illusion that life tumbles on, Bill standing there as if saying it hasn't at all, all that past is still here, living, pinned into that ice that is the whole scape of our lives, the architecture of memory. Ghosts of those dead and still living and the past all wandering through the aisles of the small grocery store in Tok, unnoticed until someone like Bill comes along and says yes, I remember you.

Carlson Lake was like Bill, if one could see all of Bill's life in his face at once clearly, as one does if the surface of the skin is reflective. Bill and the lake are age and youth at once, at once old and very brief.

When I walked on the ice with Bill, he stared down in amazement, and I ran and slid across that mirror, that image of the world. My own past, that of my whole life, lived and not-yet-lived, beneath me and distant enough that it seemed below reckoning. But I saw Bill there; his walk was more cautious. He peered in wonder at the cracks. He braced himself and walked bent, bare-faced, into the wind.

After we returned to Fairbanks, Bill bought a pulp hook to send out to Fred, who cuts all of his firewood, eight cords a year, by hand. Bill saw how the pulp hook could make the work easier for Fred, and he bought it and carved our names in its handle and sent it to Fred as a gift for our stay at Carlson Lake. As for the lake, it has pressed its image upon our memories, and that is its gift, that of memory and the latitude given us.

Bill and I talk about Carlson Lake often when we see each other, and we describe over and over the ice that was clear enough to see into its depth, and we wonder at its hold on us. We talk about it as if it were a way to speak about everything about our lives at once. About how scary it was to walk upon its surface and to trust what we knew, but the lake could not tell us or assure us. And I ask myself, Bill, what did you see in the lake's gleam?

When I see the lake in my memory, it is Bill and I on the broad, black, swept-clear ovals of ice, and I am watching Bill as he walks windward, and I am considering the cold gleanings of the ice, beautiful and strong and an intricate matrix, almost, but not, breaking.

■ ■ ■

Walking on Carlson

Lake with Bill

Charles Mason
Untitled photograph
Gelatin silver
1995
UAP98:003:001

WHAT EVERYONE
WANTS YOU TO HAVE

Jennifer Brice

BOB SPEAR'S FATHER was a Northwest pig farmer and sometime railroad man during the Depression. The old man unloaded boxcars of government-issued supplies and distributed them to families even poorer than his own. Food was so scarce back then that, more than a half century later, the taste of something sweet triggers memories in his son. For instance, Bob clearly recalls a day from his childhood when a bulk bag of sugar ripped open in transit. Neighbors walked for miles, congregating at the train station just to collect one cupful apiece.

If the five senses are the building blocks of memory, then memory is the DNA of dreams. Any vision of oneself as someone (or somewhere) else first requires a glimpse — through films, TV, literature, or travel — of a heretofore unimagined existence. Bob Spear's early years were as destitute of dreams as everything else. His wife, Helen, says that when she met him, he wanted only two things out of life: to visit Alaska, and to own a tractor. By the time he turned fifty, half of that dream had been realized. With Alaska's Wrangell Mountains rising vertiginously beyond their backyard, Helen Spear likes to tease her husband that the only thing standing between him and true happiness is a John Deere.

The Spears were scraping by in Washington state in the 1980s. One day, Helen's son, Terry, telephoned from someplace called Slana, Alaska, and asked, "If I were to build you a house up here, would you move?" Within a week, she and Bob set off on a journey to the rest of their lives. They drove up the Alaska Highway in a pickup crammed with their four youngest kids and all their earthly possessions. When Helen first clapped eyes on the muddy outpost of Slana, nearly two hundred miles from the nearest city, she muttered, "What am I doing *here*?"

On one level, the answer was simple: The federal government was offering free land, more than ten thousand acres of it near the perimeter of Alaska's Wrangell–Saint Elias National Park. Like hundreds of Americans pining for adventure and change, the Spears pictured themselves as latter-day pioneers, carving out a new and better life in the North. On virtually every other level, the answer was complicated. But then, it is an attribute of dreams always to be simpler than reality.

For the first few months, the Spear family* huddled into an ell-shaped cabin measuring roughly eight by twelve feet. They got by without plumbing and electricity, and they relied solely on a primitive wood-burning cook stove for heat. "I spent that first winter frozen to my waist," Helen told me and Charles Mason, a photographer. Our own dreams had led Charles and me to Slana, where we were documenting, over a period of several years, the lives of the last settlers on the American frontier.

History, geography, and imagination all converge at the frontier, which speaks to our distinctly American fascination with what lies on the other side of civilization—to our New World temptation to re-create ourselves in unknown territory. In some ways, the imperatives of the frontier haven't changed since the California gold rush or, for that matter, since Plymouth Rock. A degree of purposefulness, of self-reflection, arises from the decision to live outside the margins of civilization. For the settlers at Slana, Bob and Helen Spear among them, the frontier signified a fresh start; freedom from interference; and peace, prosperity, health, and happiness. These are lofty goals, but Alaska's vast wilderness demands a corresponding breadth of spirit from those who would make their home within it.

Almost immediately, Bob Spear and his sons set to work building an addition

Although this is a work of nonfiction, the names of the Spear family have been changed at their request.

to the cabin. There was no road leading to the Spears' property, so construction supplies had to be floated on primitive rafts down a nearby creek. Meanwhile, a pageant began to unfold just beyond the Spears' stoop. "First person I seen here, she had a gun like this," Helen said, coiling a hand on her hip. "They called her 'Pistol-Packin' Mama.'"

Young Daniel Spear met a prospective settler lugging an electric chain saw with a three-hundred-foot extension cord, believing he could surely plug it in somewhere. One man talked enthusiastically about his plan to farm alligators, another had a boa constrictor for a traveling companion, and yet another rode a bicycle with a parrot perched on his shoulder. Alaska has always had a knack for sorting the dreamers from the deluded: one befuddled soul staked five promisingly flat acres in the winter, only to find, come spring, that he owned a lake.

After framing in the addition to the house, the Spears set about clearing a garden. They sacrificed nearly every tree on the property in exchange for a harvest of potatoes and vegetables that runs to several tons every fall. Since then, neither the Spears nor their neighbors have had to worry about going hungry. "Homesteading is hard work," Helen said. "Good hard work, because you can see what you've accomplished."

More than a decade after the land rush, only a few dozen settlers remain at Slana, among them the Spears and their extended family. Bob and Helen's house is now a hodgepodge of building materials and styles—principally, plywood and afterthought. In this respect, it is not atypical for Alaska, even for the cities. Scattered around the exterior are torn pieces of greenhouse roofing, yellow insulation, oil cans, and the bent frame of a baby carriage.

Wispy lenticular clouds skittered across a sky so blue it looks lacquered. Seen from here, the Wrangell Mountains played a trick of perspective, seeming to balance like Buddhas atop Helen Spear's clothesline. A satellite dish bloomed like a freak vegetable in the garden out back, and the generator that powers the Spears' water pump, lights, and appliances purred rhythmically.

Charles and I knocked on the door around noon. "Well, you may as well come in," Helen said, squinting up at us. She's a tiny woman with a grandmotherly figure. In her late fifties, she has pale skin, white hair, and blue eyes with a milky sheen to them. Last time we were here, Charles startled her badly. She was in the garden, weeding potatoes on her knees, when he started snapping her picture from fifteen feet away. She tilted her head sharply, gazed right through him, and said, with alarm, "Who's that?"

Several years ago, Helen underwent eye surgery in Fairbanks. It cost six thousand dollars cash, as much money as passes through her hands in an average year. The surgery failed, and now the ophthalmologist is pressuring her to try a new procedure.

"I'm gonna have to wait for finances or God Almighty to do something for me," Helen said, with no trace of self-pity.

The interior of the Spears' house circles in on itself, like a snail's shell. Steps lead up to an outer door, the ingress to a rectangular arctic entry. A second door leads into the house proper. Across from this door is the bathroom with its Sears wringer washer. To the left, in the living room, an ancient dog snoozes on newspapers stacked behind the wood-burning stove.

The Spears save everything that was useful in the past or that might come in handy again someday, things like a meat grinder and empty NAPA filter boxes. They also accumulate stuff with no foreseeable function, such as a carved parrot swinging on a trapeze, a mobile fashioned from painted seashells, and a strand of green foil four-leaf clovers left over from a Saint Patrick's Day celebration.

A yearning for the outward trappings of the middle class is reflected in a six-foot-tall grandmother clock, an antique hutch crammed with knickknacks, and Helen's prized collection of china plates depicting scenes from such movies as *Gone with the Wind*. Despite the incongruities, the Spears possess something that eludes most people: the kind of grace that comes from wanting only small things in a society that pressures us to have it all.

Glass from the original cook stove now forms a kitchen window overlooking the sprawling garden. Scraps of brown carpet cling intermittently to the plank floor. A soiled tapestry emblazoned with a medieval hunting scene hangs on the wall above a sagging couch of threadbare velveteen. Yarn afghans have been tossed over the couch and Helen's favorite armchair. On the floor, broken toys overflow from a battered cardboard box. There is a coffee table strewn with copies of *The Guidepost* and a wall plaque that reads, "Prayer Makes a Difference." Someone has plastered a strip of wallpaper with blue seashells across one wall. Another wall is given over to snapshots of the Spears' nine children, twenty-six grandchildren, and ever-growing number of great-grandchildren.

Three of the Spears' grown children have settled at Slana: Nola and Penny live nearby with their families, and Daniel still sleeps on his parents' couch. The others, including Terry, who first staked land here, are now scattered among Washington, Oregon, Colorado, and Missouri.

Light from a bay window bathes the kitchen table, barely visible under a burden of potted seedlings. Here, in a chair next to the table, is where Bob Spear passes much of the day, tending to the seedlings, rolling cigarettes from a can of Top tobacco, watching the ceiling-mounted color TV.

Bob is gentle, bleary-eyed and slow-moving, a step or two behind his brisk wife. Helen recounted the story of how he broke his foot years ago and kept walking on it, two miles back and forth to work every day. "When he finally went to the hospital," she told us, "the doctor said both feet were swolled up, so he wouldn't X-ray it. He kept acting like Bob had had a stroke or heart attack or something."

Helen had asked Bob to turn down the volume on the TV when we arrived. Ever since, he'd been keeping one eye on the picture and one eye on us. He's pretty hard of hearing, but when Helen looked at him and touched her own foot, he guessed right away what she was talking about.

"Yup," he said. "Couldn't get the doctor to X-ray my foot 'cause it was swolled up like the other one. Wanted to check my heart instead. Wasn't nothing wrong with my heart. Foot never healed up right, though."

Bob's mother delivered him at home on April 29, 1938, without a doctor or midwife. At birth, Bob had a huge goiter on his neck and was blue from lack of oxygen. Believing him to be stillborn, his mother tossed him to the foot of the bed. The impact drove air through the baby's windpipe, and he cried out. Tenderly, his father swaddled him and laid him in the oven for warmth. Later, he sold the family's only cow to pay for an operation to remove Bob's goiter.

Bob's father died young of a heart attack, leaving his mother to work and raise the children alone. At six feet tall and three hundred pounds, she cut an intimidating figure, according to her daughter-in-law, Helen. Bob's mother worked as a nurse at an Army hospital. Plagued by cancer in her middle years, she surprised everyone by succumbing, like her husband, to a heart attack.

Bob and his siblings grew up with little in the way of adult supervision. "One grandfather gave Bob snoose [snuff] and the other one cigarettes when he was three or four years old," Helen said. The kids chopped wood to earn money, played hooky from school, and bounced between the community's two churches. On nights when the Baptists served supper, they worshipped alongside the Baptists; when the Pentecostals feasted, they made like Pentecostals.

As a boy, Bob loved doughnuts. If his mother gave him twenty-five cents for lunch, he bought a bag of sugary pastries on his way to school. He was so big in the fifth grade that he towered over his teacher. In part to compensate for this awkwardness, he began cutting classes. By the time he quit school for good in the ninth grade, Bob had only a nodding acquaintanceship with book learning. He never did learn to read.

His wife is the one who answers letters, fills out public assistance forms, and pays bills. Helen is generous in an offhand manner that makes nearly everyone she meets feel as though no request is too great. For the past several years, she has nearly single-handedly cobbled together funds to rebuild the Slana church, torched by an arsonist. Neighbors and family gather in her living room to celebrate Sunday services in the interim. During the week, her house is overrun with the children of friends and relatives. Neighbors track in and out to borrow the telephone or the washing machine or the freezer.

As the interior of the house is Helen's territory, the exterior is Bob's. With hair sticking up on the side where he slept and beltless jeans riding low on his hips, Bob showed off his plants for Charles and me. Not talkative by nature, he can rattle on for hours about varieties of tomatoes. Several years ago, he and Helen spent part of her inheritance on a used hundred-by-thirty-three-foot commercial greenhouse. The greenhouse cost three thousand dollars at an Anchorage auction; trucking it to Slana cost two thousand more, a price tag that says a lot about Helen's willingness to invest in Bob's dreams. Working with his sons and sons-in-law, Bob installed such amenities as lights, heat, and irrigation. At one end of the greenhouse, he parked the pickup that bore his family to Alaska a decade ago.

When Charles and I stepped through the door, we felt as though we'd crossed a threshold from winter into spring. We felt unaccustomed heat, smelled moist soil, saw vines twining up string ladders nearly to the ceiling. In raised beds crafted from scrap lumber, Bob had planted beans, squash, carrots, cabbage, broccoli, cauliflower. "I ain't no gardener, I just throw it in the ground," he told us, a statement belied by the lushness of our surroundings. With Helen's help, Bob once ordered what he thought were tomatoes from a seed company. What he got were packets with pictures of petunias and marigolds. Instead of mailing them back, he and Helen planted the seeds in pots and gave them to friends. No one laughed harder than Bob when the plants turned out to be tomatoes, not petunias. "In Washington, you plant your seeds, weed your garden, and wait for your plants to come up," Bob said. "Up here, you throw a seed in the ground, you nurse it, you baby it, you weed it, and it still may not come up."

Back at the house, Helen told us a story about an aunt and uncle who were fond of practical jokes. On a lark one time, they went to an unfamiliar restaurant and pretended to be deaf. They signed and pointed to items on the menu. The harried waitress brought dish after dish from the kitchen, only to have the customers shake their heads. Throughout the meal, they pretended to be immune to the commotion surrounding them. Then, as they rose to leave, Helen's uncle caught the waitress's eye, and said, casually, "Thanks. That was good."

More than once, I've felt like the waitress in the story. It's not that the Spears try to trick me into believing something that isn't true; I'm perfectly capable of doing that myself. For instance, my first and strongest impression on meeting them was one of abject hardship. Their brand of poverty evokes images of the Great Depression or Appalachia. But this is Alaska, the state with the highest median household income in the nation.

None of the conventional categories of poverty fit the Spears. Richer than many of their neighbors, they have assumed the role of local philanthropists. They are neither indigent, lazy, downtrodden, stupid, nor—the most insidious stereotype of all—poor but proud." Middle-class Americans such as myself like to label the poor in ways that let us off the hook, that create artificial distance between us and them, that—above all—help us feel better about not helping. We crave cautionary fables about the poor in America for the simple reason that, deep down, we sense we have nothing left to give them except what is rightfully ours.

There was a time, though, when we had something to give them that we didn't want. Back in 1854, columnist Horace Greeley declared: "Make the Public Lands free in quarter-sections to Actual Settlers . . . and earth's landless millions will no longer be orphans and mendicants." This brand of frontier boosterism thinly veneered the less noble sentiments of snobbery and racism. A well-known doctrine at the time, the so-called "safety valve," preached of enticing the poor from vandalism and theft with visions of riches in the West. The perennially popular labor theory of land ownership also gained currency during the nineteenth century in America. Premised on a man's right to own the soil he tilled, the theory can be traced back as far as the Old Testament Book of Psalms: "And there he maketh the hungry to dwell, that they may prepare a city for habitation."

Fueled by populist arguments that appealed to the citizenry's emotions as well as their intellects, Congress passed the Homestead Act in 1862, one year into Lincoln's presidency and the Civil War. Lawmakers introduced a host of laws modifying and expanding the Homestead Act, with its upper limit of two hundred and forty acres for farming, early in the twentieth century. The new laws proffered smaller tracts of land as a reward for independence or entrepreneurship. The Homesite Act, for instance, provided up to five acres for a private residence.

The land was never "free" in any sense of the word. A ten-dollar filing fee had to accompany the initial staking. Then, three to five years later, another ten dollars had to be submitted along with a formal application for title. If the BLM approved the claim, then the land cost two dollars and fifty cents an acre. Therefore, the total cash outlay for a five-acre homesite came to thirty-two dollars and fifty cents, a figure still substantially below market value.

In light of the (largely) philanthropic ideals behind the opening of the American frontier, it's ironic how many settlers today survive on welfare. A cynic might

Charles Mason
Untitled photograph
Gelatin silver
1995
UAP98:004:001

say their title to five acres has transformed them from mere mendicants into mendicant landowners. In fairness, however, most settlers probably never expected things to turn out this way. Jobs are exponentially more scarce the farther one gets from Alaska's three cities. Within a fifty-mile radius of Slana, only a handful of teachers, waitresses, bartenders, bakers, grocers, a postmaster, and the occasional flag person on a summer road crew can find work. Within the settlement itself, the only store is now boarded up, gone the way of such chimeras as the electric guitar factory and the alligator farm.

The land here is not conducive to yielding up a living. Temperatures in the foothills of the Wrangell Mountains range from the eighties in summer to sixty below and sometimes colder in winter. During even the temperate months, South Slana consists of a maze of narrow trails through taiga forest and muskeg swamp: fancy names for scruffy black spruce and mud that can suck the boots right off your feet.

A fissure cuts through the community of Slana, with welfare recipients on one side and virtually everyone else on the other. Charles and I visited one old-timer, a Sequoia of a man, who'd homesteaded near Slana in the 1940s. He and his wife welcomed us into their rambling log home along the Glenn Highway. As the four of us sipped cranberry juice from homemade concentrate, the old-timer regaled us with stories of how things used to be. When I tentatively raised the subject of South Slana, a vein in his neck began to throb. "Food stamp pioneers," he bellowed, banging a fist on the table. "They carry big guns and big knives, and they live off big checks from the government."

Slana is a crazy-quilt community, complex and clannish, with wilderness lodges, saunas, rusting automobiles on blocks, scratching chickens, satellite dishes, artists, ex-cons, Christians, Rottweilers, toy poodles, greenhouses with crops more dubious than Bob Spear's, and the scariest "No Trespassing" signs I've ever seen, including one that reads, "Hold still—I'm getting a bead on you."

A tourist unfamiliar with Slana's history might mistake it for a ghost town. Boards cataract the windows of a former lodge and general store. Other abandoned structures stare at passers-by like minds gone momentarily blank. In truth, however, Slana is thriving now as never before. Time has had a mellowing effect on the place, subsuming somewhat the gut-level hatreds, slander, property disputes, transiency and crime that once led a BLM agent to compare it to *Peyton Place*.

Yet there is beauty here. In late summer, for instance, nature becomes a cartographer, mapping unknown kingdoms on every hillside: golden duchies, ochre aristocracies, and red commonwealths with verdant borders of late-turning leaves. Garden flowers planted last spring now bloom hectically, as if to ward off frost with their drooping finery. Generous now, the land yields rich harvests of potatoes, mushrooms, cranberries, moose, and salmon.

As long as the fishermen continue to bring up nets full of silvers, pinks, and kings, Rod Davenport will have a job canning fish in Valdez, about one hundred and fifty miles south of Slana. Soon, though, the work will run out, and he will return home, most likely jobless, to face the winter.

Yesterday, Rod's wife, Nola Spear Davenport, invited Charles and me to call on her. Anytime after noon, she said: "I have trouble getting moving in the morning." Charles and I slept in, too, then dawdled over the task of packing up our campsite along the Glenn Highway. After lunch, we drove to Bob and Helen Spear's house and parked. One of three Spear daughters who settled at Slana, Nola lives within a couple of hundred yards of her parents.

A field separates the two dwellings. Years back, a settler cleared it for a runway to service his guiding outfit. He's gone now, just another footnote in the history of the land. Stratified layers of garbage in varying state of decay vividly related for our benefit the history of this particular clearing. There was a high-heeled sandal, a wrecked Tonka truck, a blue boot, troll dolls, tiny blue jeans, unmatched socks, smashed toys, and a pair of black boots strewn several feet apart. Just outside Nola's front door, garbage spilled from sacks that may have burst on impact or been ripped apart by dogs. What remained was either unrecognizable or inorganic. The clusters of PediaSure cans, oil cans, pop cans, and beer cans suggested someone had carried on a fleeting romance with recycling.

At the center of it all was Duke, a Rottweiler chained to the rusting hull of a snowmobile. The Davenports' house is a one-story rectangle, roughly twenty by twenty-four feet, constructed of plywood, heated by a fifty-five-gallon drum converted to wood-burning stove. The stove is surrounded by a chicken-wire fence to protect the children: Caitlin, nine; Patricia, eight; Rodney, five; and Jasper, four.

We interrupted Nola cheerfully mopping the kitchen linoleum. The smell of disinfectant hung in the air, stinging our sinuses and diluting the less savory odor of cooked cabbage. Nola was wearing jeans and a short-sleeved blue and white leotard. Of medium height and build, she is just beginning to lose her waistline, and her teeth have a slightly grayish cast to them. Her features are small and regular, and her face is unlined, childlike in its openness and eagerness to please.

Nola showed us around the house: the kitchen with its tree stumps for chairs, the bathroom with its corrugated metal washbasin in which Nola's three youngest children were bathing. While we were in there, Nola grabbed a clean washcloth and began scrubbing five-year-old Rodney, who tried to squirm away. "When I moved out here," she said, "people wanted me to have everything at once. I hear what people say: 'Her house is not that great,' or 'Her children need these things.' And one of the things they always say I need is plumbing. It's gonna cost a thousand dollars just for the tank, but this winter we're gonna have the money."

The living room and girls' bedroom are situated at the back of the house. Someone has draped a quilt over the picture window in the living room, perhaps to keep rays of light from reflecting off the television screen. On the wall hangs a realistic rendering of swans taking flight from a sapphire-tinted lake. Caitlin painted it in school last year, before her parents withdrew her. She also cut pictures of horses from magazines and tacked them up. When I complimented her on them, she warmly confided, "I rode a horse, once."

Besides the children's artwork, the only decoration is a portrait of Christ on black velvet. His eyes followed us wherever we went.

In 1994, *Life* magazine published a cover story on the ideal American home. A famous architect was commissioned to come up with a design that would meet the average American family's needs, taste, and budget. What I found most intriguing about the *Life* article was not the structure itself but the structure of thinking behind it, specifically, the myth of the Average American Family. By virtue of our common nationality, Americans in the 1990s must all yearn for the same things—split-level houses, two-car garages, air-conditioned malls, Bruce Willis movies, Dockers, diamond tennis bracelets, Classic Coke, Rollerblades, tattoos in discreet places.

Alaska is a place where the myth of the Average American Family butts up hard against the myth of the Last Frontier. The Fairbanks public schools host gun shows on weekends, and animal restraint laws are widely perceived as a communist conspiracy to erode the rights of property owners. Alaskans wear blue jeans to the symphony, and anyone with a lawn is vulnerable to charges of snobbery. Even here, though, everyone knows the difference between a lifestyle one chooses and a lifestyle one is forced to settle for. The difference between the house featured in *Life* and my own slightly sagging farmhouse on the outskirts of Fairbanks makes me want to laugh; the difference between the house on the cover of *Life* and the house where Nola Davenport lives makes me want to cry.

Nola was nearly twenty-one when she married Rod. He had just been discharged from the Army, and Nola was working as a nurse's aide. Now thirty-four, Rod has the build of a wiry adolescent. For the past few years, the only work he's been able to find has been seasonal, like the cannery job in Valdez. According to his wife, the work pays between three hundred and seven hundred dollars a month, depending on how well the fish are running. The Davenports depend on food stamps, supplemental social security, and unemployment checks to fill the gap between what Rod earns and what they need to survive.

As the afternoon unfolded, so did the story of Nola's life, unchronologically, in discrete bits and pieces that, taken one by one, seemed believable and self-aware. As a whole, however, the fragments were self-contradictory, paradoxical. For instance, Nola graduated from high school and attended community college briefly, yet she has no driver's license. She freely admits she can't read well enough to study the manual and pass the test.

For as long as Nola can remember, she's felt cut off from other people. Like her father, she was "born slow," meaning she's struggled for things that seemed to come easily to her brothers and sisters, things like a driver's license and the right to raise her own children. It's easy to feel sorry for Nola, though not always for the reasons she might think. Separating truth from its half-sister can be as harrowing for her listener as for Nola herself. It's almost as if she knits the story of her life with one hand and unravels it with the other. By degrees, I realized that Nola wasn't really lying but rather interpreting to the best of her ability a world that often seems ineffable and cruel.

"Tell me about the saddest moment of your life," I probed.

"There's lots of them," Nola replied briskly. "The saddest times were when people treated me like I was diseased because I'm different."

I pressed her for a specific example until Nola recounted in detail an incident that had taken place several months earlier. She was doing her laundry at a lodge nearby, and she was in a hurry to get home before the girls returned from school. Somehow, a soiled disposable diaper got mixed in with the clothes and went through the wash cycle. In the dryer, it exploded. Thousands of particles of padding clogged the machine and covered the floor like snow. According to Nola, the people in charge of the lodge ejected her before she could vacuum up the mess, and she's been barred from doing laundry there ever since.

"I have to watch everything I do," Nola said, blinking away tears at the memory, "because if I make the slightest mistake, that's thrown at me like it's foolin', even though it's not foolin'. I try to be perfect, but no one can be perfect."

Nola's children, the youngest three in particular, are too thin, with outsized heads wobbling on frail neck stems. Ribs jut through the fabric of their shirts, and their hair looks as though it has been cut with a hatchet. They're often dirty and almost inevitably dressed wrong for the weather. One recent day when the temperature peaked around fifty, Patty wore nothing but a one-piece swimsuit, which made her arms and legs look like popsicle sticks.

Shortly after Patty's birth, Nola underwent what she vaguely describes as a "nervous breakdown." She left the baby in her parents' care for several months. Asked what led to the breakdown, she replied, elliptically, "Not knowing whether your baby's going to live or die." Apparently, a doctor had predicted that Patty wouldn't survive six months.

"What was wrong with her?" I asked, tactfully phrasing the question in the past tense.

"Allergies."

Nola continued: "Rod and I were both working, trying to make ends meet. We never made enough money to be able to support a family together, or to get health treatment. Patty was in the hospital for years, off and on, and you can imagine how high that bill was."

"Exactly how high was it?" I asked.

Four thousand dollars, was the reply. It still comes in the mail every month, and every month Nola tears it up.

"The kids need things that are more important than paying that bill," she said.

Nola stepped into the bathroom, an unlit cigarette waggling between her lips. She scrubbed Patty's naked body with soap and water, then rubbed her vigorously with a towel. In the girls' bedroom, she rooted through a pile of clothes, coming up with a madras plaid sun suit. She laid Patty on the floor and dressed her, first in a disposable diaper, then in the sun suit. Still handling the girl like an oversized doll, she tugged her upright and brushed her hair. Patty babbled happily the whole time.

Of the Davenports' four children, Caitlin looks the sturdiest. Sometime after noon, Caitlin marched into the kitchen, where Nola and I were talking. "I'm hungry, Mom," she shouted.

Jasper was reposing in Nola's arms, dreamily stroking a breast. Rodney was on the verge of springing from the kitchen counter onto her back.

"You're always hungry." Nola sounded exasperated.

"Uh-uh. I didn't eat."

"Yes, you did." Nola loosed a shrug in my direction. "She's always doing that."

An hour or so later, when Charles and I began putting away cameras and note-books, the kids surprised us by bursting into tears. Hiccuping sobs, Jasper stretched out his arms to us. He was wearing a brown sweater and a diaper. When I squeezed him, his yellow hair bristled against my cheek. Rodney tugged on my jeans, tears tracking down his cheeks. I picked him up. Then Patty. "Hug," she said. "Patty. Hug."

Only Caitlin remained aloof, a bemused expression on her face. As we left, Charles photographed Nola in the doorway, holding Jasper, the older children

Magnus Colcord
(Rusty) Heurlin
Cabin and Spring
Oil on canvas
1963
UA88-16-10

clinging to her thighs. Nola smiled her beatific smile, and I thought how her innocence both disarms and disturbs.

Remembering something I'd meant to ask her, I went back. "Will your life be easier ten years from now?"

"Oh, yes."

"How so?"

"Because I'll have everything that everyone wants you to have. I'll have everything."

On Mother's Day 1994, the Spear children and grandchildren gathered around their matriarch, Helen, enthroned in her favorite armchair. They told familiar stories and reminisced about many things, including Helen's famous temper. One time, apparently, when Bob got together with his buddies to train bear dogs, they tried to dredge up an alley cat for bait. Failing that, Helen said, "Bob got the bright idea he was gonna use one of the kids' cats." The dogs treed the pet right outside Helen's kitchen window. Then the men began circling the tree trunk, laughing up at the mewling cat. Incensed, Helen grabbed her broom and ran outside, lighting into her husband's head and shoulders. Laughing even harder than before, Bob brushed her off like a mosquito.

Another time, Helen threw a spoon at Nola, who was ten years old at the time. She was aiming for her daughter's leg but missed. The spoon struck a sliding glass door and stuck there, leaving it intact except for a spider's web of cracks. When Bob arrived he laughed at his chastened wife, then yanked out the spoon. The glass door shattered.

An undercurrent of protectiveness, warmth and respect—even worship—runs through these stories. Hearing them retold yet again for my benefit, I recognized somehow that Helen at her worst was also Helen at her best: uncowed by Bob's displays of machismo, protective toward the family pet, quick to anger, quicker to laugh at herself.

The Mother's Day get-together in 1994 was made poignant by the events of two months earlier. On an evening in March, shortly after supper, Bob complained of chest pain. He tossed and turned all night. His daughter Penny stopped by the next morning and found her father on the floor, gripping the rungs of his chair with knuckles gone white. "Dad, are you hurting that bad?" she asked.

At the clinic in Tok, a medical technician registered Bob's pallor, blue-tinged lips, and other symptoms of heart trouble. A chartered plane flew him to the hospital in Anchorage. On the way, Bob rallied enough to enjoy his first plane ride, and to walk unassisted into the hospital. Meanwhile, Helen drove straight through, arriving in Anchorage around two o'clock Sunday morning.

"When I got to the ICU," she said, "he was sitting up in bed, wide awake. He spent all the next day sitting up and talking a blue streak."

After bypass surgery on Monday, Bob's surgeon conveyed good news to Helen: his chances of survival were good. She was with him when he woke up in the recovery room, fuzzy-headed but curious about what was happening. Helen told him what the surgeon had said.

"Well, I guess I'll have to stop smoking for a while," he told her, ruefully.

That night, Bob's heart rebelled against medical technology. Weakened by several attacks in quick succession, he died with his wife and three of his children at his side.

Helen's memory of the next week is hazy. She returned to Slana, filled out paperwork to cover Bob's medical expenses, and arranged for his hunting buddies to spread his ashes over Indian Pass. The following weekend, sixty people attended a memorial service at the Slana School. There, a preacher spoke briefly, then invited the guests to share their memories of Bob. Ten people stood up, including a child who said, simply, "I remember Bob teaching me how to plant."

A few weeks later, Helen sent word to me and Charles in a letter. We drove to Slana the next weekend, bringing potted lilies to plant in his memory. The house was quiet and dim, the curtains drawn against the spring sun, the TV silent. Bob touched so many lives, Helen told us. Fifty-one condolence cards.

"What are you going to do now?" I asked.

Well, she sighed. She'd thought of moving back to Washington to be near her aging mother. But she'd decided against it. Her children and grandchildren need her even more. And there's no point in running away from grief, she said. Besides, if heaven is all it's cracked up to be, Bob's up there gardening away. She owes it to him to finish what he started on earth.

"That's how I feel about the tomato plants," she said. "Bob'll come along and whop me in the head if anything happens to them. I have to be here for the tomatoes."

Sue Anderson
Creation Myth
Gelatin silver photograph with
photomontage and selenium toning
1978
UAP84:030:001

OUT-TAKES

Gretchen Legler

WHEN I WAS still newly arrived in Alaska, I tried to memorize the map of the state, holding my right hand up, its back to my face with all my fingers bent under, knuckles showing, the thumb straight out and down to roughly stand for the shape of the state. Anchorage—I would point to where my thumb curved into my wrist. Prudhoe Bay was on the other side of the back of my hand, and then along the edge working down to my left, Barrow, Kotzebue, Nome, Bethel; in between Nome and Dillingham was the Yukon-Kuskokwim Delta. The length of my thumb was the Alaska Peninsula and the Aleutian Chain, which stretched and curved toward another immense and faraway continent. Coming up the other side of my thumb was Kodiak, then the Kenai Peninsula. Down along my wrist was southeast—Haines, Skagway, Juneau, Sitka, and Ketchikan. I practiced it whenever I could; tucked my fingers under and spread them wide so the tissue between them whitened with the strain, and I started from the top. Right in the weathered middle of my hand, where the blue veins and scars showed through most clear, was Fairbanks, and running north from it the road to the Arctic Ocean; not far beyond that, the North Pole. I'd sketch more imaginary lines across the freckled back of my hand, indicating the great peaks, volcanoes, and mountain ranges of the Interior, which I knew vaguely from seeing them on maps, from hearing about them and from reading about them in books—the Brooks Range, the Talkeetnas, the Chugach, the Wrangells, Denali, Iliamna—and the rivers, which I knew acted as the great highways of the wild inside the state—the Noatak, the Yukon, the Kuskokwim, Kobuk, Tanana, the Copper, the Koyukuk, Susitna, Chulitna, Tokasitna. Another broad sweep and I'd cover what I'd come to learn was called "the Bush"—everything else that was out there.

By mapping the land onto my body in this way I felt I was impressing the landscape onto my self, that it would soak through me, like ink soaking deep into the grains of thick paper, and this would be the way I would find my place in a new land, a new land in which, already, I felt oddly afraid.

Like all travelers in a new landscape, I felt fundamentally divided, my material body clearly in this new place, my spirit from whence I came. When would my self become whole here? How would I make sense of it? How would this faraway place unveil itself to me, and I to it? And would I, as this place sank into me, as we became a part of each other, would I change to meet it, and how? Now north and so far west that I was almost east, would I drift away from my family and friends? Would they even be able to *find* me? Alaska, I realized only after coming here, isn't even correctly placed on most maps—instead it is tucked away in a corner, drawn to look as small as Arizona, a fraction of its true size.

Landscapes are zones of tension, sites of contact between people and the seen and unseen rest of the living world. They are the places where we work through the most pressing concerns of our lives. They are the font, the well for the stories we tell. Landscapes are where we negotiate for meaning. And in this new landscape I felt lost. How had I gotten here? I asked myself, hardly recalling the eight-day drive from Minnesota, the miles having been erased somehow from memory.

What was it to be in this enigmatic space on the globe, this Alaska, I wondered at the beginning and over and over again as my first months went by. What was it like to live in this place that still embodied so many myths of purity and wilderness and self-sufficiency? Alaska was the edge of civilization still, pushing out into the fierce wild, a place where a new friend told me about a neighbor of hers who heard a moose calf scream in the middle of a not-so-long-ago winter night and in the morning went to investigate, reading the unmistakable story in the snow of a grizzly bear's kill—a deep crater of red in the snow, the packed white, the enormous tracks—all within easy hearing distance of suburban Anchorage, of school buses and mailboxes. I had never before been in a place where what was truly wild was so close at hand; where what was truly wild dwelt so near my ordinary life.

My first summer in Alaska, in a house on a big ocean bay, where a woman I had newly met had taken me to meet her friends, I looked through a telescope out onto the water where there were big rocks that were quickly being overtaken by the rising tide. What I could see through the telescope, what was miles off, was so radiantly clear, so intimate. I saw a seal, the first seal I had ever seen, spotted, whiskered and big-eyed, lounging on top of a rock until the very last moment. Finally, as the water nipped at its lazy flippers and tail, it glided off into the ocean. I kept looking, turning the long lens to the right and left on the tripod. Through the lens, I saw otters, which I had also never seen before, cruising by on their backs, their feet crossed, as if they were relaxing on a sofa in someone's living room. And then suddenly the light of the lens turned black, then shifted colors— blue, black, brown, white. The lens was full of movement, shooting out of the sky into the telescope and up the long tube, headed for my widened eye. I stepped back and blinked, then looked again. It was a bald eagle, flown off now in another direction. I was so confused and amazed that my eyes filled with tears. I wasn't sad at all. I was overwhelmed. I had never seen an eagle in quite that way before. In fact, I'd seen only as many eagles in my entire life as I could count on two hands, most of them at great distances along the bluffs above the Mississippi River near downtown Saint Paul. I felt weirdly sure that if I had watched this eagle one moment longer, it would have met my face in a flurry of wing and broken glass.

My friend touched her hand to the middle of my back to comfort me. Her touch brought me back, out of the miracle of the telescope, into the room where we then sat to eat. Her hands were hands that knew this place. They had pulled halibut and salmon from the sea in cold, rough nets, one entire summer; built a cabin overlooking the ocean; they were small strong hands that she held in front of her face now, together; she touched them to her bowed forehead and then put her napkin in her lap, and throughout the meal I felt where she'd touched me.

It was that first summer, too, that I caught a spawning salmon in my hands. It was cool and slippery, red and green, and barely alive. When I set it down in the water again, it kept itself upright but still, over the red pile of eggs it had dropped into the gravelly stream moments before my coming. I saw clearly that it was dying. All around it were its ugly dying friends; all the way from the mouth of the stream where it entered the bay at Seldovia, where the freshwater mixed with the water of the ocean, to this place, five hundred yards upstream, there were fish falling apart, tipping onto their sides, their fins ragged, their snouts hooked and menacing, their backs humped like monsters. There were gulls everywhere, pulling the dead fish apart, eating their fill; half-eaten fish carcasses littered the banks. I had never seen fish like this before; never seen birds act like this before.

Once I had seen spawning rainbows filling a stream in central Utah, and my brothers and sister and I had stepped into their midst and touched them, cradled them in our hands and then let them go. But that was nothing like this scene of noise and stench. Nothing. The next day I tried to fish for the salmon with a fly rod and every big colorful fly I had in my fly box, casting in front of them, on top of them, but they ignored me. I had heard that you can't get a spawning salmon to eat anything, but you can get them to strike in annoyance. As I fished I listened to a conversation on the bridge above me. Someone visiting Alaska from North Carolina, who, like me, had also never seen salmon spawning, was being educated by a local man who had just ridden up on his bicycle. "They come back from years away at sea to the place where they were born," he said. "Who knows how they know their way." Later a friend would tell me, "It's as if they come back home to a place they never really knew."

Another day in that same first summer, I walked alone around Kasitsna Bay, a secluded bay across from Homer, on the other side of Kachemak Bay. My destination was McDonald Spit. The spit reached out into the ocean, just a thin strip of land with a few trees, separating tiny Kasitsna Bay from the bigger water. And behind the spit, far away but seeming nearby, were three huge volcanoes—Augustine, Iliamna, and Redoubt—that at night turned black, backed by the setting orange sun.

Charles Janda

Composite Island, 1968

Gelatin silver photograph,

selenium toned

1968

UAP84:117:001

I walked from the marine laboratory where I was staying over to the spit, expressly with the idea of finding sand dollars. The tide wasn't low enough for me to pick my own, but some fishermen pointed out a pile of them, already collected and neglected by children who lived on the spit year 'round. "Take some," they urged me. "They don't mean much to those kids. Those kids see sand dollars every day of their lives."

On the way back along the shore, I ran across a brown and white rabbit, with mottled, thick fur and two long ears hanging down, sitting near a tuft of long, flat-bladed sea grass at the edge of the beach. I was startled at first to see a rabbit there on the other side of the bay from Homer, but was told by the caretaker that rabbits had been introduced there, found it to their liking, and had multiplied, so that now there were brown ones and black ones and white ones hopping all over the place, scuttling under the boardwalks, sitting by the sea grass, sunning themselves beside the equipment sheds.

The grass this rabbit was eating was about a foot high, and the rabbit was chewing rhythmically, shortening the grass stalk by the inch. As I watched, the grass disappeared into the rabbit's mouth and the rabbit moved slightly to its left and began anew on a fresh stalk. The rabbit ignored me. I was fascinated by its confidence and its lack of fear. Its brown eyes nearly reflected me in their brightness. It was placed here and was not really meant to be here, but it made this place its home.

Toward the end of that first summer, I took a job as a deckhand on a small charter boat. I was amazed at my good fortune, having met the captain earlier in the summer on a salmon fishing trip. She had been the first to welcome me to this state. "Welcome to Alaska," she'd said, opening her big arms wide and holding me close and tight. And then she asked me if I'd like to be her deckhand. I looked forward from the start to the physicalness of it, to the smell and feel of fish, to sun, to saltwater, to wind. In fact, I imagined a whole life of it—being a teacher for nine months of the year, a fisherwoman, a boatwoman for the rest. I would put my sweat into it and have Alaska, this new place, written onto my body in the best way.

I learned fast on the boat that this was no easy job, no job for anyone who thought slow or moved slow or took directions slow. And whatever the captain said, went. There were reasons for everything, but they weren't for me to know.

There was a reason, for instance, that the captain insisted one day on my restacking the halibut white-side-up, dark-side-down in the fish box. More of a reason than that she said so, although that was what counted most. The reason, I learned later, was so that the blood would drain down into the dark side of the fish, leaving the white side dense and pale.

We had just hauled up the last halibut, thick and heavy like a kite pulled against the wind, and on deck I had worked ineffectually for several minutes trying to bash it to death. I was beating a body nearly as large as mine—as big a fish as I had ever laid hands on. Blood spattered out onto the deck, onto my rubber boots, into my face. The deck was slick with fish slime. The captain, impatient, threw open the cabin door, flew out, took the metal baton out of my hand, and with one swift, hard hit the fish was still. I put the halibut in the box and listened to it come alive again and then slowly thump itself into quietness.

I had never fished like this before. I had fished for trout—lithe, silver fish that would fit, head and tail attached, into a large frying pan. I had fished for walleye and northerns, bluegills, perch and crappies. I hooked a sturgeon once, caught some bass. There wasn't enough blood in any of those fish to fill a teacup. But these halibut, so large they needed to be gaffed and hauled over the side of the boat, they wrestled and bled.

After I restacked the fish, the captain came out of the cabin again to check my work and teased me. "You got blood on your rain suit," she said.

She said she loved to harpoon them—"'poon 'em," she said—and I saw how excited she got for the first big fish that day. She readied the gleaming sharp point, tied the rope to the boat cleat, raised the wooden pole ready. The woman reeling up the fish was having a hard time. She called the fish a "son-of-a-bitch" and someone else yelled out "sucker." The captain took off her jacket and rolled up her sleeves, turned her baseball hat backwards. The woman lost the fish, then, just as we could see it through the thick green, just as the captain was about to slam the harpoon home.

In the afternoon, when things were a little slow, someone on board entertained the rest of us by eating a herring, like a person in a circus swallowing a sword, except she didn't really eat it, she just turned one side to us and slowly acted as if she were stuffing it down her throat. I could see the herring's eye come out on the other side of the woman's head.

Dockside, at the end of the day, the captain gave more instructions in how to wash the fish and how to pose it, white-side-out, so everything looked nice, as if nothing bad happened there, as if nothing had died and there was no blood shed, as if fishing were the clean and fun sunny afternoon sort of thing I was used to, not a thing full of harpoons and sometimes, I learned, even pistols when the fish were truly big.

Later she'd help fillet the fish, peeling away the great white slabs of flesh, tossing guts to the gulls. Her hands, despite the ropes, the saltwater, cuts from bait knives, and the crease of fishing line, were soft and tan—the kind of hands you'd want touching your forehead, checking for fever, smoothing your hair.

It was fall and a new friend and I were sitting on the beach at Homer as the tide was coming in. We let the water creep as close as it would, pulling our feet up to stay out of its way. In the cool sun, she told me a story about when she'd come to Alaska, a story about a hawk, a story that made her cry.

She was young when she first came to Alaska. She was living with a couple in a remote cabin in the Chugach Mountains. There was a hawk that kept getting at the chickens. One day the woman who owned the cabin with her boyfriend finally caught the bird—stoned it first and then threw a net over it. The woman decided rather than wring its neck, she would drown it, so that the bird could be stuffed as a fine gift for her lover. My friend marched along with the woman to the water barrel.

She told me how the hawk fought under the woman's hands to live, and then, right there on the beach with me, my friend started to cry. She'd never told anyone that story, she said. She was embarrassed by it and disgusted with herself for going along with it, for letting the woman drown that beautiful bird. I touched her hair, pulling it back from her face, tucking it behind her ears, and she leaned her head into my shoulder. I was comforting *her*, who'd been here longer than I. Already, I, who was so newly come, was listening to someone else's story about this place.

It was late fall and my neighbor had been talking about the Alaskan moon to strangers on the Internet. He wrote, "Hey, has anyone seen the moon tonight?" Computer users far and wide responded. "Wait, I'll go look," someone wrote, and rose from a computer screen in New Jersey and looked out to see and wrote back, "Beautiful."

Not long after, I was walking with my students back from the coffee stand across the parking lot from our classroom during a break in class at the University of Alaska in Anchorage. We had gloves on and mittens and coats just for the short walk. Our breath was steaming; the coffee was steaming. Outside the science building we saw two telescopes set up with their platter-sized lenses facing what I had earlier, on the walk to get coffee, not even seen—the moon, full, or nearly so.

There were two bearded men in parkas with clipboards fiddling with dials and jotting down numbers, and I asked if we could look at the moon, and they said, "Sure, why not." I put my eye to the most obvious lens and saw only black. "No," one of the men said, "look here." I moved to another lens and peered into the telescope, disoriented. How could I see outward and upward if I was looking downward? But of course, my eye was directed by the mirrors and configurations of the telescope toward the amazing light above me.

At first I didn't understand what I was seeing. The lens was blocked by blue-white light. I pulled my eye back, then started again and saw more clearly. It was the moon; the moon, with its enormous craters and seas. The moon, rising over the library, rising over the heating plant, over the moose calves and grizzly bear, over the mountains, over the trees, over the sleepy deep-water halibut and whiskered seals, over the eagles and whales and rabbits and otters, over the roads and streams, over me and over the entire state, all that vast wild country I had first mapped on the back of my hand.

The same moon that shone over New Jersey, over Seattle, over Santa Fe, over

Virginia K. (Kathy) Marchlinski
Bright Night
Oil on paper
Undated
UA88-13-15

Minnesota, shone over me as I stood there. It linked me to those familiar places, this moon, with its surface of mottled gray and deeper gray blue. I reached for that comfort, the comfort that Alaska was only an extension of that other, more known, more understood, more civilized world. But it was thin comfort. I shivered, then stepped aside so someone else could see.

James Kuiper

Untitled painting

Oil and alkyd on canvas

UA84-3-143

A PIECE OF
THE BROOKS RANGE

Carolyn Kremers

ROB AND I go back a long ways. Occasionally I wonder whether we will just drift apart someday, like ice on a river. Somehow, though, I don't think so. Not everyone gets to pick up the pieces after a really bad thing happens, let alone try to fit those pieces into a new configuration. Maybe that's what we will always be doing—I don't know. I'm just glad that I understand both of us better now.

Rob is a doctor. He leads what I consider a charmed life. He rents a modest apartment in Atlanta, Georgia, and works as an epidemiologist for the U.S. Centers for Disease Control. For the past three years, however, he has spent much of his time in Bolivia, directing cholera research projects of his own design, making friends with the Indian people of the high altiplano, listening to Andean folk music in village squares and local cafés, and exploring the rain forests of the Amazon River.

What Rob loves best about his work are the Bolivian people. I could see this in his gray-blue eyes, as he showed me his photos last summer at the round table in my cabin in Fairbanks, the morning before I took him to the airport to fly back to Atlanta. He says that Bolivian faces remind him of the Yup'ik Eskimos in the Yukon-Kuskokwim Delta. Glancing between the photos and his eyes, I could understand. That is what I love most about the Delta, too: the people.

Another charmed part of Rob's life, in my view, is the fact that he gets paid to fly every year from Atlanta to Alaska to work for two weeks in the hospital in Bethel. This is one way the federal government encourages talented clinical doctors, hired to do research, to continue to work in public health. Rob could work for two weeks at any public hospital in the United States, but he always chooses Bethel. This is because he lived there from 1986 to 1990, serving as medical director of the Yukon-Kuskokwim Health Corporation, and like so many other *kass'aq*s and me, he fell in love.

Rob's annual hospital stint, and my invitation, are what have spurred him to join me on my fourth trip to the Brooks Range. For not much money, he can tack on a round-trip flight, Anchorage to Fairbanks, at the end of his Bethel stay. This is good, because it can be expensive to get up north—from outside or inside Alaska.

I live in a small log cabin on the northwest side of Chena Ridge, seven miles west of Fairbanks. Rob and I led parallel lives until we were both forty, but neither of us knew it. We grew up in adjoining neighborhoods in South Denver, went to neighboring high schools, and majored in English at the same university in California. We both graduated in 1973, began working in jobs related to social change, and, thirteen years later, found ourselves three thousand miles north in Alaska, living in the Y-K Delta. Still, we had not met. Later we both left the Delta, and we might never have met if Rob's best friend from medical school, Davida, had not flown to Alaska in the summer of 1991 to raft the Copper River. I had been invited to accompany the trip and to write about then-governor Walter Hickel's illegal Copper River highway. As the group rafted and camped together, Davida and I became friends, and she began to realize that Rob and I had parallel lives. She decided to introduce us by mail. But that is another story.

The Brooks Range. It, too, seems charmed. For me, the name conjures a hundred bell-like sounds, silver tinkling sounds like the ones made by a wand drawn down the length of a Chinese bell tree. The sounds sparkle, slip through cracks, and break down barriers between reality, imagination, and the spaces between that humans call magic or the spirit world.

I like to think that Bob Marshall heard similar sounds. Born in 1901 in New York

City, he spent childhood summers in the Adirondack Mountains and later completed a master's degree in forestry and a doctorate in plant physiology. In his late twenties, he made the first of what would become four trips into the central Brooks Range, exploring twelve thousand square miles that had never been mapped and climbing twenty-eight major peaks. Like many white explorers, Marshall wanted to quantify, conquer, and name. What he discovered, however, involved more. Until his death of a heart attack at thirty-eight, Bob Marshall strongly advocated wilderness preservation. He helped Aldo Leopold found The Wilderness Society, and his relationship to the Brooks Range has been compared with that of Henry David Thoreau to Maine and of John Muir to the Sierra Nevada.

I expect that Bob Marshall would agree: to go to the Brooks Range—even if only once a year—is to encounter God.

The Brooks Range stretches east and west seven hundred miles, linking Canada's northwest Yukon Territory with the edge of the Chukchi Sea. This huge chain is the northernmost major mountain range in the world. Getting there is a challenge, even from Fairbanks, which is close by Alaska standards.

The cheapest way to reach the Brooks Range is to drive. One heads north out of Fairbanks on the Steese Highway and keeps driving north on the Eliot Highway to the Dalton Highway and on up to Coldfoot and the Arctic Circle. The route is not a highway, but a well-kept two-lane gravel road—nicknamed "the Haul Road"—used mainly by red Alyeska trucks. These trucks supply and maintain the Trans-Alaska Pipeline, which carries oil from Prudhoe Bay eight hundred miles south to Valdez.

After rattling four or five hours north on this gravel road, one enters the Endicott Mountains, the major chain in the central Brooks. Jagged and multicolored—gray, white, brown, pink, yellow—these peaks thrust up from the earth's crust at odd angles. About 225 miles north of Fairbanks, the Haul Road reaches the Dietrich River, which marks the rugged eastern boundary of Gates of the Arctic National Park. This is the only part of the park near a road, but the area is difficult to enter. Unless the Dietrich River is frozen, it is treacherous to cross on foot, and in times of high water—at breakup, after rainstorms, or on warm sunny days—it is impassable. The Haul Road parallels the Dietrich for about fifteen miles, then leaves the valley and climbs 4,800 feet to the top of Atigun Pass and the Continental Divide. At last, its thin gravel strip descends into the Arctic coastal plain.

This drive up Atigun Pass I have made twice.

An even more spectacular—and daunting—way to reach the Brooks Range is to fly in. I first did this in August 1991 with my friends Rick and Susan. We flew in a fifteen-seat Beechcraft 99 from Fairbanks north to Bettles, a village of about fifty-five Koyukon Athabaskan and non-Native people. From Bettles, we flew north in a floatplane and were dropped on a small lake in Gates of the Arctic. We hiked from the lake up into the Arrigetch Peaks and over two mountain passes to Walker Lake, backpacking for six days.

Choosing an area to visit in the Brooks Range can be as challenging as bushwhacking through an alder thicket. There are many trunks and branches, and each section promises difficulty and surprise. For the trip with Rob, I have again chosen Gates of the Arctic.

Not much written information is available about visiting "the Gates." This I know from the trip with Rick and Susan, so I pick up the telephone and begin gathering oral history.

The ranger I reach in Bettles is reticent to recommend any particular route. He tells me that he is not a backpacker and that he has mostly floated in the park, meaning rafted or canoed. Understandably, he is unwilling to share any information about wolf packs and where they might be seen, saying only that wolves may be found in any portion of the park but are most easily seen "in open country"—along river bars or on high alpine tundra. He also tells me not to expect many caribou in July, since they migrate through the park in August and September.

"Doonerak is a hard mountain," he says, when I ask about this 7,457-foot peak, which Bob Marshall called the "Matterhorn of the Koyukuk" and which he thought was the tallest peak in the Brooks Range. Roger Siglin, a former superintendent of Gates of the Arctic, has told me about his own climb up Doonerak, and I know that the first recognized successful climb was in 1952.

"Lots of willow and alder patches up Bombardment Creek," says the ranger. "And, yes, it's a technical climb at the top. Steep, loose rock. You'd need ropes and pitons."

We talk about other areas that I have studied on maps, and the ranger reminds me, "Any place with a wide valley is going to be pretty tussocky." The area east of Anaktuvuk Pass around Summit Lake, though, he admits, "is beautiful country."

I telephone two pilots in Bettles—one with Brooks Range Aviation and the other with Bettles Lodge—and they concur. Summit Lake is beautiful country. Both are eager to describe additional drop-in and pickup places, however, where they have flown backpackers before, on guided trips. They fill my head with names of rivers, passes, and lakes—scattered across the 7.2-million-acre park— and they inspire me to buy eight more topographical maps. At home, I spread all of the maps—eleven now—over my cabin floor, sofa, and table. Pondering possible routes along waterways and over mountain passes, I note elevation gains and losses, and search for clues of steep deadends, rude alders, mud bogs, and tussocks.

Topo maps are a challenge and an art to read. My skills have improved, though, over the last nine years, and now I know better than to believe everything I see. The absence of green does not mean the absence of willow or alder thickets, and a traffic jam of zigzagging brown parallel lines does not necessarily mean that a steep slope is unclimbable, up or down. Most important, "creek" does not mean wadeable, and "river" usually means braids.

I think and dream for days, while continuing to teach my world literature class at the university and to work part-time as a data-entry clerk in the basement of the university museum. I am glad that I chose to become a writer and a teacher, but, unlike Rob, I am not paid well for my work. I earn just enough to cover my small bills and am not able to set aside money for savings. Rob, on the other hand, makes donations each month to nonprofit organizations, sharing his wealth and lowering his tax bracket. He can afford to do many of the things he wants most. Is this another reason that, to me, his life seems charmed?

In free moments, I crouch over the maps on the cabin floor, and at night I lie on one elbow in bed in the loft and read John M. Kauffmann's book *Alaska's*

Brooks Range: The Ultimate Mountains. I decide to stick with my original plan: something in the area around Anaktuvuk Pass.

Anaktuvuk Pass. Its name, its history, and its photographs (which I have seen in books and magazines) have intrigued me ever since I moved to Alaska. It is a village in the northeast portion of the park and home to about 365 Nunamiut Eskimos. The Nunamiut, an inland people whose seminomadic ancestors in Alaska date back to 500 B.C., settled permanently at Anaktuvuk Pass in the early 1950s. This area is part of a major caribou migration route. Today, as a result of ANCSA, the Alaska Native Claims Settlement Act, the Nunamiut hold title to about 175,000 acres in the northeast region of Gates of the Arctic.

Because I lived for three years among the Yup'ik Eskimos in the Yukon-Kuskokwim Delta, the most subsistence-based population in Alaska, I am curious to learn more about these Inupiat Eskimos in the Interior. I want to spend some time in their part of the Brooks Range. I know that I will learn more about myself and my own ancient connections with the natural world. Perhaps I will also learn more about my connections with Rob.

I call up a friend's friend named Patty, who works as a ranger in the Gates of the Arctic National Park office in Fairbanks. Patty says that she will be happy to meet with me, and we make an appointment. A few days later I drive to the glass building downtown, near the Chena River, and spread out the maps again, this time on a long rectangular table. I have decided on the area between Summit Lake, west of Anaktuvuk Pass, and Chimney Lake, to the south.

Talking by phone with the two pilots in Bettles, I have learned that Chimney Lake is not an easy pickup place. It fills most of the strip of tundra that tops 2,400-foot Chimney Pass. This pass is sandwiched between Whiteface Mountain (almost six thousand feet) and Chimney Mountain (more than four thousand feet). One pilot says that it is easier to drop off people at Chimney Lake than to pick them up. If the winds are calm and the day is hot, it can be difficult to get enough lift in a Cessna 185 fully loaded with a pilot, two passengers, and two backpacks. It seems best to be dropped at Chimney Lake and to be picked up twenty-five miles north, at Summit Lake in the Oolah Valley.

Patty has not backpacked between these two lakes herself, but she knows a few rangers and others who have. Park employees fly in with a park pilot, but private individuals must charter a plane. Patty does not know of any pilots in Anaktuvuk who fly commercially, so Rob and I will not be able to fly there and then south. We'll have to fly to Bettles.

Studying the maps, Patty and I discuss several routes over the mountains that separate the Clear River from the north fork of the Koyukuk. We conclude that Saint Patrick's Creek looks like the best way to get from one major river valley to the other.

"The views of Mount Doonerak should be spectacular," Patty says. "If the weather is clear."

I promise to report back with my opinions of the route and to show her our photographs when we return. Now it is time to make plane reservations and to call Rob in Atlanta, to make sure that he still wants to pay for the tickets. The commercial flight from Fairbanks to Bettles with Frontier Flying Service will be $212 each. The charter flight from Bettles to Chimney Lake with Brooks Range Aviation will be $358, and the charter from Summit Lake back to Bettles will be $495. That comes to $638.50 each, total flight costs.

The deal was that Rob would buy the plane tickets if I planned the trip and bought the maps and food. This was his idea, and it seemed simple enough—and more than advantageous—to me. I have never backpacked with Rob, but four and a half years ago when we thought we knew each other better and were trying to find a way to live together in the same town, we went back-country skiing and telemarking several times. That was when I learned that Rob's stamina is at least equal to mine. I also know that he has a fair amount of Alaskan wilderness experience—river-rafting, canoeing, and backpacking with his former wife—and that he can read topo maps. Between the two of us, we should be able to find the route. This is my biggest concern. I don't want to get us lost or into something we can't handle.

According to the topo maps, there will be only four major water crossings: the Clear River, Saint Patrick's Creek, Amawk Creek, and Alinement Creek. There are several other unnamed, solid blue lines on the map, which we will need to cross, and numerous dotted blue lines to cross, too. But our biggest challenges will probably be the river and the three named creeks, depending on the weather. If it rains a lot, water levels may be high. If the sky is clear, or overcast but not raining, the crossings may be easier. We will see.

This is one of my favorite aspects of wilderness travel in Alaska: the "we will see" factor. It is much higher than in Colorado, where Rob and I grew up and where I first learned how to survive in the outdoors. I backpacked in Colorado as a teenager and an adult, but this was usually on established trails. The few times that route-finding was involved, there were no major river crossings and few wild animals. The route was always a loop, starting and stopping at the same place, and a car or truck would be waiting dutifully for me at the end, to be driven away on a road. Summer weather in Colorado could be as unpredictable and deadly as in Alaska, but clouds rarely socked in for days, and sunburn and thin air were more common than wet feet and alder scratches. The biggest summer threat to humans in the Colorado Rockies was lightning strikes. The thunderstorms that brought these, however, usually rolled out as quickly as they rolled in. Best of all, Colorado had few mosquitoes.

In Alaska, nature occurs on a larger scale. Distances are greater, people are few, animals are more diverse and occur in greater numbers, and waterways are wider, deeper. Rain is more, mosquitoes are more, and help can be unlikely and far away. I cannot say that the rewards of wilderness travel in Alaska are greater than in Colorado because, to me, they are not. They are just different. Certainly, the "we will see" factor is part of that difference.

"We'll see," I say, when at last Rob is sitting on the sofa in my cabin, not too close to me, and we are scrutinizing the maps, learning how to relax again with each other. We've been discussing how many days may be needed to reach Summit Lake. "It depends on the tussocks and the weather, and how long it takes us to cross all the creeks, and whether the route is as direct as it looks on the map."

"And what we find to look at along the way," Rob adds. "I'd love to see a grizzly or a wolf. And catch some fish."

"Well, I've got my backpacking rod and a fishing license," I say. "So, we'll see."

When I read back over my trip journal—the little blue four-by-six-inch spiral notebook carried in the top pocket of my fifty-eight-pound pack for eight days—I am struck by how little those forty pages, covered in small handwriting front and back, can capture. It is almost as little as the two hundred color photographs that Rob and I took with my three-pound Nikon camera. The journal and the photos capture many things, but not enough. Often, they do not show the dangerous or the difficult and confusing things. Or the revelations. What they do well is jog the memory, so that when I read my notes or look at the pictures, a flood of sensations comes back. This is the magic of journals and photos, and one of the reasons that I think they are always worth the hour of writing each night; the extra weight of film, camera, and notebook; and the cost of the film and its development. What they leave out, though, is also important. Perhaps that is why, when a trip has ended, I remember certain moments—like mountain pools—and I try to look more deeply in and dive down.

It's safe and fun to start with colors. The emerald ponds and grasses dotting the ground as we fly north of Bettles into the mountains; the silty gray braids and tan gravel bars of the north fork of the Koyukuk, meandering south to join the Yukon River and the Bering Sea; the brilliant green tundra slopes right next to our wingtips, as we drop into the bowl of Chimney Pass, tilt, and circle before landing; the two brown ducks on the lake and the white wavelets, as we motor, then glide on the plane's floats into cattails, looking for a place in the mud to hop down.

After the pilot has handed us our two red canisters of bear spray and four Coleman fuel bottles—three silver, one red—from the cubbyholes inside the aluminum floats, and after we have hoisted our packs to dry ground, he calls, "Good luck!" and motors back out to the center of the lake to lift off. What is the color of silence, when the blue and white dot that is the plane disappears beyond the rust-colored monolith topping Chimney Mountain?

It isn't silent, though. The whine of mosquitoes—several hundred mosquitoes—assaults our ears as Rob and I search quickly for our headnets and Deet. Then we are looking at the fuzzy ball of the sun in the overcast sky, noting its angle, and glancing at the face of my black plastic watch, five o'clock, and studying the first of our six maps, deciding which way to go. The approach by air has helped. We cannot see beyond the bowl we are in, but we know that not far to the east, just over the horizon, is a pond with a bull moose feeding in it, and beyond that, miles of tussocks that drop to the Clear River valley floor.

We set out, Rob in the lead.

No people. No car, plane, or boat noise, just wilderness. And signs of animals: huge moose tracks; smaller caribou tracks; droppings from ptarmigan, caribou, moose, bears; and numerous animal trails. We follow one that skirts the pond, take distant pictures of the moose—velvety brown against brilliant green, elegant, wary, king-like—and continue through bogs, tussocks, creeklets, and willow patches. Whenever possible we walk on the dry, yellow-white "reindeer" lichen.

After about two hours the rocky face of a very tall mountain looms out of the clouds, to the northwest. We take the map out of its Ziploc bag and compare the rock formations and waterways around us with ovals and lines on the paper. Yes, that must be Doonerak—disappearing now, back into clouds. We will be walking right past it in a few days, provided we can identify the large drainage that is Saint Patrick's Creek and can cross the Clear River.

Will Doonerak reveal his face again, then?

Up here, the latitude is about the same as at the Inupiat Eskimo village of Kivalina on the Chukchi Sea. We are about seventy-five miles north of the Arctic Circle. It stays light all night here in July, and there are zillions of mosquitoes. I have lived nine years in Alaska, but this is the first time that I have resorted to a headnet. Even on the Seward Peninsula, where I worked one summer on a construction crew north of Nome, the mosquitoes were not this thick. My new light-green headnet dangles over the cheap white visor cap that I received last year at the Fairbanks Equinox Marathon relay. I was tempted to give the visor away (I never wear visor caps!), but now it has come in handy.

After Rob and I have walked over tussocks for two more hours—not talking much, just drinking in these new dimensions of space and time—black clouds

Carolyn Kremers

284

Arthur William (Bill) Brody

Guardians of the Valley

Oil and alkyd on canvas

1993

UA93:024:001

roll down fast from the direction of Doonerak. A camping spot magically appears: fairly flat, padded with reindeer lichen, on a slight rise by a clear creeklet. We roll out the blue dome tent, set it up quickly, shove the packs inside, and dive in just as the rain pelts down. Water drums hard on the tent for more than an hour, accompanied by thunder and lightning. Against our etiquette regarding bears, we eat gorp inside: golden raisins, cashews, pecans, walnuts, sunflower seeds, M&Ms. I like the new blue ones. And the chocolate stars.

Around ten o'clock the rain quits, and we go outside to boil water for soup and rice. Mindful again of bears, we find a place a hundred yards from the tent and crouch down to cook dinner on the one-burner Coleman backpacking stove. This green stove has accompanied me to many places in Colorado and Alaska and is worth every ounce of its three pounds. Rob pumps the stove and touches his Bic lighter to the burner, producing a bright yellow flame. I think thanks for this flicker of warmth, harbinger of nourishment, and turn to measure water into pots.

When I glance up again, a space alien is tending the stove! He sits on the fluorescent reindeer lichen in a navy-blue windbreaker, his bulging triangular head silhouetted against an orange and black sky. Hundreds of tiny dark satellites whine and whir about his face.

It has been four years since Rob changed his mind about wanting me to move to Atlanta, four years since he chose Patti, then Linda, over me. Happy to be backpacking with him, at last—alien or not—I am laughing and laughing out loud.

Each of the next seven days will be different from this one, but partly the same. We will often be wrapped in rain: pelting rain, misting rain, threatening rain, cold rain. It will become difficult to remember how it is to live beyond the weather.

Except for soaked feet, I will be dry inside my fleece cap, neoprene rainjacket, and Gore-Tex pants, and Rob will be partly dry. He earns a good salary but spends little on himself, and is particularly proud of his prehistoric camping gear. He wears, for instance, a 1960s style orange plastic poncho instead of a rainjacket. The poncho rides up under his backpack shoulder-straps, and the long ends flap around his six-foot-three figure in the wind. When it rains hard enough, Rob switches to his navy-blue nylon windbreaker, which fits better than the poncho but is less water-repellent. His Colorado-style, all-leather hiking boots are threaded with thin tennis-shoe strings, and each of his wool socks has a hole or a near-hole in the heel and toe. He has not yet graduated from polypropylene long underwear to Capilene, which is softer against the skin and doesn't get so smelly (we laugh!). And he could use Capilene glove liners—I wish I had brought some for him—for his hands get cold first. He says he is grateful, however, that I convinced him over the phone to buy a nylon raincover for his pack. And I am relieved that he took my advice ("This is serious country," I said) and brought a new sleeping bag instead of his old one with the broken zipper.

Each day, we will set up or take down the tent in rain, and each night we will light the stove—often in strong wind—and gratefully warm our hands and hungry stomachs with one instant Nile soup between us, one and a half shared pouches of instant Lipton pasta or rice, cocoa with peppermint schnapps, ginger tea, and sometimes one macadamia nut cookie or one brownie. Then we will quickly wash the dishes near a stream, hang the food bag in a tree or bury it in rocks, stash the stove and dishes far from the tent, and filter two liters of water, for thirst in the night and milk in the morning. Sliding into our fiberfilled sleeping bags—Rob's royal blue, mine purple—we will write in our journals and read for awhile, the tent flapping or rain tapping on the igloolike tent, a creek singing, or everything quiet. Then, usually before Rob, I will close my book and slip into deep sleep.

There will not be many animals, but many signs: droppings, tracks, moose trails, and long narrow caribou trails—like highways, Rob says. Ground-squirrel holes have been torn up by grizzly bear claws, and large wolf tracks show in the mud by the Clear River. The water is nearly transparent, with just a trace of glacial silt. This is day 2, in the afternoon, and the river looks easily fordable. We waste no time scouting a crossing place and exchanging our boots for tennis shoes. Rob takes the upstream side and we hold elbows, our waist-belts and chest-belts unhooked. The middle of the channel is a little less than knee-deep for me, and there are only two braids to cross. The water rushes—cold!—but my thin Capilene liners and thick red-violet wool socks are pulled up high over my calves. This helps.

As with all major water crossings, I shout with joy and relief when we reach the other side.

"Piece o' cake!" Rob yells, too. "Maybe they'll all be this easy."

The air temperature is almost warm—mid-fifties—and a light wind discourages mosquitoes. As we head up the glacial moraine on the west side of Saint Patrick's Creek, leaving the Clear River valley below, Chimney Mountain is lost behind us. Ahead, we are greeted with a canvas of wildflowers: dark purple monkshood; fuschia dwarf fireweed, called river beauty; pink candlesticks known as whorled lousewort; and a few delicate, powder-yellow Alaska poppies. We stop to look more closely, and see the tiny pink bells of kinnikinnick, some poisonous purple-blue larkspur, and frigid arnica, dark yellow and daisylike.

"This is the Arctic!" Rob exclaims. "And look at this . . . flowers! The most gorgeous profusion of flowers. Some of my friends in Atlanta think there's nothing up here but snow. I've got to take some pictures."

He removes the camera from the top pocket of my pack and I smile, half wishing we shared more friends, half wondering who Rob's friends are. The flowers *are* gorgeous. And there will be more.

Purple, daisylike Siberian asters with yellow centers; blue and yellow alpine forget-me-nots, the Alaska state flower; glaucous gentians, which remind me of Colorado's red Indian paintbrush, but are blue-green; yellow paintbrush; white Alaska cotton; delicate "frigid" shooting stars; and the white stalks—one or two feet tall—of the alpine meadow bistort. Also pushing out of the soil are giant red mushrooms and white mushrooms, and red toadstools spattered with white dots. These toadstools are poisonous, I know, but I cannot remember their name. There are leathery, green bearberry leaves, blueberry bushes and wild currant bushes, and thousands of not-yet-ripe salmonberries. Such diverse and remote canvases. I think of them as handiwork—of an invisible God?

Here in the Brooks Range, the waterways and rock formations are so big that, if we just pay attention to where we have been and where we are going, it is not difficult to locate ourselves on the map. This is fun, bit by bit to put ourselves into the landscape—marking an X on the map every evening—instead of envisioning the topography from the safety of the cabin floor. Saint Patrick's Creek pours down a narrow canyon, steep walls on either side. Clear brooks spill down the walls, as do rockslides. Like Joseph's coat, the rocks are many-colored: green, pure white, red with white stripes, black, orange, metallic pink, metallic lavender. This is one of my favorite things about the Brooks Range: the kinds and colors of the rocks. I could look at rocks all day. I was like this as a child. I gathered rocks, then constructed boxes to keep them in. Rocks were easier to relate to than people.

We alternate between walking along the gravel bars and willows of the creek bottom and traversing the mossy tundra above—whichever seems easiest. Sometimes we are silent, and sometimes we talk about Bolivia, or teaching, or subtitles for my book, which Rob has read in manuscript and which will be published in the fall. Part of the book is about living in the Yukon-Kuskokwim Delta, and what I learned.

"I'm proud of you," Rob says. "You worked hard to write that book. And to get it published. I knew you could do it, though."

I didn't. Often, I wished I had someone close, to talk with about it. A few times, I talked with him.

This is one of our connections, Rob's and mine: our love of literature and of trying to write things down.

"I want to write a novel someday," Rob says, as he has said before. "I think I can do it. But there are other things I need to do in medicine, first."

I know that feeling. I want to write *now*, though. This is hard, much harder than I ever thought, this effort to write *now*. Especially living alone.

I want to talk with Rob about living alone: how it feels, when it's not what I wanted, at all. But I don't know how. I want to tell him the things that are hard and the things that are missed, living alone. How I wanted to share my life with someone who could understand it, who loves *the seeking* as much as I. But I am afraid. I know that Rob needs time—he has said so—to sort out what went wrong between Linda and him. But does he ever think anything, now, about what happened between him and me?

Like many things I want to ask, I don't.

When the creek curves east, toward the pass, we enter high alpine tundra, and rugged peaks move in and out of the clouds. The names on the map beg to be spoken. To the south and east: Midnight Mountain, Wien Mountain, Boreal Mountain, Whiteface Mountain. To the west and north: Amawk Mountain, Apoon Mountain, Twoprong Mountain, Inclined Mountain, Snowheel Mountain. And, of course, Doonerak. He remains hidden by clouds. His power is felt, however, whether he is visible or not. We know that we are walking just below his rugged face, as we head toward the pass that will drop us into the plain of the north fork of the Koyukuk.

In a collection of Bob Marshall's journals and letters, edited by his brother and published as *Arctic Wilderness* when Rob and I were five years old, Bob Marshall describes his experiences in a section called "Toward Doonerak." Like most wilderness travelers in this area, Marshall was drawn to Mount Doonerak. He described the mountain as a "towering, black, unscalable-looking giant." In a style common among white male explorers of his day, he wrote of his thoughts in 1938:

> For seven years I had been longing to return to the arctic Koyukuk. I had been thinking of the most glorious year of my life which I spent up there. I had been recalling thousands of square miles of wilderness scenery, large creeks and even rivers unvisited by man, deep canyons and hanging valleys glimpsed from a distance but never explored, great mountains which no human being has ever ascended. But most of all I had been thinking about Mount Doonerak. . . . The Brooks Range is one of the six major mountain systems in United States territory, but whereas the highest peaks in the Appalachian, Rocky, Sierra, Cascade, and Alaska mountain ranges have long since been climbed, no one is known to have ever been even part way up Mount Doonerak. Since I had discovered the mountain, had made the first map of it, and had named it during my trips in 1929 and 1930-31, I wanted to complete the job and also make the first ascent.

■ ■ ■

Bob Marshall did not succeed. In fact, he and his three companions nearly lost their lives on that trip in August and September of 1938, when their boat overturned in a flood on the north fork. This was on the west side of Doonerak, opposite where Rob and I stand now. At that time, little more than half a century ago, Marshall and his friends estimated that probably "no more than twelve white men had penetrated [this part of] the magnificent Koyukuk country."

Rob and I cannot see Doonerak now. But there will be other days.

At the top of the pass lie two lakes edged with lily pads. A wind has come up, and it is raining again. This is the highest elevation we will reach—3,900 feet—and the wind chill is bringing the temperature down to forty. We decide to pitch the tent beside a large boulder at the north end of the second lake. We hope the boulder will provide shelter from the wind. We pile stones around the stove, and, after several tries, Rob lights the burner with his magic Bic. I am reminded of other wilderness trips and stoves, and other partners. A pair of shrikes dive along the trail.

The next morning we begin to pick our way down the pass. Rob is a strong, dependable backpacking companion, and he is good-natured about the weather and the necessarily limited food. He likes to do things his way, but I am accustomed to that with men in the outdoors. I usually defer to my companion's decisions and try not to disagree, unless his choices frighten me or seem mistaken.

On this morning, slip-sliding downhill, I am afraid. The route that Rob has chosen seems terribly steep. We argue, not raising our voices, but each trying to make a case, and Rob suggests that I take whatever route I want and meet him at the bottom. Splitting up in such difficult terrain is not my idea of safety, however, and I tell him so. The argument intensifies. After a few minutes, Rob defers. We climb back up the slippery rocks hidden in moss, and choose another route: unstable scree, but less steep.

Eventually, we drop down into a creek nameless on the map, ford it in boots that have been wet since day 1, and climb back out in order to avoid getting trapped in the steep canyon (revealed by the map) further down. Above the creek again, this time on the other side, we follow caribou trails dotted with bear scat— and once with wolf scat—down a smooth long slope, half a mile to Amawk Creek. What other spirits have walked this perfect hillside, I wonder, besides bears and wolves and us?

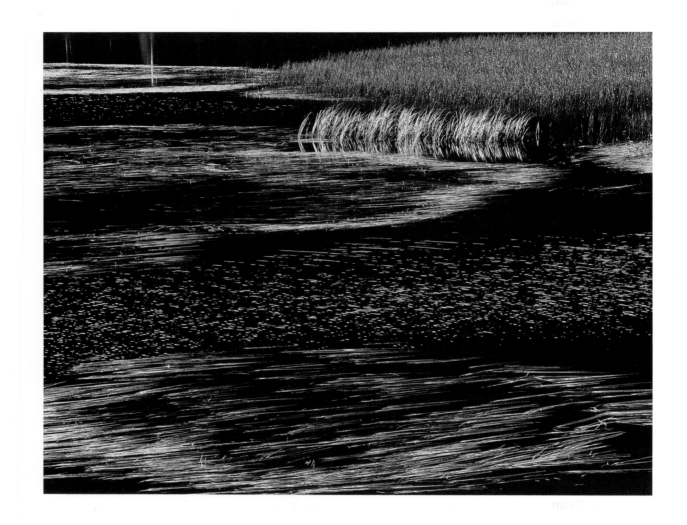

John Charles Woods

Wind-Rippled Pond Near Portage

Gelatin silver photograph, selenium

toned

1983

UAP84:004:001

We cross the shallow Amawk and another nameless creek in our boots and come out, at last, onto the broad plain of the north fork of the Koyukuk.

It is late afternoon of day 4. We have walked about fifteen miles since Chimney Lake. This is good progress in the Arctic, where the often difficult terrain may allow backpackers to cover only three to five map-miles per day. Ahead lie more tussocks—some, two feet tall—and wet tundra, willows, blueberry bushes, and mosquitoes. It's Deet time again.

Walking across the broad plain toward the river, we see three caribou antlers and many bones. This is our first intersection with a major caribou migration route. The silver backs of four marmots flash against green.

"Rodents eat antlers and bones for calcium and phosphates," Rob says. "Luckily. Otherwise, this area would be buried in antlers and bones."

I chuckle, lost in the wide plain and my imagination, and tickled at the magnitude of so many unseen things.

When we reach the first gravel bar of the brown-colored north fork, we find big moose tracks, huge bear tracks, two sets of bootprints, and a blue Spam can. Clear water for a campsite is not evident, however, and we swim through alders for ten minutes, pushing aside stubborn branches with our arms and legs, before reaching the next nameless creek on the map.

We sit on rock seats beside the clear creek that spills into the melodious brown river, and Rob lights the stove. Cooking without rain for a change, we relax and enjoy the peaceful, bright evening. Surrounded by rounded rocks of all sizes, I feel as though I am seated at an intricate stone altar. A breeze keeps most of the mosquitoes away, and Rob tells of the total solar eclipse that he observed last year at Salar de Uyuni in Bolivia. He says he traveled there by train, alone, and that Linda, who was living with him then, did not want to go.

"Black shadows erased the white floor of the desert," he says. "And the desert was a plain of salt."

The next morning we wake at eight o'clock to steady rain. We decide to stay inside our bags and read until the weather lets up. Rob chuckles with a novel, *The River Why*, and I read an issue of *Creative Nonfiction*. After waiting an hour and a half, we pack up our gear under remnants of rain and have a fine breakfast — on the rock seats — of granola, golden raisins, and powdered milk.

We do a little willow and alder swimming to find a place to cross the creek without wading, so our wet boots and socks won't get wetter. Then we stay high, walking on tundra.

At Alinement Creek, we see bootprints where two people have crossed, but after days of rain, the water must be higher than when they were here. Rob tosses one boulder into the current, then another. The water is too noisy and swift, though, for us to hear how deeply the boulders fall or to tell whether they sink to the bottom, or roll. Rob wades in to test the route, but the creekbed drops off quickly.

"Jesus Christ, this current is fast!" he yells, returning to the bank.

This seems an impossible place to cross, so we head up the rushing creek away from the river, still wearing our packs. We walk a mile and a half, wading several braids and hopping many rocks, looking and looking, but there is no good route. The creekbed narrows into a steep-walled canyon, and it becomes impossible to walk further. After almost an hour, we hike back down, nearly to the place where the others apparently crossed.

"Well," Rob says, over the noise, "this is the widest place, with the shallowest areas on both sides. I guess this is it."

We have to cross this creek. There is no choice, no going back to Chimney Lake. This is the ultimate "we will see."

Without saying much (I'm trying not to feel scared), we zip a few survival items into our rainjacket pockets (or, in Rob's case, into his soaking wet windbreaker pockets). Hypothermia is what we don't want. If either or both of us falls in, we will need to build a fire quickly after getting out. We take all of our matches, the Bic lighter, some toilet paper for fire starter, the two remaining maps, our Swiss Army knives, and a Ziploc bag of gorp. Trying not to imagine my pack or myself floating downstream, I put plastic bags around my sleeping bag, my two stuff-sacks of dry clothes, and the camera, and tightly zip each inside the pack again. I take my bear-spray canister off the hip-belt and tuck it inside the pack's top pocket. Then I take off my Gore-Tex rainpants and roll up my black nylon pants to the knees.

Back when we neared the Clear River, before our first water crossing, Rob told me a story about fording a creek with friends. This was the summer after he and his wife had moved to Alaska to work in Bethel. They crossed crab-style, he said.

"That's the most stable way two people can cross without a rope."

Now, with our hip-belts and chest-belts unbuckled, Rob and I face each other, grasping both arms above the elbows, and step in.

We move like one creature: me one leg, Rob one leg, me one leg, Rob one leg. The current is powerful, and Rob stands rooted on the upstream side, blocking some of the creek's force. Water cascades off the backs of his knees like a fan. It comes to about mid-thigh—his? mine?—impossible to tell, because of the fan effect. I know that the water is cold, but I am concentrating solely on getting a good foothold with each step, and my brain does not register temperature.

Rob has not held me for years, but this is a different embrace. It has nothing to do with one kind of love, and everything to do with another.

Like a synapse, this other love is instantaneous and recurring, impossible to see. It has brought us to this place, and it will take us out of it. Tenacious, arcing, it has tensile strength. It extends backward beyond lovers, schooling, neighborhoods, birth, and it shoots forward past the Delta and Bolivia, books and maps, past my cabin, this place.

One big boulder on the creek's bottom causes Rob's foot to slip and almost upsets our crab configuration. We keep concentrating, though, and manage to plant our feet firmly again, among the invisible rocks in the foaming brown water. We make steady progress. The shore we have left recedes. Near the creek's center, the water does not get deeper—*Hallelujah!*—but remains swirling at mid-thigh. Then it begins to shallow out. We move more easily toward the opposite shore, and soon Rob has released my arms and we are scrambling up the bank to rocky ground.

"We did it!" I yell. Rob yells, too. "Ahright! Goodbye, Alinement Creek!" We drop our packs to the ground and look across the quick water toward where we were just standing. There's no turning back now, that's certain. *The shortest dis-*

tance between two points is a synapse. Alinement Creek lies behind us, and a heady sense of freedom hangs ahead. It's five o'clock—long past lunchtime—and we can sight down the river and see the rocky clear creek by last night's campsite. Only one mile away, according to the map.

Rob shrugs, then grins. "Well, that's travel in the Arctic," he says.

We climb onto boulders, wring out our freezing socks, and pour water out of our boots. It's time for wheat crackers with cheddar cheese and peanut butter, swigs of filtered cold water, and our precious daily ration of half a Ziploc bag of gorp. When we each begin to shiver from sitting still, we put our wet boots back on and hoist our packs to our backs. Then we head into a thick grove of willows that blocks the slope up the next mountain.

As if a gift to us, a trail dotted with large droppings leads beneath the otherwise impenetrable thicket. Bending low, we walk like short bears, hoping not to meet other bears. After several minutes, the leafy tunnel nudges the hillside, and we can grab onto willow roots in the soil above our heads and pull ourselves up with our packs, onto the tundra slope above. This is the area on the map where the young guide we met in Bettles, at the airstrip, told us to be sure and stay high.

"Otherwise," he said, "you'll run right into a big waterfall at the end of a dead-end canyon. That's what I did the first time, and we had to turn back and hike all the way out and around."

Looking at the map, we probably would have decided to stay high here anyway, but remembering the guide's advice, we climb extra high: about a thousand feet in one and a half hours.

The backs of my shins are screaming.

"At least there's plenty of oxygen," Rob says, looking down at me from several yards up. "Not like in Bolivia, hiking at fourteen thousand feet."

"Right," I reply, out of breath anyway. My back is tired, my legs are tired, the bottoms of my feet are tired. We are walking like upside-down L's, backs bent almost perpendicular to legs, as we negotiate the steep, uphill climb. At least there are plenty of animal trails. These make it easier to walk without thinking. Anything to conserve energy.

I imagine how hilarious this would look to someone videotaping us from the air. We turn up in the most unexpected places. It would have been funny, for instance, to see a fat blue pack and a body, then another fat blue pack and a smaller body, emerge from the *top* of a willow thicket, as we pulled ourselves up by those roots below onto the side of this mountain.

Nothing but ground squirrels and caribou droppings up here. No trees. Spectacular views, though, as the mountainside levels out and we climb into high alpine tundra. Jagged peaks move in and out of the white clouds and gray rain that cloak the world all around. Magnificent rock slides and waterfalls are alternately revealed and obscured on the opposite side of the valley. If things look this good now, I wonder, what do they look like on a sunny day? And which of those peaks to the south, unmasking, is Doonerak?

We make camp at 3,600 feet on a sliver of level ground covered with reindeer lichen and pink wildflowers. The north fork of the Koyukuk pounds somewhere below, but we are so high, we cannot see or hear it. On the opposite side of the valley Barrenland Creek seems to hang suspended in the sky. It winds like a rock serpent, downhill for miles, swallowing the seam between the cloud-hidden, six-thousand-foot peaks of Twoprong Mountain and Inclined Mountain.

The next (and last) map shows that the shelf holding Summit Lake and the Continental Divide may be just a four-and-a-half-mile "walk" up the tundra-lined valley of the north fork, below. We should be able to make a base camp at the lake tomorrow and have two days to relax and explore, up the Oolah Valley.

This is the ultimate in backpacking. A "black-belt national park," John Kauffmann calls Gates of the Arctic, in his book about the Brooks Range. I have to agree. But this piece of wilderness is more than a national park, and this trip—though "black-belt"—is more, too.

I feel fortunate to travel with Rob. He is generous to have paid for my plane tickets.

"I was poor once, too," he says, "and others paid for me."

He loves days and places like these as much as I, and that is another thing that draws us together. He moves fast, though, dauntlessly advancing toward goals. He does this in life, too, I have learned. Often on this trip, I have found myself hiking fifty or a hundred yards behind. I've begun to get used to it, though.

Once we led parallel lives, and now I see that perhaps they remain so. Rob walks faster than I because he is taller and stronger, and his goals are different from mine.

"Don't mind me," he says. "I'm just off in my own reverie."

But so am I. I lag behind because I am six inches shorter and, by nature, slower. Each of us likes to look closely at things—lichen, pebbles, and views; writing and books, people's faces; where to live and what to do with our energy; whom to trust with our innermost thoughts; whom to spend time with outdoors. Rob has more tolerance, though—and, perhaps, more need—for spontaneity and quick decisions. He seems less meticulous and thorough than I, less process-oriented. More able to drive forward without delay.

"But science is meticulous and thorough," he says, "and process in science is key."

Still, I search out reasons that he is a doctor and research scientist, and I am a writer and teacher. Or that he rents an apartment and I have bought a cabin, and he shuttles between Atlanta and Bolivia and I have settled, like snow.

These are the things I consider, while walking fifty or a hundred yards behind. Equally curious is the question why the two of us may never become more than just friends. Why our earlier attempts failed. Why the writer continues to connect and wants to jump parallel lines. Why the doctor connects, too—perhaps feels what is there—but prefers to fly away. And why both of us, in the videographer's camera, love so much the same places and things.

The sky is clear on the afternoon of day 6, when we reach Summit Lake on the Continental Divide. We pitch the blue tent on the flattest piece of tundra we can find above the lake, dwarfed in the broad sweep of the Oolah Valley. This campspot turns out to be a wind tunnel for three nights and two days, but the wind dries our wet clothes, which we tie to the tent strings and spread on the tundra with rocks. Even our boots and tennis shoes get dry, and we revel in happy, warm feet.

To the southeast Doonerak glints like a lighthouse, its tilting rock summit silver-gray and sharp in the sun. Fog rolls in, but the next morning its white curtain dissolves, and we decide to hike north up the valley. Walking on the sturdy, high alpine tundra with slim day-packs, we cover six miles before stopping for lunch, in sight of Oolah Lake.

The pilots were right, and so is the name. Oolah Valley is paradise.

While munching the last of our crackers and cheese—Rob wiping the peanut butter container clean with his finger—we spot a single caribou, perhaps a half-mile away, moving down the Itkillick River. It is eating lichen, and does not notice us.

Through my binoculars, the caribou looks young. Its body and antlers are small, beside the wide valley and rugged mountains. Some sixth sense tells it to look up, and it sees us.

Startled, it runs.

The young caribou runs and runs in the valley, against a backdrop of rock and green, stops to scrutinize us, and runs again. It runs and stops, runs and stops, until it feels safe, perhaps, or has forgotten why it is running. Then it is bending again its mottled brown neck to the ground, nibbling lichen, and nudging toward water. Rob and I try to put our pleasure into words.

This is the only live caribou we have seen on this trip. Is it lost?

A loner?

A messenger of what is to come?

Not long from now, in the red and deep purples of autumn, this valley and its lakes will be flooded with caribou moving down from the north. Thousands of old and young animals will pour through this place in their rhythmic and cyclical search for food, shelter, and time. They will eat and sleep, run and walk, hooves clicking, noses snorting, leaving tracks, droppings, antlers, and some weak animals, to cross over parallel lines. And from Anaktuvuk the Nunamiut Eskimos will come, part of this ancient rhythm, to hunt with guns and skill.

In a realm somehow similar, day after tomorrow, day 8, I will sit again with Rob in the blue and white Cessna. He will be strapped in the co-pilot's seat and I behind, with my pack beside me, his stowed in back. Both packs will be almost empty of fuel and food. We will wait more than an hour inside the small plane for the fog—which has settled thickly over the lake and the valley—to lift and let us fly. Rob and the pilot will talk, in front, of regulations and radar, visibility and ceilings, while my mind—like the caribou—drifts away.

I will be thinking of an unspoken closeness and of the bright orange flesh of an arctic char, splayed open and placed on a rock, before cooking. How Rob cast with my rod into a small school of fish at the mouth of a stream feeding Summit Lake. How he hooked the fish on the second cast and filleted this fine thing with my Swiss Army knife (sharper than his), then cooked it with margarine and care. How we smiled upon eating. How Rob threw the head, tail, and entrails back into the lake, with a prayer, and how we washed the pan and the knife and our hands carefully with soap, so not to attract any bears. How the gift of the wild orange fish melted in my mouth—like wilderness—and I hoped to remember it, back at the cabin, where it is easy to turn on propane to heat tea, pull dry socks from a drawer, switch on the Monitor oil stove to get warm.

Images of caribou—the song-cycles of their migrations—will be strewn upon my memory and my imagination. Here and there, large and small, seventy-five, one hundred, some tips broken and some not . . . caribou racks. Some will be sinking into the wet tundra and bogs, others will hide beneath lichen and mold. Hoofprints, deep trails, shriveled droppings; the remains of two kills: cracked bones, broken skulls; parts of a brown and white hide.

I will see again, in my mind's eye, the mares' tails, streaking across blue sky with their wild, white spikes—fifteen or twenty, all parallel—in high-wind cloud formations that I will not remember ever having seen before. These mares' tails will herald the drone of a plane, coming through fog, droning between the rock peaks of the long and sweeping valley. Then I will see how the slick face of Doonerak, shining for two mornings beyond the flapping blue tent, has been swallowed again in clouds.

I will think it is clear why the Nunamiut, the "people of the weather," did not consider human beings the center of things. They lived out here with each other and with the cold and the caribou, the lichen and the stunning orange fish, year-round. And like the Yup'ik Eskimos in our beloved Yukon-Kuskokwim Delta (Rob's and mine), the Nunamiut were aware of what the center is.

Standing on the tundra hill above the lake, attempting to trace the drone of the plane to its source, through fog, I will hear two voices. And I will not be startled. One voice will come from my memory, something difficult, extraordinary, and still.

Rob flies back to Atlanta tomorrow.

The other voice will come from the mares' tails, high above the hill. This voice will whisper . . . beyond reason, distance, and time . . . telling me things I have known since childhood, things I want to believe:

This is not the center
this is not the center

This is the center
this is the center

Stay
Listen, listen, listen

CONTRIBUTORS

BRIAN ALLEN   A Fairbanks resident, Brian Allen is a graduate of Harvard University and received his M.A. in studio art in 1989 from the International Center of Photography at New York University. He has had solo exhibitions at the Alaska State Museum and the Anchorage Museum of History and Art, as well as in San Francisco, Seattle, and Philadelphia. He received an Individual Artist Fellowship from the Alaska State Council on the Arts in 1982. Allen curated eight shows for the Photographic Center in Seattle in 1990–91 and served as president of the Photography Council of the Seattle Art Museum from 1990 to 1992.

ALVIN ELI AMASON   Originally from Kodiak, Aleut artist Alvin Amason received his B.A. and M.A. in art from Central Washington University and his M.F.A. from Arizona State University. He has taught at the University of Alaska Fairbanks, where he heads the Alaska Native Art Center, since 1992. Amason is a nationally recognized Native American artist who has participated in invitational exhibitions in Arizona, Michigan, Oklahoma, Montana, and Washington, D.C. His work is in the collections of the Nodjyllands Kunstmuseum in Denmark, the Indian Arts and Crafts Board, and the U.S. National Collection of Fine Arts.

SUE ANDERSON   Born in Minneapolis in 1949, Sue Anderson lives in Anchorage. She received her B.F.A. in photography from the San Francisco Art Institute in 1983. Her work has been shown in group shows in Alaska and California, and published in *Portfolio* (Aperture Press, N.Y.). She received a Purchase Award in the 1984 Alaska Positive statewide photography competition and is a cofounder of the Alaska Photographers' Guild.

JAMES BARKER   Alaska's foremost ethnographic photographer, James Barker visited the Yukon-Kuskokwim Delta for the first time in the winter of 1970. He moved to Bethel in 1975 and lived there until he moved to Fairbanks in 1987. Barker received his photographic training at the Los Angeles Art Center School of Design. Solo exhibitions of his work have been held at the Anchorage Museum of History and Art in 1992 and at the University of Alaska Museum in 1993. His large volume of photographs and commentary, *Always Getting Ready, Upterrlainarluta: Yup'ik Eskimo Subsistence in Southwest Alaska* (University of Washington Press, 1993), was published to widespread acclaim.

JOHN BARTLETT   Born in 1948 in Mount Edgecumbe, Alaska, John Bartlett is currently a resident of Fairbanks. He graduated with a B.F.A. in art from the University of Alaska Fairbanks. *Standing Raven* was created for the *Bending Traditions* exhibition sponsored by the Institute of Alaska Native Arts in 1990.

JENNIFER BRICE   When asked to talk about the process of writing about Alaska, Jennifer Brice uses the metaphor of bifocals: "For me, the trick is juggling just the right amount of distance (to see clearly and unsentimentally) with the right amount of closeness (to write authoritatively and compassionately)." Born in Alaska, she lives on the outskirts of Fairbanks with her husband and three daughters. Her essays have appeared in *Manoa, American Nature Writing 1994* (John Murray, ed.; Sierra Club Books), and *The Island's Edge: A Sitka Reader* (Carolyn Servid, ed.; Graywolf Press, 1995). "What Everyone Wants You to Have" is a selection from her book *The Last Settlers* (Duquesne University Press, 1998).

ARTHUR WILLIAM (BILL) BRODY   A longtime professor of art at the University of Alaska Fairbanks, Bill Brody received his B.S. from Harvey Mudd College in Claremont, California, in 1965 and his M.F.A. from Claremont Graduate School in 1967. His recent exhibitions include a 1993 show at Shepherd College in West Virginia and a 1991 exhibition at Queensborough Community College in New York. Since 1990 his work has been seen in group exhibitions at the Vorpal Gallery in New York, Wenninger Gallery in Boston, Newman Gallery at Bryn Mawr, Pennsylvania, and Wetherholt Gallery in Washington, D.C. In the last several years he has joined groups of Fairbanks artists on painting trips to the Arctic National Wildlife Refuge and other portions of the Brooks Range.

CHARLES CROSMAN   Born in Fairbanks in 1945, Charles Crosman currently resides in North Pole, Alaska. He made *Abandoned Dreams* with a Bronica S2A camera in Circle City, Alaska, in 1986. Crosman has been an active member of the Camera Arts group of Interior Alaska photographers. His work has been included in the annual 64th Parallel Juried Exhibition in Fairbanks, and he has shown his work in Anchorage as well.

NINA CRUMRINE Nina Crumrine (1889–1959) was born in Indiana and trained at the Art Institute of Chicago. In 1923 she moved to Alaska to live with her uncle, H. V. McGee, in Ketchikan. She later acquired land in Haines where she lived and from which she was a peripatetic traveler through every region of the state as well as South America, Africa, Europe, and Asia. She is best known for her portraits of mid-century Native Alaskans, twenty-four of which were purchased by the Alaska Territorial Legislature in 1941.

DAVID DAPOGNY Born in Berwyn, Illinois, in 1945, David Dapogny received his M.F.A. from the Rhode Island School of Design in 1976. In addition to solo shows at the Alaska State Museum and Lavender-Grey Gallery in Juneau, he has exhibited in Washington, New York, Texas, Pennsylvania, Oklahoma, California, New Mexico, and Ohio. He received an Individual Artist Fellowship from the Alaska State Council on the Arts in 1983. His work is included in numerous public collections, among them the Alaska State Museum, the Alaska Contemporary Art Bank, and the Chicago Historical Society.

MARK DAUGHHETEE Longtime Juneau artist Mark Daughhetee's exhibition record includes solo exhibits at the George Brown Convention Center in Houston; Cliff Michel Gallery in Seattle; Ventura College in Ventura, California; the University of California at Santa Barbara; the Anchorage Museum of History and Art; and the Alaska State Museum. His work is included in the collections of the Houston Museum of Fine Arts, the Seattle Art Museum, the Eastman Kodak Company, and Microsoft Corporation, in addition to each of the three major museums in Alaska. He received an Individual Artist Fellowship from the Alaska State Council on the Arts in 1984.

CLARICE DICKESS Clarice Dickess has lived in Fairbanks going on ten years. A provincial Alaskan from head to pinkie, she has dedicated herself to a protracted exploration of the Alaska Range and the hills and rivers immediately surrounding the Fairbanks area: "Writing while in the wilderness and about my visits to Alaska's wild places generates an energy I'm not completely responsible for. . . . I suppose I can justify my right to the drama of Alaska's outdoors by virtue of physically carting myself there, sometimes literally risking my carcass in doing so." Clarice Dickess's essays have appeared in the collections *Another Wilderness: New Outdoor Writing by Women* (Susan Fox Rogers, ed.; Seal Press, 1994) and *Alaska Passages: Twenty Voices from Above the 54th Parallel* (Susan Fox Rogers, ed.; Seal Press, 1996).

HENRY WOOD ELLIOTT Henry Wood Elliott (1846–1930) is best known in Alaska as the savior of the state's fur seal population, but he was also one of the finest watercolorists to visit Alaska in the late 19th century. A Cleveland native, Elliott first visited Alaska in 1867 with the Western Union Telegraph Survey, two years before serving as official artist for F. V. Hayden's U.S. Geological Survey expedition to the western United States. He was sent north again in 1872 as U.S. Treasury agent supervising the Alaska Commercial Company's management of the fur seal industry in the Pribilof Islands, and he visited Alaska regularly thereafter, spending much of the rest of his life fighting in Congress to reverse the practices that had led to disastrous declines in the northern fur seal population.

LESLIE LEYLAND FIELDS Leslie Leyland Fields lives with her husband and four children on Kodiak Island, where she teaches English at the University of Alaska's Kodiak campus and in the summers joins an extended commercial salmon-fishing operation on a nearby island. She writes, "Alaska's writers labor under several burdens, I think. The one I am most conscious of, apart from the isolation, is the very extremity of our landscape. There is not a lot of subtlety here, in topography or climate. . . . Dramas seem almost daily occurrences, yet here is the caution: it is easy to dwell there, to be moved simply to the script of this vast outdoor drama, but the real drama is interior." Her two books are *The Water Under Fish* (Trout Creek Press) and *The Entangling Net: Alaska's Commercial Fishing Women Tell Their Lives* (University of Illinois Press, 1997).

EDMOND JAMES FITZGERALD Perhaps the finest watercolorist to work in Alaska in this century, Seattle artist E. J. FitzGerald (1912–1989) was a frequent visitor to the territory. He first came to Alaska in 1928 as a crewman on a telegraph-cable repair ship in southeast Alaska and returned to the territory seven times in the 1930s with the U.S. Geological Survey. His work for the Survey as a boatman, field assistant, cook, and packer afforded him the opportunity to see many regions of the territory, and he did sketches in oils and watercolors wherever he went. In 1970 the artist traveled to the Brooks Range, North Slope, and Interior regions of the state while making illustrations for a Humble Oil Company article on the proposed trans-Alaska pipeline. FitzGerald was president of Allied Artists of America (1960–63), a member of the National Academy and the American Watercolor Society, and author of two books on watercolor instruction.

GARY L. FREEBURG Born in Minneapolis in 1948, Gary Freeburg completed his M.F.A. in studio art and photography at the University of Iowa in 1978. He was head of the Photography Department at Islands College, Sitka, from 1980 to 1982 and has taught since 1989 at the Kenai Peninsula campus of the University of Alaska Anchorage. A frequent exhibitor and award winner in statewide juried art competitions, he received an Individual Artist Fellowship from the Alaska State Council on the Arts in 1983.

ROBERT SWAIN GIFFORD R. Swain Gifford (1840–1905) was one of the many prominent artists and naturalists retained by Edward Harriman for the last great exploring expedition to Alaska, the Harriman Expedition of 1899. Along with artists Frederick Dellenbaugh and Louis Agassiz Fuertes, photographer Edward S. Curtis, and such well-known scientists and naturalists as John Muir and John Burroughs, Gifford traveled up the coast of Alaska and as far as Plover Bay in Siberia. A number of Gifford's paintings are reproduced in the first two volumes of the thirteen-volume account of the expedition (*Harriman Alaska Expedition* series, Smithsonian Institution, 1910–14).

NELSON GINGERICH Born in 1938 in Iowa City, Iowa, Nelson Gingerich was educated at Bethel College (B.S.), Oregon State University (M.S.), Rochester Institute of Technology, and the University of Oregon. His work was frequently included in Alaska juried exhibitions throughout the late 1970s and 1980s and was featured in *Visions of Alaska*, an invitational exhibit of Alaskan photography at the University of Alaska Museum in 1982. He had a solo exhibition at the Anchorage Historical and Fine Arts Museum in 1979.

JANE GRAY Born in 1947, Jane Gray received a degree in fine arts from the University of New Hampshire in 1969. She moved to Juneau in 1970 and taught printmaking in Adak and Kenai before moving to Anchorage in 1977. She is best known for her *Kagamil's Children* series of mixed-media drawings and her *Kradula* series of mixed-media sculptures, produced throughout the early and mid-1980s. These sensitive, highly acclaimed works were inspired by the remains of mummified Aleutian children found by Smithsonian anthropologist Ales Hrdlicka in 1936 within caves on Kagamil Island in the Aleutians. Gray's work was featured in solo exhibitions at the Anchorage Museum of History and Art in 1981 and 1990, the Alaska State Museum in 1982, and the Visual Arts Center of Alaska in 1983. She moved to Sydney, Australia, in 1991.

DIANA HAMAR Both an accomplished photographer and one of the most highly respected nonrepresentational painters in Alaska, Diana Hamar received her B.F.A. and M.F.A. from the University of Washington. She has lived in Alaska most of her life, and she has often split her time between Juneau and France. A recipient of an Individual Artist Fellowship from the Alaska State Council on the Arts, she had a solo exhibition at the Anchorage Museum of History and Art in 1990.

MAGNUS COLCORD (RUSTY) HEURLIN One of Alaska's most beloved historical artists, Rusty Heurlin (1895–1986) was born in Christianstad, Sweden, and raised in Massachusetts. After studying at the Fenway School of Illustration in Boston, he arrived in

Valdez in 1916. He served in World War I in Europe and worked as an artist/illustrator in Connecticut and New York for a time after the war. Returning to Alaska in 1924, Heurlin made his home in Ester, in the Fairbanks area, where he spent the rest of his life. He produced several series of large-scale paintings chronicling Alaska's history and Native people, and received an honorary degree from the University of Alaska Fairbanks in 1971.

MARYBETH HOLLEMAN Marybeth Holleman's essays and poetry have appeared in the *North American Review, American Nature Writing 1996* (John Murray, ed.; Sierra Club Books), *National Wildlife*, and *Alaska Magazine*. Her commentaries on environmental issues have aired on National Public Radio's *All Things Considered*. She has lived the last decade in Alaska, spending as much time as possible at Prince William Sound learning how to live. "I believe a change for the better is happening—that our words, spoken alone and together, aloud and in silence, are nurturing a change in the way we humans live."

JOHN HOOVER Born in Cordova of Aleut heritage in 1919, John Hoover currently lives in Grapeview, Washington, where he works as an artist and as a commercial fisherman. Influenced by local artists in Cordova as he grew up, Hoover painted for twenty years before turning to three-dimensional work. He later studied with Leon Derbyshire in Seattle. He served as an art teacher with the U.S. Air Force school system in Japan, Taiwan, and the Phillipines and taught at the Institute of American Indian Arts in Santa Fe and in Saint Paul, Alaska. His work has been included in museum exhibitions in London, Phoenix, Montana, Oklahoma, Washington, D.C., Oregon, and Alaska, and he has completed commissions for the Washington State Arts Commission and Anchorage's Egan Convention Center.

CHARLES JANDA Born in Chariton, Iowa, in 1934, Charles Janda captured *Composite Island, 1968* with a Hasselblad 500C camera in Alaska's Glacier Bay National Monument. Janda served a fourteen-year tour of duty as chief ranger of the area, during which time he produced many memorable images. His exhibition venues include Equivalents Gallery in Seattle in 1980 and the Alaska State Museum in 1984. His work was included in the annual American Photographers in National Parks exhibits from 1979 through 1984.

SAM KIMURA Youngest brother of important Alaskan painter Bill Kimura and husband of prominent Alaskan painter Joan Kimura, Sam Kimura (1928–1996) was as well known and highly regarded in the Alaskan art community as either. Born in Anchorage and educated at the Art Center, College of Design in Los Angeles, Kimura was one of the true progenitors of fine arts photography in Alaska. He operated a portrait studio in Anchorage before running a photography studio in New York in the mid 1950s. Subsequently returning to Alaska, he became a leader in the Anchorage art community and was a key figure in encouraging serious fine-art photography in the state. He taught for many years and served as art department chairman at the University of Alaska Anchorage.

CAROLYN KREMERS Carolyn Kremers's recent book *Place of the Pretend People: Gifts from a Yup'ik Eskimo Village* (Alaska Northwest Books, 1996) tells of her move from Colorado to Alaska in 1986 to teach in Tununak, on Nelson Island. In her essays and poems, Kremers explores how people learn and don't, and the ways in which Native and non-Native people connect with each other and the world. She says, "I write to figure things out and to bear witness to things that I feel are wrong, complex, or beautiful."

JAMES KUIPER Born in 1945 in Roseland, Illinois, James Kuiper received his M.F.A. from Michigan State University in 1976. Coming to Fairbanks as a one-year sabbatical replacement for a University of Alaska painting professor in 1983, he remained in Alaska for several years, becoming one of the state's most prominent abstract painters and serving as visual arts director and head of Alaska's Percent-for-Art program with the Alaska State Council on the Arts. During his several years' stay in Alaska, he won numerous awards in statewide juried competitions, and his work became a part of most of the state's major visual arts collections. He currently teaches at Chico State University in California.

THEODORE ROOSEVELT LAMBERT One of Alaska's most admired historical painters, Ted Lambert (1905–1960) traveled more widely throughout Alaska than did any other artist of his day, working for lengthy periods in numerous locations from McCarthy and Kennicott to Bethel, Lake Clark, and the North Slope. He spent almost twenty years in Fairbanks. A onetime pupil, friend, fellow traveler, and artistic collaborator with Eustace Ziegler, Lambert was also highly regarded by Sydney Laurence, who told an Anchorage reporter in 1937 that Lambert was a great artist and might someday be Alaska's greatest painter. Unlike Laurence and Ziegler, Lambert never abandoned the rough life of the Alaskan sourdough, and his paintings are widely sought after in part because they reflect his ongoing personal involvement with the details of pioneer life.

SYDNEY LAURENCE Alaska's most widely beloved historical painter, Sydney Laurence (1865–1940) was the first professionally trained artist to make Alaska his home. Born in Brooklyn in 1865, Laurence studied at the Art Students League in New York and exhibited regularly in that city by the late 1880s. Settling in 1889 in the artists' colony of Saint Ives, Cornwall, England, over the next decade he exhibited at the Royal Society of British

Artists and was included in the Paris Salon in 1890, 1894, and 1895, winning an award in 1894. Laurence moved to Alaska in 1904 for reasons still unknown. Living the hard life of the pioneer prospector, he painted little in his first years in the territory, but between 1911 and 1914 he began to focus once again on his art. He moved from Valdez to the budding town of Anchorage in 1915 and by the early 1920s was Alaska's most prominent painter.

GRETCHEN LEGLER Born and raised in Salt Lake City, where she learned how to fish, backpack, climb, and ski, Gretchen Legler came to Alaska in 1994 to teach in the Creative Writing Program at the University of Alaska Anchorage. She says of her adopted state, "From the very beginning, Alaska was to me an enigmatic landscape, and still I struggle to make sense of it. I don't see myself as an Alaskan yet. I don't know if I ever will. I don't know what that takes." Her essays have appeared in *Orion, Another Wilderness: New Outdoor Writing by Women* (Seal Press, 1994), and numerous other publications. Her work is collected in *All the Powerful Invisible Things: A Sportswoman's Notebook* (Seal Press, 1995).

MALCOLM LOCKWOOD Born in New Britain, Connecticut, in 1936, Malcolm Lockwood came to Alaska in 1958. First nationally published in 1953, Lockwood's photographs have appeared in *Modern Photography, Sunset, Time, Wilderness, National Parks, Popular Photography, National Geographic,* and *National Wildlife,* among other prominent contemporary photographic journals. His work has been shown in Maine, Montana, California, Alaska, Switzerland, Germany, and Australia. He is currently a fine art and commercial photographer in Fairbanks, where he and his wife, Hope, own and operate Image House, a custom photography business.

NANCY LORD Nancy Lord is actively engaged in conservation and environmental issues, both as a community activist and as a writer. A resident of Homer since 1973, she has written two collections of short stories, *The Compass Inside Ourselves* (Fireweed Press, 1984) and *Survival* (Coffee House Press, 1991). She wrote the text for the Pratt Museum's catalog accompanying its traveling exhibit *Darkened Waters: Profile of an Oil Spill* (1992). "Alaska . . . seems to me, in its scale and extremes, to provide not just intriguing situations and attractive background but a wealth of metaphor for commenting upon modern life," Lord writes. "Under the Tides, Under the Moon" is excerpted from her latest book, *Fish Camp: Life on an Alaskan Shore* (Island Press, Shearwater Books, 1997).

HOWARD LUKE Howard Luke, a Tanana Athabascan elder, was born in Nenana in 1923. After attending a mission school for a few years, he worked as a logger, gandy dancer, riverboat deckhand, and navigator. He has always lived a subsistence lifestyle, acquiring in-depth knowledge of lands and rivers; of weather; of hunting, fishing, and trapping; and of plants, herbs, and medicines. In the 1960s Luke began his Spirit Camp on the Tanana River to teach Native traditional knowledge. His autobiography, *Howard Luke: My Own Trail* (Alaska Native Knowledge Network), is forthcoming. Luke writes in collaboration with Ann Oury Lefavor.

FRED MACHETANZ Born in 1908 in Ohio and educated in art at Ohio State University, Fred Machetanz came to Alaska in 1935 to visit his Uncle Charles Traeger's trading post in Unalakleet. After a two-year stay, he worked as an illustrator in New York and served in the Aleutians in World War II before settling in Alaska for good in 1947. With his wife, Sara Dunn, whom he met and married in Unalakleet in that year, he worked on books, films, and lecture tours until becoming a full-time painter in 1962. He has become the most popularly acclaimed artist to continue the traditional, romantic image of pioneer Alaska into the present day. His work is widely reproduced and is collected by individuals and museums throughout the United States and abroad.

VIRGINIA K. (KATHY) MARCHLINSKI A longtime Fairbanks resident and prominent local painter and graphic designer, Kathy Marchlinski moved in the late 1980s from Alaska to Savannah, Georgia, where she completed her M.F.A. at the Savannah College of Art and Design. She has subsequently settled near Flintville, Tennessee, where she continues to make art and create intricate designs for lace embroidery.

CHARLES MASON A resident of Fairbanks since 1984, Charles Mason has taught photography at the University of Alaska Fairbanks since 1990. He is also an Alaska stringer for *Time* magazine, the Associated Press, and the *Anchorage Daily News*. He received his M.S. in documentary photography from Illinois State University in 1988. His work has been widely published in such prominent journals as *Audubon, Outside, Geo, National Wildlife*, and the *New York Times Sunday Magazine* and was included in *Time* magazine's *1989 Pictures of the Year* and in *Life* magazine's *1988 Pictures of the Year* and *1980's Pictures of the Decade*. His many solo exhibition venues include the Alaska State Museum, the Anchorage Museum of History and Art, and the University of California, Berkeley.

CLARK MISHLER Born in Trenton, Michigan, in 1948 and educated at Ferris State College, Clark Mishler has been a prominent Alaskan fine art photographer, media producer, and publication designer since the 1970s. His photography and design have regularly been featured in major commercial productions in Anchorage and throughout Alaska, and his individual photographs have won numerous awards in statewide juried exhibitions.

Alaska Wildlife #1 was included in his solo show, *I Shoot Wildlife Also*, at the Anchorage Historical and Fine Arts Museum in 1982.

ROBBY MOHATT   One of Alaska's best-known abstract painters, Robby Mohatt was educated at Beloit College, Black Hills State University, and the University of Alaska Fairbanks. She has been a working professional artist and teacher in Fairbanks since 1983. Her work is included in the collections of the Anchorage Museum of History and Art and the Alaska State Museum, both of which have featured solo exhibitions of her paintings. She received an Individual Artist Fellowship from the Alaska State Council on the Arts in 1992.

Mohatt's work features dense, mysterious grounds on which float forms and symbols often reminiscent of signs from various Native American cultures.

DAVID MOLLETT   David Mollett grew up in Fairbanks from the age of ten and went on to study at Reed College in Oregon and the New York Studio School. He is the progenitor of much of the interest in on-location landscape painting among Interior Alaska artists in recent years. Known by the mid-1970s for his Fairbanks cityscapes, Mollett began working in the hills and river valleys around town, moved on to the more dramatic scenery in and around Denali Park, and since 1988 has worked frequently in the Brooks Range and other areas of arctic Alaska. He has had solo exhibitions in virtually every major public exhibition space in Alaska and has been represented in group exhibitions throughout the United States. He was awarded Individual Artist Fellowships by the Alaska State Council on the Arts in 1982 and 1988 and a Camargo Fellowship for a residency in Cassis, France, in 1992.

JOHN MORGAN   John Morgan used to think of himself as the only New York poet in Alaska, but after twenty years in the state, he has given up the title. He lives with his wife Nancy and their two sons in a house overlooking the Tanana River. His collections of poetry include *The Bone Duster* (*Quarterly Review of Literature* Poetry Series), *Arctic Herd* (University of Alabama Press, 1984), and *Walking Past Midnight* (University of Alabama Press, 1989).

RICHARD NELSON   A cultural anthropologist by training, Richard Nelson spent twenty-five years studying and writing about the relationship between native people and their environment. His books include *Shadow of the Hunter* (1980), *Hunters of the Northern Ice* (1969), *Hunters of the Northern Forest* (1973), and *Make Prayers to the Raven* (1983; all published by University of Chicago Press), the last of which was developed into an award-winning PBS television series. His essays have appeared in *Antaeus*, *Orion*, and *Harper's* in addition to many other magazines and journals. "The Island's Child" is a selection from his book *The Island Within* (Vintage Books, 1989). Nelson's latest book is *Heart and Blood: Living with Deer in America* (Alfred A. Knopf, 1997).

GAIL NIEBRUGGE Gail Niebrugge began her career as a professional artist in 1972, painting the landscape of the U.S. Southwest, Baja, and Mexico. Her search for new subject matter brought her in 1976 to Alaska, where she found her life's work painting the Wrangell–Saint Elias region. Since that time, more than 650 of her original paintings have been purchased by collectors throughout the world. In 1989 she was named official Artist in Residence of the Wrangell–Saint Elias National Park. Her work has been included in many national and international exhibitions, among them the Vancouver (British Columbia) *International Wildlife Art Exposition* (1994), the U.S. *Arts for the Parks* (1988, 1989, 1994), and the *Pacific Rim Wildlife Art Show* in Tacoma, Washington (1991–94). She currently lives and works in Palmer, Alaska.

MARY ODDEN Mary Odden came to Alaska from eastern Oregon in 1977 to fight fires for the BLM. She has lived in the Brooks Range and in Nelchina, Fairbanks, Galena, and McGrath. She writes, "I want to tell other people's stories to the extent that is possible, though the result is that I tell mine. It's tragic that everything changes all the time, very funny that the rug is always being pulled out from under us. Alaska has an attractive big screen for this action, but the good stuff is in the minutiae. A can of Carnation milk or a shoe can be such an amazing thing in its own story." Odden's essays have appeared in the *Georgia Review*, the *Northwest Review*, and other journals.

DAN O'NEILL Dan O'Neill first hitchhiked to Alaska in 1972 and moved up permanently in 1975. He has trapped a bit, built log cabins, and run long-distance mushing trips with his wife of twenty years, Sarah Campbell: "a month on the trail, nylon mountain tent, no heater, temperatures to minus thirty." His award-winning book *The Firecracker Boys* (St. Martin's Press, 1994) tells the story of a thwarted attempt by the Atomic Energy Commission to create a harbor with nuclear devices and illustrates his attraction to nonfiction as a form where, "in response to public issues, I hope to make both a humane or political contribution and a literary one."

CHARLES OTT Born in Milwaukee in 1913, Charlie Ott lived and worked in Denali Park for many years. In his long career as a nature and fine art photographer, he has gained the respect and admiration of wildlife photographers throughout the United States. He was awarded an honorary doctorate by the University of Alaska Fairbanks in 1989. *Nenana River with Sugar Loaf Mountains* was shot with a Linhof Teknika 4″ × 5″ camera.

TONY RUBEY   As manager of the printmaking studio at the Visual Arts Center of Alaska in Anchorage in the early 1980s, Tony Rubey was one of the state's most influential and innovative printmakers. Perhaps his best-known body of work is a suite of twelve original color lithographs produced for the Anchorage Pioneer Home through Alaska's Percent for Public Art program in 1982. Collectively titled *Camera Obscura*, the prints in the suite combine a variety of photographic images largely drawn from the personal collections of elderly residents of the Pioneer Home. The project is widely regarded as one of the most successful public art pieces produced in Alaska. The University of Alaska Museum is fortunate to own a full set of the prints. Like the other images in this beautiful suite, *On the Porch, In the Store* juxtaposes cultures and worldviews in a seemingly casual but often provocative way.

AL SANDERS   A prominent Anchorage photographer throughout the 1980s, Al Sanders participated in numerous statewide juried exhibitions and worked with the Anchorage Photographic Center. His untitled image of two rowboats, taken with a Mamiya 645 camera, was shown in the 1985 *Rarefied Light* statewide juried photographic exhibition.

EVA SAULITIS   A marine biologist by training, Eva Saulitis says of her last ten summers at Prince William Sound studying the habits of killer whales, "My time spent at the Sound has changed me in nearly every possible way and has been the inspiration for much of my recent writing. The natural world is the lens through which I examine troubling questions in my own life." She has published her work in *American Nature Writing 1995* (John Murray, ed.; Sierra Club Books).

SHELLEY SCHNEIDER   A 1977 graduate of the University of Michigan, Shelley Schneider has, since her arrival in Alaska in the early 1980s, become one of the state's best known and most widely exhibited photographers. An active promoter of serious contemporary photography in Alaska, she served as director of the Alaska Photographic Center in Anchorage from 1986 to 1990. Twenty solo exhibitions of her own work since 1985 have been mounted at such wide-ranging venues as Samuel Fox Museum in Dillingham, Alaska (1989); Anchorage Museum of History and Art (1987); Extension Center Gallery at the University of California, Berkeley (1988); and the Chicago Public Library Cultural Center (1990). She has more than fifty juried and invitational group exhibitions to her credit.

JAMES SCHOPPERT   A Tlingit artist born in Juneau, James Schoppert (1947–1992) was one of the leading members of a new generation of university-trained Alaska Native artists. Schoppert received his B.F.A. in art from the University of Alaska Anchorage and his M.F.A. in sculpture and printmaking from the University of Washington. A talented speaker, writer, and teacher as well as a skilled and well-known artist, he taught, lectured, and wrote widely on contemporary Alaska Native art. His work has been included in a number of major national exhibitions of contemporary Native American art, at the Philbrook Art Center in Tulsa, the Heard Museum in Phoenix, the Yellowstone Art Center in Billings, and elsewhere, and he completed a number of public art commissions in Alaska and Washington state.

CAROLYN SERVID   One of the founders of the Island Institute in Sitka, Carolyn Servid serves as codirector, developing public literary arts and humanities programs that deal with social and cultural issues. Sitka has been her home since 1980, and her essays have been her way of coming to terms with the strength of her attraction to the Alaskan landscape and of making a commitment to a place: "Making such a commitment is, in a sense, an entry into history through the acknowledgment of one's relationship to the social, cultural, and natural evolution of that place." Servid's essays have appeared in *Alaska Quarterly Review*, *North Dakota Quarterly*, *Great River Review*, and other journals.

TODD SHERMAN   A faculty member in the art department at the University of Alaska Fairbanks since 1990, Todd Sherman has been an exhibiting professional artist working in painting, drawing, and printmaking for more than fifteen years. His exhibitions include seventeen solo shows and more than seventy-five juried and invitational exhibitions. His work was included in the 1978 Smithsonian Institution exhibition *Contemporary Art from Alaska*. Sherman was trained at the University of Alaska Fairbanks, where he received his B.A. in art in 1979, and at Pratt Institute in Brooklyn, where he received his M.F.A. in printmaking in 1985. *Silent Forest V* was displayed in the Anchorage Museum of History and Art's twenty-fifth anniversary exhibition and was reproduced in the May 1993 *Alaska Magazine* issue devoted to wolves.

PEGGY SHUMAKER   Peggy Shumaker is the author of three collections of poetry: *Esperanza's Hair* (University of Alabama Press, 1985), *The Circle of Totems* (University of Pittsburgh Press, 1988), and *Wings Moist from the Other World* (University of Pittsburgh Press, 1994). She was a visiting teacher at the University of Alaska Fairbanks in 1985–86 and returned to Alaska for good in 1988. Shumaker writes, "Years ago, a respected writer and scholar warned me, 'Don't bury yourself here.' What he saw I can only guess. But what

I feel is only vastness, in land and in people, an openness. Every day is a risk, as it should be. Every day is a gift."

GLEN SIMPSON   Born in 1941 in Atlin, British Columbia, Glen Simpson is of both pioneer Canadian and Tahltan Indian heritage. In addition to solo exhibitions at all three major Alaska museums, his work has been included in numerous national and international exhibitions, among them *Craft Today, Poetry of the Physical*, at the American Craft Museum in New York (1986); *American Crafts: A Pacific Heritage*, in Sacramento, California (1982); and *Remains To Be Seen*, at the Kohler Arts Center in Sheboygan, Wisconsin (1982). He is professor emeritus of art at the University of Alaska Fairbanks, where he recently retired after more than twenty-eight years of teaching.

SHERRY SIMPSON   Sherry Simpson has lived in Juneau, Petersburg, and Fairbanks and has traveled to many places in Alaska, though not nearly as many as she would like. She explains, "Writing about Alaska is like undertaking an archaeological expedition. You scrape away at layers of event and history and landscape, sift through debris looking for evidence of what lies hidden, turn strange artifacts in your hands, trying to figure out what they do, what they mean. Growing up here, as I did, requires setting aside the familiar explanations in favor of the unknown." Simpson's essays have appeared in *Creative Non-Fiction Journal* and *American Nature Writing 1994, 1996* (John Murray, ed.; Sierra Club Books). Her first collection of essays won the Sasquatch Books Chinook Prize and is forthcoming in 1999.

FRANK SOOS   Frank Soos moved to Alaska in 1986 to teach in the creative writing program at the University of Alaska Fairbanks. An author of short stories and essays, he has yet to move fully into the country as a writer. "I remember standing on the rocky edge of the Copper River, looking over a quarter-mile torrent of water, taking in the rock bluffs leading to the mountains climbing up into the sky, and thinking, I have no words for this. Nothing in my background or education has prepared me for this." His first book of short stories is *Early Yet* (St. Andrews Press, 1998). His second book, *Unified Field Theory* (University of Georgia Press, 1998), won the 1997 Flannery O'Connor Award for Short Fiction.

JAMES THOMPSON   Born in Chicago in 1951, James Thompson received his A.B. in art and art history from Ripon College in Wisconsin in 1973 and his M.F.A. in painting and printmaking from Washington University in 1977. One of many talented artists who have come to Alaska for short stints as workshop instructors, visiting professors, and the like,

Thompson served as a one-year replacement for a professor on sabbatical at the University of Alaska Fairbanks in 1983–84, teaching the department's printmaking courses. During his stay, Thompson encouraged development of mixed-media and collagraphic printing techniques, participated in juried exhibitions, and produced work that was collected by both institutions and individuals.

JANEL THOMPSON A longtime Fairbanks resident, Janel Thompson received her B.F.A. from the University of Alaska Fairbanks in 1985. She served from 1989 to 1996 as executive director of the Fairbanks Arts Association, continuing to produce paintings, prints, and mixed-media work during that time. She had a solo exhibition at the Alaskaland Civic Center Gallery in 1983 and has been included in juried and invitational exhibitions in Alaska since 1982. She lives in Fairbanks, where she is a productive printmaker, painter, and worker in mixed-media.

JOHN CHARLES WOODS Born in Inglewood, California, in 1952, John Woods was trained in photography at California State University, Fullerton and Long Beach. He has had solo exhibitions in Kansas City, Missouri, Longview, Washington, and Carmel, California, and has participated in group exhibitions in Alaska, Pennsylvania, and California. Among the permanent collections holding examples of his work are the Contemporary Center for Photography in Tucson, Arizona, and the Photographic Studies College in Melbourne, Australia.

KESLER WOODWARD Kesler Woodward has been an Alaska resident—first in Juneau, then in Anchorage, and lastly in Fairbanks—since 1977. A painter who teaches art at the University of Alaska Fairbanks, he has had solo exhibits at the University of Alaska Museum, Alaska State Museum, and Anchorage Museum of History and Art, as well as at galleries on both coasts. He is author of *Sydney Laurence, Painter of the North* (Anchorage Museum of History and Art and University of Washington Press, 1990), *Painting in the North: Alaskan Art in the Anchorage Museum of History and Art* (Anchorage Museum of History and Art, 1993), *A Sense of Wonder* (University of Alaska Museum, 1995), and *Spirit of the North: The Art of Eustace Paul Ziegler* (Morris Museum of Art, 1998). He says of his work, "For me the most challenging thing about painting in Alaska is finding a way of celebrating the beauty and magic of this landscape without mimicking it, competing with it, or trivializing it. I try to make paintings that walk a fine line between being completely about paint on the surface of the canvas and completely about how it feels to be in the great Northern forest."